ORIEL IN THE DESERT

for

Katharine
(my Zipporah)

ORIEL IN THE DESERT

An Archangel's Account of the Life of Moses

Robert Harrison

ORIEL IN THE DESERT
Published by Scripture Union, 207–209 Queensway, Bletchley, MK2 2EB, England.

✆ **Scripture Union:** Scripture Union is an international Christian charity working with churches in more than 130 countries providing resources to bring the good news about Jesus Christ to children, young people and families – and to encourage them to develop spiritually through the Bible and prayer. As well as a network of volunteers, staff and associates who run holidays, church-based events and school Christian groups, SU produces a wide range of publications and supports those who use the resources through training programmes.

Email: info@scriptureunion.org.uk
Internet: www.scriptureunion.org.uk

First published 2004
ISBN 1 84427 091 2

British Library Cataloguing-in-Publication Data: a catalogue record for this book is available from the British Library.

Cover design and photography by David Lund Design, Milton Keynes.

Internal design and typesetting by Servis Filmsetting Ltd of Manchester.

Printed and bound in Great Britain by Creative Print and Design (Wales) Ebbw Vale.

Foreword from the author

Oriel in the Desert is both the last and the first book in the Oriel trilogy. Last, because it is the third to be written, and first, because it takes us to an earlier stage in the work of Oriel and his fellow angels. Each of the three books focuses on one person in the divine Trinity. *Oriel's Diary* retells the life of Jesus. *Oriel's Travels* shows the Holy Spirit living in and through the first Christians. *Oriel in the Desert*, as well as telling the story of Moses, is about God the Father, or 'the Boss' as Oriel describes him.

Those who have read *Oriel's Diary* or *Oriel's Travels*, will appreciate that this book is a careful weaving together of biblical fact with imaginative fiction. Those who are starting the Oriel story at this beginning will need to know that my presentation of heaven, and the lives of angels, though inspired by insights from the Bible, is unashamedly humanesque. The idea that angels are afraid of water, for example, is entirely my own device; the idea that humans ultimately have a higher place in God's plan than the angels, though, is inspired by 1 Corinthians 6:3. Angels, in truth, are beyond words, so any book that attempts to describe them as they really are would be inevitably incomprehensible!

If you watch history programmes on television, you will probably be familiar with the idea of historical reconstruction. A historian takes the ruins of an ancient castle and, with the help of computer technology, years of study, and some imaginative guesswork, shows what the building might have looked like in its prime, buzzing with activity. This is what I have tried to do with the Bible's account of Moses (though without the technology). *Oriel in the Desert* cannot presume to tell you what Moses *was* like, but I have tried to describe what he *might* have been like.

I would like to thank Oriel's regular support crew – Lin Ball, editor; John Grayston and Martin Davie, theological advisers; Naomi, Grace and Isaac, to whom I read the first draft; and Katharine, my wife – for their gracious support. In addition, my thanks to Stephen Mort, Dave Hopkins and Liz Sands who have furnished me with an assortment of obscure scientific facts.

Finally, as I bid a fond farewell to Oriel and turn my attention to the story of King David, I urge you to pick up the Bible itself and allow its treasury of stories to excite your own imagination.

Robert Harrison

PART ONE

The Sinai Desert

I had assumed that it would be easy to find a human being in the middle of a desert.

My Boss called Archangel Gabriel and me into his office and announced, 'The time has arrived to take Abraham's descendants away from living as slaves in Egypt. I shall now give them the territory that I promised Abraham I would give them.'

'Good!' Gabriel said, cheerily. 'They've been praying about it for centuries.'

I looked anxiously at my colleague. Gabriel is responsible for the department that records every prayer ever offered by any human. But he was dangerously close to criticising his Creator. My Boss also looked at Gabriel, his gaze as steady as eternity.

'Not one of those prayers has been wasted, Gabriel,' he said. 'They have been planted in my People's love, and watered by their tears. The fruit is now ripe.'

'What do you want us to do?' I asked, drawing my Creator's intense gaze from Gabriel.

'I have chosen who will rescue the Israelites from their slave masters,' my Boss explained. 'I would like you two to deliver a message for me.'

'Who is it for?' I enquired.

'A child of Hebrew slaves, an Egyptian prince and a Midianite shepherd.'

I carefully recorded this information.

Gabriel asked, 'Which one should we visit first?'

Our Boss smiled. 'You will find him in the Sinai mountains.'

'Who's in the Sinai mountains?' Gabriel responded.

'The man I have chosen.'

Gabriel was confused. 'You said there were *three*.'

We both looked enquiringly at our Boss, who told us, 'His name is Moses.'

'So this is the *Egyptian*?' Gabriel asked, uncertainly.

My Boss looked at me while I hurriedly reconsidered the information he had given us. 'Explain it to him, Oriel,' he said.

'If I understand this correctly, Gabriel,' I said, carefully, 'Moses, the Egyptian prince, is the son of Hebrew parents and – if we are to look for him in Sinai – I assume that he is now working as a shepherd among the Midianites.'

I looked across to my Boss: 'How did I do?'

'Very well, Oriel.'

Gabriel was quick to re-seize the initiative. 'An excellent choice, Lord,' he declared with limited sincerity. 'Understands the Egyptians, identifies with the Israelites, and is familiar with the territory they will have to cross.'

Our Boss was unmoved. I glared at Gabriel, imploring him to show more respect towards his Maker. He noticed my irritation and apologetically asked our Boss, 'What shall I tell this Moses?'

'Tell him I have seen the misery of my People in Egypt, that I have heard their cries for help. Tell him to speak to the Pharaoh and then lead the Israelites out of Egypt to the place where Abraham lived – the land of the Canaanites.'

'Sounds simple enough,' Gabriel said. 'Come on, Oriel, let's get on with it.'

I stayed where I was, looking into the eternal eyes of my Creator. If it is so simple, I wondered, why did he ask both Gabriel and me? Gabriel usually goes alone when delivering messages.

My Boss's ageless face bore the same steady look he had maintained throughout our conversation, a look tinted with a gentle smile. He said nothing, and no Angel can read his thoughts. But I knew that he had invited me for some reason. I joined Gabriel.

*　　*　　*

Angels do not see Creation the way humans see it. The substance of the physical Universe is dim to our eyes. What we see, primarily, are the solid, spiritual realities of love, faith and hope. In a place as sparsely populated as the Sinai Desert, a man who loves and trusts my Boss would stand out like an elephant on an anthill. It was with that expectation that we arrived on Earth. However, but for one moderately bright Midianite priest, the desert was as devoid of spiritual life as it was of vegetation. Straining our sight to the limit we spotted a few gerbils going about their business, an assortment of nomads and three camel trains led by merchants who were brightly dressed but spiritually dim. There was no sign of the kind of person who might fit into Abraham's sandals.

'He's scarpered!' Gabriel exclaimed.

8

'No he hasn't,' I replied.

'How do you know?'

'If our Boss says he's here,' I assured my colleague, 'he's here . . . somewhere.'

'I'll go back and ask for better directions,' Gabriel suggested.

'No,' I replied firmly. 'He told us everything he intended to tell us.'

We both scanned the horizon, searching for a clue.

'How good are you at spotting sheep?' I asked Gabriel.

'I've never tried.'

'This man is a shepherd,' I said. 'If we work our way through every flock of sheep in Sinai, we should find Moses – eventually!'

It was tedious work. Even though all our Boss's creatures reflect something of their Creator's life, sheep have a minimal spiritual presence. Gradually we learned to recognise the telltale Heavenly resonance of the desert flocks. Our enquiries with some of the hardworking Angel guardians of the shepherds led us to a bleak and craggy mountain near the southern tip of the desert. There we found a modest-sized flock of sheep clambering over the mountainside and, some distance from the animals, there was an Angel. Neither Gabriel nor I could see a shepherd. The Angel was intently studying the corpse of a dead locust.

'Angel!' Gabriel called abruptly, 'where's Moses?'

The Angel did not look up from his studies, but said vaguely, 'With the sheep.'

I was irritated. I am responsible for all Angel guardians and it is their duty to maintain a continuous and careful watch over their charges. This Angel was neglecting his task. 'What's your name, Angel?' I asked sternly.

He looked up with the serene calmness of a startled sloth. 'Ah, hello Oriel. Hello Gabriel.'

'Where . . . is . . . Moses?' I laboured to contain my anger.

The Angel stared intently into the flock of sheep and then said, 'Over there.'

I was shocked to see a shepherd whose spiritual light was no brighter than that of his sheep. I turned on the Angel.

'You are supposed to look after that man, Angel. What's happened?'

'He's been like it ever since he ran away from Egypt.' The Angel paused for a moment and then said, 'Look at this locust, Oriel. It's fascinating.'

'You look at me, Angel,' I exploded. He turned slowly to face me. 'This Moses has been carefully picked for a supremely important mission. Which idiot put you in charge of so valuable a human?'

The Angel did not reply and his mind was so calm that reading it was a slow process. Eventually I saw the answer that he had chosen not to say.

Gabriel saw it too. 'Perhaps you should re-phrase your question, Oriel?' he suggested, repressing a giggle.

I concentrated on the unusual spirit before me. 'What is your name, Angel?'

'Hushael.'

'And what was your task in Heaven before you came here?'

'I was a singer in Archangel Raphael's choir.'

That explained his incompetence as a guardian.

'And how, Hushael, did you end up as guardian to Moses?'

'If you remember, Oriel,' Hushael said softly, and with no hint of criticism, 'the old Pharaoh ordered that all Hebrew boys be murdered at birth. You gave some of us a brief taste of guardianship, knowing that our charges would not live for more than a few hours.'

Gabriel gave up trying to restrain his amusement. 'What went wrong?' he chortled.

Hushael continued. 'Moses' mother hid him for three months and then placed him in a basket among the reeds in the river, where Pharaoh's family washed every morning. Pharaoh's daughter found the baby and adopted him. I have been his guardian ever since.'

That explained Moses' royal connections and his Egyptian name. 'You said he ran away from Egypt,' I remembered. 'Why?'

'Moses' Hebrew mother was employed as a wet-nurse by the Princess, and she cared for Moses in her own home until he was weaned. After that he lived in the royal household with Pharaoh's daughter. When his Egyptian mother eventually told him that he was a Hebrew by birth, he took great interest in the plight of the Israelite slaves. One day he found an Egyptian beating a Hebrew man. He was furious and killed the Egyptian.'

Gabriel muttered, 'Our Boss omitted *murderer* from the list of Moses' qualifications.'

'Carry on,' I said to Hushael, ignoring my colleague.

'When Moses' Egyptian uncle, King Seti, found out, he drew

up an execution order and Moses fled to Midian. He has been dangerously depressed ever since.' Hushael paused and carefully placed the dead locust on a smooth stone. 'I took Moses to the brightest human in all Midian, a priest, and arranged for the brightest of the priest's seven daughters to fall in love with him. The couple have two handsome and healthy sons – but none of these things has resolved the mess inside Moses' brain.'

I revised my opinion of this Angel's competence. 'You have done well, Hushael,' I said. 'Now, if you will excuse us, Gabriel has a message for Moses.'

Gabriel and I approached the dull shepherd, closely followed by Hushael. Moses was crouching among his sheep, gazing over the featureless landscape of his own thoughts. All that he could see there were his own failings: he is not a good husband, not a good father and not even a good shepherd; he has been disowned by the Hebrews, disinherited by the Egyptians and is now distrusted by the Midianites. I was astounded that my Boss should consider using such a person.

Gabriel's observations were similar. 'Here goes,' he said with resignation. He called into the shepherd's mind, 'Moses! Moses!' There was not a glimmer of response.

'MOSES!' Gabriel called more loudly. Nothing.

Gabriel further increased the intensity of his call. Moses' unfocused eyes did not even flicker.

Heaven's chief messenger looked at me while he considered what to try next. 'This probably won't work,' he said, 'but let's have a go at all three of us calling together – full volume.'

He counted us down and Hushael and I joined our voices with Gabriel's in a great howl that only vaguely approximated to Moses' name. Our call bounced back to us from every surface in the vicinity but it disappeared into Moses' brain like a single raindrop into a dried sponge.

'I don't know if this idea will be any use to you,' Hushael said quietly. We both looked at him expectantly. 'But . . . he tends to be less depressed when he's *asleep*.'

'Hmm . . . then you could try what you did for Jacob,' I suggested to Gabriel. 'It would take some planning, though.'

'One thing at a time,' Gabriel replied impatiently. 'I'll show myself to him visibly, and appeal to his eyes and ears together.'

Gabriel dimmed his Heavenly brightness until it was only slightly stronger than that which is usual in loving humans. Thus transformed, he stood in front of Moses and called his name. Moses yawned, stretched his arms, stood up and walked among his sheep, routinely counting them.

'Did I make him do that?' Gabriel asked me, a spark of hope in his voice.

'Try again,' I said, 'and I'll watch closely.'

Gabriel dimmed his brightness a second time and called to Moses. The shepherd redirected his sheep count to the area around Gabriel.

'You're not going to like this,' I told my colleague. 'I'm pretty certain that he can hear you – but he can't see you at all.' I paused, before adding, awkwardly, 'He thought he heard the frightened bleat of a new-born lamb. That's why he started counting the sheep.'

Gabriel scowled. 'This is ridiculous!' he exclaimed. 'I'll just have to appear to him more brightly.'

'I don't think you should,' I advised. 'You might damage him.'

Gabriel accepted my advice reluctantly.

'The problem is not with you, Gabriel,' Hushael observed calmly. 'Moses does not really believe in Heaven.'

'There must be *something* that will work,' I insisted, 'or our Boss wouldn't have sent us here.' I had an idea. 'Gabriel, what if you dimmed yourself down to a less than human brightness.' I could see that he did not like the idea. 'We need to meet Moses on his own level.'

'Are you asking me to appear as a *sheep*?' he asked indignantly.

'Not exactly, but . . .'

'Too dangerous,' Gabriel declared.

'Why?'

'It could cause me permanent damage.'

I pursued the idea. 'But, that aside, Moses might *see* you. What do you think, Hushael?'

'I am *not* doing it,' Gabriel insisted. 'If it's wrong to risk Moses' life by appearing too strongly, it's just as wrong to risk mine by appearing too faintly.'

'Could it work, Hushael?' I asked, ignoring Gabriel's objection.

He was not exactly quick to answer. 'It . . . might.'

'Then *I'll* do it,' I said.

'Don't, Oriel, it's not safe,' Gabriel implored.

'Our Boss does not ask us to do things that cannot be done,' I stated.

'If you insist,' Gabriel said, with an apparent change of mind – looking around at the rocky mountainside – 'I suggest you do it over *there*.'

'Why?' I asked.

He grinned. 'I don't want you to make a mess all over Moses if you explode.'

He was not taking this seriously. But I decided to follow his instructions rather than begin an argument. I went over to the very dead desert shrub he had indicated.

'No Angel has ever done this before,' Gabriel warned me. 'It isn't brave, Oriel. It's reckless.'

'Obedience is neither brave nor reckless,' I asserted, and began to dissipate my Heavenly life down to the gloomy level of Earthly existence. I reached and passed the state in which Angels usually appear to humans. My sights were set on the dull glimmer of Moses' sheep. I could feel my spirit becoming slow and my mind becoming leaden. I concentrated hard on the nearest sheep and steadily approached its level of blank stupidity. Suddenly, I was distracted by a light beside me and I could hear Gabriel laughing.

'Look what you've done!' he was shouting. He seemed to be talking impossibly fast.

I turned myself slowly round and saw that the desert shrub beside me had caught fire. The bush was being illuminated by my dissipating spirit and was shining with bright Heavenly light. Beyond the bush, Gabriel quivered with laughter. I wasn't sure what to do next. Then a Heavenly voice emerged from the middle of the incandescent bush. It was not Gabriel's voice. This voice was slow enough for me to hear every word, despite my near-animal state. It was my Boss.

'Well done, Oriel,' he said. 'Look!'

I turned towards the flock of sheep. Moses was walking towards me. I had no opportunity to enjoy my success because it took all my concentration to maintain my life at such a dangerously low pitch. I knew I would not be able to hold it there for long. Once Moses had reached the edge of his flock, I discovered that he was not heading towards me at all, as I had supposed. It was the bush that had caught his attention.

'Moses! Moses!' my Boss called from within the fiery plant. The former prince heard the divine voice and instinctively stooped to remove his sandals.

Assuming that my job was now done, I was about to return to

my usual state when my Boss said, 'Stay there, Oriel. You are doing an excellent job.'

'I don't know how long I can maintain this,' I said honestly. My entire being was throbbing, and all my senses had become dull.

'Trust me, Oriel,' he replied.

Moses was now standing barefoot before the shining bush. My Boss introduced himself as 'the God of Abraham, Isaac and Jacob', and began to pass on the message he had entrusted to Gabriel. Moses heard every word. But he was not impressed.

'I d . . . don't think I could do that,' he mumbled. 'In f . . . fact, I am qu . . . quite sure I couldn't. The th . . . thing is . . .'

'I will be with you, Moses,' my Boss replied. Moses stared forlornly into the flaming branches. He had long ago abandoned all meaningful belief in any gods.

'Who are you?' he asked.

'I simply am!' my Boss declared.

The voice from the bush continued, 'I want you to bring the Israelites here, Moses, so they can meet me on this mountain. Then you must take them to Canaan.'

Moses was not convinced. 'The . . . the Hebrews – I mean the Israelites – will never believe me,' he complained. 'Neither will Ra . . . Ra . . . Rameses, I mean King Rameses – the new pharaoh. Well, not so new now . . .'

My Boss was patient. 'What are you holding in your hand, Moses?'

Moses looked at his shepherd's staff. 'It's my . . . well, it's . . . it's really just a stick.'

'Throw it on the ground.'

Moses was still struggling to accept that he could actually be in conversation with one of the gods that he had so resolutely denied. He pushed away his staff. The moment it touched the desert dust, it transformed into a brightly coloured snake which hissed and spat at him. Moses took one look and ran. He vaulted the nearest sheep, pushed aside the next few and cowered in the middle of his flock.

'Come back, Moses,' my Boss instructed.

He returned warily.

'Pick up the snake.'

Not taking his eyes off the writhing reptile, Moses stopped at a safe distance from it.

'You can do it, Moses,' my Boss urged. 'Pick it up.'

Cautiously, Moses leaned forwards and then, with remarkable

dexterity for such a slow being, he grabbed the snake's tail and snatched it up. Instantly it turned back into his old wooden staff.

My Boss said, 'If you do that in Egypt, Moses, then they will believe that I have appeared to you.'

I was beginning to panic about the amount of time I had spent at such a low level of life. 'I can't do this any longer,' I yelped.

I could not see my Boss at all. I could only hear his voice as he gave Moses two further demonstrations of his limitless power and I forced myself to trust my Creator's judgement.

Moses was not so trusting. 'As you w . . . will have noticed,' he muttered, 'I'm n . . . not very good at talking. What I mean is, I . . . I can never g . . . get across what I want to say. It's just that . . .'

He was interrupted by a Heavenly voice that was faster and more furious than my Boss's.

'Who gave you your mouth, you ungrateful man? Who gave you your ears and your eyes and your slug-like brain? If your Creator asks you to do something . . .'

'Thank you, Gabriel,' my Boss said firmly. Then, to Moses, 'He is quite right though. But you do not need to worry. I will help you to speak clearly, Moses, and I will tell you what to say.'

Moses looked down at his wooden staff. He was afraid: afraid of his own People, the Israelites; afraid of his Egyptian cousin, the pharaoh; afraid to leave the familiar comfort of his flock and his small family; and quite terrified to discover that there really was such a thing as a God. He mustered his sparse mental resources, and demanded, 'Lord, send someone else.'

I have known Angels to refuse my Boss's service. None of them have ever been invited into it again. They have drifted into the clutches of Lucifer and his Opposition. I expected that Moses would now face the same fate and be cut loose, abandoned to drift through his life until finally trapped in unending Death. I waited for my Boss's irresistible wrath to condemn the man.

He was most certainly angry, but he was patient. 'What about your brother, Aaron?' my Boss asked quietly.

'What brother?' Moses replied blankly.

'Your Hebrew mother's son,' my Boss explained. Deep in the farthest reaches of Moses' memory there sparked the faintest re-collection of not being entirely alone.

'Aaron will do the talking for you,' my Boss told him. 'If you tell Aaron what to say, he will say it. He will be your voice.'

Moses said nothing.

'Take your staff with you, Moses,' the voice from the bush told him. 'Now go to Egypt. Aaron will meet you.'

As soon as Moses turned to leave, I struggled back to my usual form. Gabriel caught me as I swooned from exhaustion.

'Oriel, Gabriel,' my Boss instructed, 'your next job is to find Moses' brother Aaron and bring the two of them together.'

Goshen in northern Egypt

While Moses returned the sheep to his father-in-law – who turned out to be the same, faithful Midianite priest I had noticed when we first arrived in the area – Gabriel and I proceeded to the Nile Delta in search of Aaron.

We looked down on the great swarms of slave labourers being used to build the new Egyptian cities of Pi-Rameses and Pithom. They come from numerous nations, including an assortment of Egyptian peasants and petty criminals. Wherever they come from, these people work under the condescending eyes and blood-stained whips of the Pharaoh's master builders.

'How will we find one man in this tear-drenched swamp of humanity?' Gabriel asked me.

'Is this Aaron a Hebrew?' I asked. 'Or is he from Moses' Egyptian family? He might be a prince.'

'He isn't,' Gabriel replied, still taking in the misery of enforced labour on an industrial scale. 'Aaron is an Israelite name. We are looking for a slave. I suggest we split up.'

I wandered among the callous-handed, scar-backed slaves of Pi-Rameses, while my Angelic eyes acclimatised to the shadowy shapes of the physical Universe. In addition to their abused bodies, they all had something else in common: every slave I saw was devoid of hope. Many are second or third generation slaves, and know nothing other than brutal slavery. The rich and varied cultures of their homelands have long since been forgotten. These pale-spirited people have nothing to look forward to, nothing to dream about. Their muted minds harbour just one desire: for a swift and pain-free death, which is their only prospect of freedom. How little they understand these things.

I stopped and spoke with the Angel guardian of one of the slaves. 'Do you know an Israelite called Aaron?' I asked.

'Race and name mean nothing here, Archangel,' the Angel replied. 'They are all called *Habiru*, wherever they come from. The Egyptians deliberately mix together slaves of different races and languages to stop them from hatching plots against their masters.'

I moved on and asked another Angel. His human, a young girl, was struggling to carry the same load of bricks as the adult men in her group. I watched as she fell, scattering her burden, and was lashed by her Egyptian driver. Bleeding from the assault, the girl piled the bricks back into her hod and rejoined the line of silent slaves.

I spoke to her guardian. 'Why have you not taught her to pray?'

'To whom would she address her prayers?' he asked, dismally. 'The gods of Egypt are the masters of her masters – she would never pray to them. The gods of her ancestors are defeated and forgotten.'

'Teach her to pray to our Boss,' I suggested.

'Whips make poor teachers,' the Angel replied. 'The weight of those bricks has flattened her spirit.'

He watched the faltering progress of his human and offered his own prayer on her behalf. Then the Angel asked me, 'What brings you here, Oriel?'

'I am looking for an Israelite called Aaron,' I explained.

'I think the ones who make the bricks are called Israelites,' the Angel said.

'Where can I find them?'

'Go to Pithom,' the Angel told me. 'Beyond the city, follow the track that leads to the clay pits. The Angels there may be able to help you.'

Along the road I passed numerous groups of slaves, all carrying bricks, all watched over by whip-wielding Egyptians. I saw one old woman who had been left to die alone by the side of the road. I realised how potent the fantasy of a painless death must be to these tormented shadows of humanity.

I travelled through the building site that would be Pithom. Beyond the city, the road opened out into a vast yard – almost a small plain – filled with bricks. There were stacks of bricks waiting to be transported. Behind them were row upon row of newly moulded ones, laid out to dry. Behind those, at regular intervals, there were round tanks of wet clay into which slave women mixed bundles of straw, using their feet. These women sang a dismal

17

song as they worked; a song addressed to whichever god had abandoned them to slavery. They were pleading for him to rescue them. They sang in rhythmic but passionless voices. The song may have alleviated the boredom of their work, but it had little value as prayer. Nonetheless, as I looked across the plain I could see a faint spark of hope in some of the slaves, in those who still trusted that their god heard their prayers. I concentrated on these hopeful slaves, waiting – and hoping – for one of them to pray. At last one woman looked up from her work. She prayed to the God of Joseph and Jacob and Isaac and Abraham. I had found the Israelites!

I went straight to the praying woman, and spoke to her Angel guardian. 'Are these all Israelites?'

The Angel stared at me. His Heavenly spirit had become dull through the systematic suffering of his charge. The same was true of many of the Angels. There was a bleakness in their eyes which said, *What are you doing here?*' Eventually, the woman's guardian nodded.

'Why are the Israelites kept together here?' I asked. 'I understand the slaves who transport the bricks are routinely mixed up with other races.'

'The Israelites have a long history in Egypt,' the Angel told me, 'but they were only shepherds, so the new Egyptian kings left them alone – at first.'

Another Angel took up the story. 'When this building work started, they needed high quality bricks. So they did a deal. The Hebrews were allowed to stay together, as long as they provided well-made bricks.' There was a sombre quietness. 'Anyway, Oriel, what are you doing here? Have you come to rescue them?'

'Not exactly,' I said, 'I'm looking for a man called Aaron.'

'Most of the men dig in the clay pits,' a third Angel told me, directing my attention to a series of vast holes in the ground.

The Israelite men were standing up to their waists in murky water, scooping clay onto wooden boards with their hands. When they dragged the clay to the mixing tanks, they were accompanied by an Egyptian to ensure that they did not stop to talk to their women. They were sent back to the pits as soon as they had delivered the clay.

Again I asked after Aaron and was directed towards one of the hundreds of clay-caked workers. Like the women, some of these men still had a genuine hope that the God of their forefathers would rescue them. I was greatly reassured to see that this hope was particularly bright in Aaron.

I recognised Aaron's guardian, an Angel called Ahoshal.

'What brings you here, Oriel?' he asked me.

'I have come to collect Aaron,' I said. 'Our Boss wants him to go into the desert to meet his brother.'

'Do you mean Moses?' Ahoshal exclaimed. 'I thought he was dead!'

'You're almost right,' I told him, 'but our Boss has chosen Moses to lead the Israelites away from all this and take them to the land he promised to Abraham.'

'The last time I saw Moses,' Ahoshal mused, 'he was wanted for murder.'

'You know about that?' I asked.

'It was their hatred for Moses that held the Israelite men together at one time,' Aaron's guardian told me. 'Those were difficult days for Aaron. It's not easy for a slave when your brother is the king's nephew. But that's all in the past now. Since Rameses became Pharaoh and this hard labour began, they have been too tired to hate.'

Ahoshal's melancholy was evident. I looked around at the Hebrew slaves and thanked my Boss that they had the energy for a little hope, even though they had none for hatred. Then a bright light invaded our mutual gloom. It was Gabriel.

'Oriel,' he boomed. 'How did you manage to beat me?' He seemed quite untroubled by the suffering around him. 'Ahoshal, get your man out of that water – he could drown in it. I've got a message for him.'

'Gabriel, please, not now,' Ahoshal pleaded, 'not while he's working. If he stops work, even for a moment, he will be beaten. Tell him tonight when the others are asleep.'

* * *

Gabriel successfully informed Aaron that his younger brother is alive, and travelling across the desert to meet him. Then, while Aaron slept, Gabriel, Ahoshal and I worked on the harder part of our task: a plan to slip Aaron away from his slave masters without him being beaten or killed for desertion. We quickly agreed that the first phase of this escape would involve infiltrating the cruel labour of the brick-carrying gangs. That decided, I fetched the Angel I had spoken to earlier – the guardian of the young Habiru slave-girl who had collapsed prayerlessly under her load. He informed us that, in order to stifle potential rebellion, the brick carriers are shuffled into different groups every time they collect and deliver their cargo. This made things easier for us because Aaron would not be recognised as an impostor as long as he was not caked in clay or wearing the distinctive striped cloth of the Israelites.

Ahoshal woke Aaron while it was still dark, and escorted him to a deserted clay pit. During the night the clay had settled, leaving a layer of clear water on the surface. Aaron used this clean water to wash off all traces of the sticky mud that usually adorned his skin night and day. I watched in horror as he relished the opportunity to wash his wrinkled body in the suffocating liquid. (Angels hate water.) It took a considerable time for Aaron to scrub off the residue of his time in the clay pits. All the while, Egypt was turning steadily towards the yellow rays of Earth's Sun. It was vital to our plan that Aaron hide himself before the Sun cast its spotlight on the only clean Israelite in the whole of Goshen.

He only just made it.

Scurrying between piles of bricks to avoid the gaze of the ever-suspicious Egyptians, Aaron made cautious progress towards the large heap of straw delivered that day to be mixed with clay for bricks. He burrowed into the pile and waited there. I settled myself on the top of the straw and looked out for Gabriel, who was scheduled to arrive with the Habiru girl later in the morning. Ahoshal was busy linking together the chain of Angels and humans whose co-operation was essential to our plan.

I watched and waited. Waiting is a tedious business that most Angels never experience. To wait requires time, and time only exists within the cramped boundaries of the physical Universe. I pondered the fact that Angel guardians, and others whose work is in the Universe, must become accustomed to such constraints. I am not. While Earth's time crept by, I studied Aaron's mind, searching his memories for information about his brother. Aaron remembers Moses' birth and the excitement of keeping the family's secret as his baby brother was hidden for three long months. He remembers that whenever the baby cried he – Aaron – was slapped hard to make him cry, so that his crying would cover up Moses' noise. Aaron's adult mind is unable to access these early memories clearly. He feels deep anger at the trouble his brother caused him. His later memories are snatched glimpses of an awkward-looking Egyptian prince who, his mother claimed, was his brother.

Each one of these memories reinforces Aaron's resentment of Moses. Crouching beneath me, covered in straw, the long-enslaved elder brother can only imagine that meeting Moses again will bring more humiliation. He would rather return to his mind-numbing labour in the clay pit. I struggled to keep his mind focused on my Boss's message.

Eventually I saw Gabriel. Beside him was the Habiru girl. Her hod was empty on this return trip, but she was being driven at a speed that was as much of a struggle to maintain as the weight of the bricks. Ahoshal gave the signal for a group of Israelite women to leave their mixing tank and fetch more straw. They were more than a little startled to find themselves pulling Aaron out of the heap along with armfuls of straw. After some hurriedly whispered instructions, they bundled him onto their wooden sledge, covered him up and dragged their unusually heavy load towards the slaves' water jars. The women arrived at the jars at exactly the same time as the brick-carrying group.

Next came the most delicate phase of our operation. The water station is always watched very closely by the Egyptians, as are all places where slaves gather. However, Gabriel had done his work well. The driver who had brought the girl's group of brick-carriers complained loudly to one of his fellow drivers about the pampered privilege of the Egyptians who oversee the water station. The over-seers defended themselves, asserting what hard and unrewarding work theirs was. Gabriel danced from Egyptian to Egyptian, high-lighting these petty grievances. Within a remarkably short period of time they were in the full flood of an argument.

During this dispute, the Habiru girl 'fainted' and the group of Israelite women tended to her. At the same time, Aaron slipped out from under the straw, dropped his striped Israelite kilt, crawled naked between the water jars, picked up the girl's dis-carded sarong, tied it round his waist and stood up in the middle of the growing group of brick carriers. The Israelite women quickly restored the girl's modesty using Aaron's striped garment. They then smuggled her back to their mixing tank where, I hope, she will be loved, and taught – among other things – to pray.

Aaron was soon counted into a brick carrying group and lashed twice before he located the girl's hod. Blood dripping from his shoulder, he loaded up with bricks and followed his new companions in miserable slavery. His heart, however, was pounding with the prospect of freedom.

The next phase of our plan followed a suggestion from the Habiru girl's Angel guardian. It required that we synchronise our arrival at the building site with the disappearance of the Sun around the curvature of Earth's surface – not easy for two Angels who are strangers to time. Ahoshal, being more familiar with the vagaries of time, took charge. My task was to keep Ahoshal informed of our progress between the moment we entered the Sun's rays to the time when we would leave them. Gabriel's job was to update him on our progress between the brickyard and the building site. It was up to Ahoshal to ensure that both journeys ended at the same point in time. His intention was to achieve this by causing Aaron to fall over whenever necessary, thus regulating the progress of the whole group. It was a crude plan, but fallings and beatings were about the limit of the Habiru girl's experience, so her Angel did not have much to work with.

As the plan proceeded, Aaron did not require Ahoshal's help to fall over. He did it on his own – numerous times. Muscles that were accustomed to bending over and scooping out clay were quite unsuitable for carrying a hodful of bricks. Every time Aaron fell, he was whipped. The more he was whipped, the more he fell. Every time he fell, his driver grew more angry. The more angry the driver became, the more vicious the whippings.

It was a terrible day. Our assumption that Aaron would be stronger and fitter than the girl had been quite wrong. The light of his newly rekindled hope quickly faded. Like his fellow carriers, Aaron's only intention was to survive. However, unlike the Habiru slaves around him, he reserved some energy for anger, and that anger was directed at his brother Moses.

'If it were not for Moses,' Aaron reasoned, 'I would be enjoying the safety of the clay pit and the company of my fellow Israelites.'

His anger was raw and brutal. The only thing that kept it in check was hope, his People's hope, that the God of Abraham and Isaac and Jacob – their forefathers – would somehow rescue them. Since Gabriel's message last night, Aaron has connected that hope with his calling to meet Moses. It didn't quench his hatred for his brother but, if this humiliation was part of God's escape plan, he could not afford to let it be ruined by thoughts of a treacherous brother.

22

There were too many falls. Their progress was too slow. As I reported our distance from Earth's approaching shadow and Gabriel reported our approach to the building site, Ahoshal switched his attentions to the task of keeping Aaron upright. Gabriel and I abandoned our posts and joined him. Ahoshal took the weight of the bricks and Gabriel spoke words of encouragement into Aaron's mind. For my part, I quietly panicked, wishing I was in the familiar surroundings of my office and wondering how we might set Aaron free from this trap that we had lured him into.

As the Sun floated down out of the sky, Aaron's slave driver became almost hysterical at the prospect of having to spend another night in the open, watching over a group of hated slaves. Our plan had failed. The Egyptian halted the brick carriers near a settlement of houses that were already completed and occupied. He tied the slaves to a thick wooden post and went off in search of enough wine to smother his anger. He provided food for his slaves, only because his pay depended on the number of bricks safely delivered. He sent a child with bread and water. There was almost no communication between the slaves. They ate, they drank and they slept. We Angels planned.

We decided to leave Aaron to sleep to allow his body to recover as much as possible from the assaults of the day. Two hours before dawn we untied the ropes that bound the slaves. We had decided to liberate the whole group, though the other slaves' guardians were anxious about it.

'You can't free them,' they told us. 'They have nowhere to go. Sooner or later they will be captured and then they will be beaten even more severely and put to still harsher tasks.'

'Is there more punishing work?' Gabriel asked.

I was shocked to discover how traumatised the Angel guardians had become through the sufferings of their humans, but there was little I could do to help them. We left the slaves to accept or reject their liberty as they chose. Ahoshal woke Aaron, and Gabriel guided us by the shortest route to the edge of the part-built city and into the receding darkness.

Back at my office

As soon as Gabriel and I returned to Heaven, leaving Ahoshal to guide Aaron towards the Sinai desert, I went to see my Boss. There were several matters that concerned me.

'You have done very well, Oriel,' he said. 'Tell me what is troubling you.'

One of the great joys of serving my Boss is that, although he always knows exactly what I am thinking, he lets me express my thoughts in my own way. In his company, an Angel, even an Archangel, could be swept along like a feather in a tornado, but he accommodates our weaknesses, and delights to involve us in his plans.

'This Moses worries me,' I ventured. 'He doesn't appear capable even of looking after himself. He certainly couldn't lead a nation. And you are expecting him to shape a new one.'

My Boss said nothing.

'I have studied your Israelites,' I continued. 'All they know is threats and violence. When you take away their oppression, they will be like a tree without a trunk. They will collapse.'

My Boss still said nothing. I had more.

'They will need a strong leader. Aaron is strong . . . '

'Except when it comes to carrying bricks,' my Boss interrupted.

I looked up in surprise. He was smiling, but I was distracted by the reminder of Aaron's hideous experience. As I understood the situation, Aaron's strong hope was the one light in an utterly dark night.

'Oriel,' my Master said, patiently, 'do you remember Abraham?' I nodded. 'How well qualified was *he* to be the father of many nations?'

I said nothing. Abraham was extremely old and his wife incapable of having children when my Boss called them and, indeed, Abraham had fathered the nation of the Israelites.

'I have chosen Moses – just as I chose Abraham.'

I backed off from the leadership issue. I had another concern.

'Aaron hates Moses,' I said.

'I know,' my Boss concurred. His face became grave as he considered thoughts deep in his mind, far beyond the sight of any Angel. Then he said quietly, 'Aaron must learn the cost of forgiveness before he can administer it to the Israelites.' There was pain and a sadness in my Boss's eyes. Then he looked straight at me and his smile returned. 'Oriel,' he said cheerfully, 'I would like you to help me in this.'

I basked in the blaze of unbridled love shining from my Boss, as he drew me into the unspoken secrets of his plan for the Universe. He directed my attention towards the nearly soulless shepherd who was leading his young family across the Sinai desert towards the wealth and pride of Egypt. He also showed me the angry and resentful elder brother who was crossing the same desert to meet them. I could see my Boss's love for both these crippled souls, and for all the tortured slaves in Egypt.

'What would you like me to do?' I asked.

'Assemble a team of Angels, Oriel, that I can call on to help with developments in Egypt.'

'What will you require us to do?' I asked, wondering what sort of Angels I might need.

'Anything.'

I had hoped for a smaller answer. My Boss warmed my uncertainty with a vast smile. He knew that I wanted the comfort of specific information. I knew that he wanted me to trust him.

* * *

So here I am, sitting at my desk considering a list of Angels to invite onto my team. It's a very short list at present. It has one name – Gabriel – and I have just crossed that out. My Boss had purposefully asked both Gabriel and me to visit Moses; he had just as purposefully asked only me to form this team. I replaced Gabriel's name with my own to prevent the list from being totally empty.

Next

Archangel Raphael called into my office on his way to a choir practice. I explained my latest commission. Raphael's responsibilities are almost all focused on the affairs of Heaven, especially its worship. As his involvement in our Boss's other creations is minimal, he was able to offer some unprejudiced advice about the skills and specialisms I might need for my team.

'There is a limit, my dear old friend,' he said, 'to the number of voices that can enrich a harmony. Too many of them, and you produce only noise.'

His musical allegory was detailed and comprehensive; I will not repeat it in full. Raphael returned to his choir leaving me with much to think about. Most valuable of all his wisdom was his insight into the way that our Boss works. I have decided to start with a group of just three Angels – myself and two others. I will need two very different talents: inspiration and industry – one Angel who reflects something of my Boss's boundless creativity, and another who can focus all his attention on one particular task without being distracted by imagination.

* * *

I have visited many Angels, and held long discussions with them all, but only one of my vacant posts was filled when my Boss came into my office and said, 'Moses and Aaron are within a day's walk of one another, Oriel. I would like you to organise their meeting and ensure that it goes smoothly.'

'How do you suggest that I do that?' I asked, looking up from a comprehensive list of all the Angels who have experience of working within the Universe. He had gone. I leapt up and dashed into the corridor in time to see my Boss disappear into his own office. 'I haven't appointed my team yet,' I shouted.

There was no reply. I was just about to return to my desk when my Boss's bright face lit up the space between us. 'A day's walk, Oriel,' he repeated merrily.

I did not return to my desk but went directly to Archangel Gabriel's office to collect the one Angel I had chosen.

'What's wobbled your foundations?' he asked.

'I need Jeshaphael immediately,' I stated, my mind preoccupied with the impending disaster of Aaron and Moses meeting.

'Then you shall have him, my friend,' Gabriel declared with some amusement, sending a Cherub to fetch the head of his prayer collation department. 'Oriel, you may just be the answer to Aaron's prayers,' Gabriel added, filling an uneasy silence.

'What do you mean?'

'Aaron has been praying for some assistance in locating Moses,' he explained. 'He is reluctant to ask too many questions of people he meets on the road, for fear of being taken back to Egypt. But how else can he locate a man he hasn't seen since childhood?'

'A very good question.'

'I assume, from the look on your face, that you haven't found any inspiration to go with Jeshaphael's perspiration?' Gabriel asked.

Jeshaphael entered the room. He is a neat and ordered Angel whose task in Heaven is to painstakingly cross-reference all prayers that are received, matching them up with prayers from other people concerning the same matter. Such convergence of prayer makes the work of Angels much easier. Finding and recording convergent prayer is a thorough and detailed business. Removed from his exquisitely ordered desk, he was now awaiting instructions.

'Jeshaphael,' Gabriel said breezily, 'your new employer has arrived to collect you.'

'Gabriel tells me,' I said, 'that Aaron has been praying for help in locating his brother.'

Jeshaphael nodded economically.

'Has Moses, by any chance, offered any similar prayers?'

'Who?' Jeshaphael answered.

I was about to repeat the question, a little irritated by the bluntness of Jeshaphael's reply, when Gabriel explained.

'Moses never prays, Oriel.'

The studious Angel nodded his agreement.

'Is *anyone* else praying for the meeting of Aaron and his brother in the middle of the Sinai desert?' I asked.

'Zipporah,' he replied immediately.

'Who's Zipporah?' I asked.

Gabriel knew. 'Zipporah is Moses' wife.'

Jeshaphael nodded thoughtfully. 'She prays for her husband at least three times a day.'

'I thought you hadn't heard of Moses,' I observed, trying to get the measure of this unusual Angel.

'Firstly,' he explained, 'there are currently 2,427 men called Moses alive in Egypt and none of them are praying for a meeting with Aaron. Secondly, Aaron's prayers for help in finding Moses, and Zipporah's prayers about what the two men will think of each other, are not convergent.'

'I will work along the lines of Aaron's prayers,' I said. 'Thank you for your help, Jeshaphael.'

'What would you like me to do?' he asked.

'I would like you to draw up a list of the most creative and imaginative Angels currently in Heaven who have experience of the workings of the Universe.'

'Creative and imaginative?' Jeshaphael repeated questioningly. I could see that these classifications meant very little to him.

Gabriel rescued the situation. 'Jeshaphael,' he said, with playful solemnity, 'make Oriel a list of the Angels who most *irritate* you.'

Jeshaphael looked to me for confirmation of this revised instruction, his serious expression contrasting with the mischievous Archangelic grin beside it.

'It will be a start,' I said.

Back in the desert

I found Aaron quickly and located Zipporah the moment she paused from organising her children to pray for her husband. The desert tracks along which they were each travelling crossed in the middle of a broad featureless plain. I would have to arrange for them to meet at the crossing. With help from the Angel guardians involved, I calculated that Moses and Zipporah were likely to reach the crossroad first, so I travelled with them. Hushael briefed me on the current state of Moses' mind and spirit.

'He has shut himself up in the far recesses of his mind,' the Angel told me. 'He's been continuously repeating his conversation with our Boss, engraving it into his memory . . .' Hushael seemed to be about to say something else, but stopped abruptly.

When I realised that the Angel was going to say no more, I spoke with Zipporah's guardian, Yashenel. I learned that it had been Zipporah's father, Jethro, who had recognised that Moses had an encounter with our Boss. Jethro encouraged his daughter to go to Egypt with Moses. He also advised her to start praying to the Israelites' God. Zipporah has a clear and beautifully honest faith.

As we approached the crossroad, I asked Hushael, 'Do you think Moses is any more likely to hear me now?'

He didn't reply. He was completely absorbed in his charge's recitation of my Boss's instructions. I was reasonably confident that I would be able to communicate with the family through Zipporah, if necessary, but I wanted to try Moses first.

I went ahead to the crossroads and dimmed my Angelic substance down to a dullness near that of a human spirit. I was interested to see what effect his encounter with my Boss had had on the slave/prince/shepherd. When the little procession of people and donkeys arrived, I called out as clearly as I could, 'Moses! Stop!'

It worked.

Moses stopped right where he was. I don't think he had any understanding why, but he obeyed the impulse that resonated through his spirit.

Zipporah took advantage of the halt to lift her young sons down from their donkeys and let them play for a while. Moses stood motionless where he had stopped and his wife did not interfere.

I ascended to a higher vantage point and looked for Aaron. He was on his way. I rejoined Moses and was intrigued to find that he was looking intently down the road along which his brother was walking. I wondered: had he sensed something more than my command to stop? Was he, at some level, aware of my presence, and had he picked up my interest in that one of the three desert tracks before him? Perhaps it was a coincidence. I tried discussing this with Hushael. He was thoughtful. For a while I thought he was about to say something, but no. I asked Yashenel to ensure that the travellers did not move on until I returned, and set off down the road to meet Aaron.

Aaron's anger at his brother seems to have run its course during his long journey. He has accepted now that this family reunion has some significance in the Divine plan to liberate the Israelites. That liberation is his personal goal.

'If I have to meet Moses along the way,' he reasons, 'so be it.'

Aaron's path came over the crest of a slight rise in the featureless landscape and there before him, still stationary at the crossroads, stood Moses. For the first time I noticed the contrast in the physical characteristics of these two men. Aaron is gaunt and slightly bent by decades of hard labour. Moses is tall and broad; his body has been well cared for by his devoted wife. The brothers' mental health is quite opposite.

As Aaron approached the crossroads, I was preparing to introduce the two men. There was no need. What Aaron saw, waiting for him on the desert track, was the image of his father. His memories of Moses were of a smooth-faced young man wearing an expensive braided wig. The figure he now saw had thick greying hair and a full beard, just like the man who had tucked Aaron into bed when he was a child, filling his head with stories of his ancestor Abraham. Aaron walked right up to his brother and looked closely into those familiar eyes. He remembered how the same eyes – the last time he had seen them – had been adorned with dark Egyptian make-up. It was a memory that caused Aaron's latent anger to rumble in the rarely visited pathways of his mind. His old resentments were roused once again.

Zipporah was preoccupied with the necessary business of human motherhood when the stranger arrived. She watched from a distance as the two men stared at each other, and was anxious to join her husband, to help him.

Before Aaron's resurgent hatred had a chance to infect his actions, he leant forward and kissed Moses on both cheeks. It was not a show of affection; it was little more than a respectful greeting for a fellow countryman in a foreign land. But then he clutched Moses' shoulders and planted a third kiss in the middle of his brother's forehead. That kiss, as Aaron understood it, was not for his estranged sibling at all, but for the memory of their beloved father.

For Moses, however, the kiss was like rain on a parched desert. He had watched the approach of the lone traveller with interest. He recognised Aaron to be an Israelite by his features and had considered the possibility that this Israelite *might* well be the elder brother his God had appointed to be his spokesman. These thoughts were dull – like all the machinations of Moses' mind – but Aaron's third kiss unleashed long-repressed memories of their mother. Moses had not been finally separated from his Hebrew mother when Pharaoh's daughter found him among the bullrushes. The princess had unknowingly employed Moses' mother as a wet-nurse to care for the child until he was weaned. The experience of forgotten lips pressed gently against his forehead caused the desert of Moses' emotions to erupt into flower. He threw his arms around Aaron and began to sob uncontrollably.

Once the emotional sluices had been raised, long years of suppressed sadness hurtled down the channels of his mind. He gripped Aaron tightly and howled into his shoulder. Zipporah ran towards the two men. When she was close enough to see that Moses was crying, she stopped. She had never seen him cry before. She watched in wonder as her husband emptied his reservoir of sorrow onto the shoulder of a total stranger, met – apparently – by chance on a desert track.

Aaron's anger was subverted by his younger brother's response. The Moses of Aaron's memories cared nothing for him. The infant Moses had cost Aaron many tears; the baby Moses had distracted his mother's attention away from the rest of the family as she treasured those few precious months with her youngest son;

the boy Moses had only ever ridden past, looking down with disdain on the Habiru peasants; the young man Moses had been far too busy milking the pleasures of Egypt to look twice at any Hebrew slave. Aaron had not considered for a moment that the grown Moses might embrace him with such desperate passion.

Back in Heaven

I was keen to share this news with one of my colleagues, and did so with Archangel Raphael. I waited outside the practice room while the long line of Heaven's most musical spirits filed out. I then pushed open the door to discover that Raphael was in animated discussion with an Angel I did not recognise. This Angel was delivering a detailed complaint about the limitations of the choir's repertoire.

'There are so many other ways to combine the intervals and cadences of music,' the Angel was claiming.

I did not expect to understand much of this conversation. In demonstration of his point, the energetic Angel sang a variety of outrageous rhythms, all of which Raphael considered with his usual patience.

While I winced and grimaced at yet another snatch of irreverent noise, I became aware that someone was standing behind me. It was Jeshaphael. He sombrely handed me a document entitled, 'Those Angels who most irritate me – as requested – listed from the most to the least irritating'. I thanked him briefly and asked if he knew the Angel chorister who was forcefully dominating Archangel Raphael's attention.

Jeshaphael grimly directed my attention to the name at the very top of his list: Maphrael. I looked at the Angel with renewed interest. He was expounding a musical theory that meant nothing whatsoever to me, but Raphael was nodding with keen interest. I turned to Jeshaphael. 'When Maphrael has finished, could you please both come to my office.' Jeshaphael did not question my instruction, even though he understood its implications, and the prospect clearly terrified him.

I returned to my office and read up everything I could find about Maphrael. He seems to have worked in most of Heaven's various departments and his habit of questioning his superiors has been the primary cause of almost all his transfers. I paused to consider the delicate care with which my Boss would have created this unmanageable Angel and I smiled. Maphrael was just what I needed.

The two Angels arrived in my office – one smiling, the other very solemn. I looked at the smiling maverick. 'Will Archangel Raphael be putting in a request for you to be transferred?' I asked.

'He promised that he would try out some of my ideas,' Maphrael replied confidently, showing none of the customary deference to the seniority of an Archangel.

'Maphrael,' I began formally, wanting to gather his full attention before inviting him to join my team.

'Maff,' he corrected me. This did not bode well. I had only said one word and he was already disagreeing with me.

'Your name is Maphrael,' I insisted.

'I am called Maff.' His tone was polite but firm.

I had no trouble understanding why this Angel had served in so many very different functions, but I was determined not to overreact.

'Our Boss named you Maphrael,' I said calmly, appealing to the highest authority.

'Our Boss calls me Maff.'

I was out-trumped. I looked intently at this precocious Angel and pondered the fact that Raphael, my fellow Archangel, had acceded to his suggestions.

'Maphrael,' I said firmly, determined not give in, 'I have a new job for you. You and Jeshaphael will join me in a special operations team working directly for our Boss on planet Earth.'

Jeshaphael's face had not changed in any way since he met me outside the practice room. Maphrael looked at his new companion and then at me. 'When do we start?' he asked.

'You started the moment you walked into this office.'

When I had fully briefed Jeshaphael and Maphrael, our Boss called the three of us in to see him.

'Jeshaphael, Maff,' he began – at this point Maphrael shot me a quick *I told you so* look – 'Welcome into our team. Oriel calls it a *special* operations team, and it is – for him. But you must not forget that to me, every creature, from Archangel to amoeba, is celebrated for fulfilling its own task in Creation. This team, for you, for now, is your given task.'

I had heard similar words from my Boss many times. He was

entreating the two contrasting Angels to respect each other. He held their gaze long after he had finished speaking, watching his message reverberate into the very centre of their spirits.

'Now,' he announced, his voice suddenly brighter, 'when Moses and Aaron arrive in Egypt, they need to meet with the elders of the Israelite community and share their news.'

'What exactly is their news?' I asked.

'Moses has been rehearsing it daily since he left Sinai,' my Boss replied.

'I thought Aaron was supposed to do the talking?' said Maphrael.

I shuddered at such a blunt outburst coming from a creature to his Creator.

My Boss looked at Maff and then at me and again at Maphrael.

'You seem to have a good grasp of the situation, Maff,' he smiled.

Goshen, on the Nile Delta

We arrived in Goshen ahead of the brothers. I set Jeshaphael the task of identifying, gathering and briefing the Israelite leaders' Angel guardians. Maphrael and I returned to the desert to monitor the progress of Moses and his family.

Moses, Aaron and Zipporah are all highly nervous at the prospect of arriving in Egypt, each with good cause. Zipporah's people, the Midianites, have been at war with Egypt all her life; Aaron is an escaped slave; Moses is still, technically, wanted for murder. They each face the possibility of arrest and execution. Moses' sons, on the other hand – encouraged by the irrepressible Maphrael – are greatly excited at the idea of living in the richest and most powerful nation in their world.

It was night when we led the family through the part-built grand city of Pithom and into the shabby, sprawling shanty town where the Hebrew slaves are kept. They knocked quietly at the door of Hur, the chief spokesman for the Israelites. Jeshaphael had done his job well and before first light all the elders of Israel were assembled in Hur's small home. Aaron introduced himself; some of the elders remembered stories of an escaped slave. Then he introduced his brother. Without exception, the Israelite leaders considered Moses with great suspicion. His Egyptian name and Midianite clothes did not help. I watched as the Angel guardians in the crowded room struggled to implement Jeshaphael's instructions to illuminate positive responses in the minds of their charges.

Eventually one Angel succeeded. His human remembered the incident when Moses killed an Egyptian slave driver who had been mercilessly beating an elderly Israelite. Admittedly, the man's memory of Moses was of a reckless fool, but his story stimulated a modest acceptance that Moses might be one of them in some convoluted way. A number of the elders requested that Moses speak for himself. This was not a good idea. Neither his faltering speech nor his aristocratic Egyptian accent would help his cause.

Without consulting me, Maphrael took control of the situation. He made Moses pass his shepherd's staff to Aaron. Aaron stood up and threw the staff on the ground. It instantly turned into a writhing snake. All demands for the former prince to give an account of himself were quickly forgotten. The elders recoiled to the edges of the room, leaving only Aaron and Moses in the centre, looking down at the miraculous creature without a hint of concern.

'The Lord, who is the God of Abraham, the God of Isaac and the God of Jacob,' Aaron announced, 'has appeared to my brother in the mountains of Sinai.' He bent down and took hold of the snake, which assumed its usual form. Aaron leaned on the staff and repeated in full everything that my Boss had said to Moses.

Suspicion gave way to excitement. The thin hope that had united the Israelite slaves through their years of oppression was finally taking a definable shape. Even though that shape bore the name of an Egyptian prince, the clothes of a Midianite shepherd and the physique of a well-fed Israelite (a sight that had not been seen for many years), it was a welcome development.

The leader of the Levite clans, Izhar, a cousin of Aaron and Moses, spoke up.

'The God of Israel has heard our prayers. We must praise his name.'

Immediately he led his fellow elders in a song which, coming from their aged and mistreated bodies, sounded like little more than an elongated groan. I looked at Maphrael. He had a particularly pained look on his Angelic face, but I knew that my Boss would not be so fussy.

The singing – I name it according to its intention rather than its sound – was brought to an early conclusion by frantic knocking at Hur's door. The elders were gripped by sudden fear, assuming that their Egyptian masters had come to break up the illegal gathering. Aaron and Moses were silently hidden in the far corner of the single room of the house while Hur, slowly and with trembling hands, pushed back the wooden bolts. A middle-aged woman stepped over the threshold; her clothes caked in the red clay that dominates the lives of all the Israelites.

'Where are they?' she demanded, breathless from running.

'Who are you looking for?' Hur asked cautiously, fearing that she might be spying for the Egyptians.

'They told me my brothers are here,' the woman announced, still breathing heavily.

Aaron emerged from behind a storage box. The woman looked at him, her face aglow with excited anticipation.

'Aaron,' she asked, 'is it true? Has he come home?'

Aaron looked at the woman, his face lined by a lifetime of struggle.

'Yes, Miriam, it's true.'

Moses unfolded himself from underneath a low table and stood beside his shorter brother. Miriam's face was transformed from excited glow to radiant joy.

'The Lord be praised!' she exclaimed, making her way through the elders to embrace her long lost brother. She had not touched Moses since the day of his second birthday – the day that she delivered him to Pharaoh's daughter. (Their mother had been too distraught to take him there herself.)

While Moses introduced Miriam to his wife and children, Hur dismissed the elders, sending them off to their day's labour. I turned to my two Angel colleagues.

'Watch, listen and learn,' I instructed them. 'You need to know everything about these people that it is possible for an Angel to know.'

A week later

Moses and Aaron followed Miriam to her rough shack and waited there until she returned, exhausted, from her day in the clay mixing tanks. Miriam brought other members of their family with her. Tired though they were, they all brought extra rations of food to celebrate Moses' homecoming and Aaron's safe return. Moses was greatly moved by this humble but heartfelt feast. It was much more to his liking than the complex choreography of Egyptian royal banquets.

The next morning, when Miriam went to her work, the brothers laid low to avoid being spotted by the Egyptian slave drivers. I reminded them that they must now deliver their message to Pharaoh. Aaron guided Moses back to Hur's home. Hur led them to the dwelling of Abihu, the deputy spokesman of the Israelites. Together with Abihu, Hur took them to the headquarters of the building works at Pithom to seek a meeting with Pramessu, the man responsible, under Pharaoh, for the new cities.

Very gradually, the four Israelites worked their way up the Egyptian hierarchy. At every step they were obliged to wait: a deputation of Habiru slaves are a low priority to any Egyptian. Every middle-ranking official they met asked what Hur and his companions wished to discuss with the chief official. Hur was careful not to answer this question directly, only saying that it was a matter of great importance regarding the successful completion of the cities. It took three whole days to arrange a meeting with Pramessu.

Today, after two days' walking, the Israelites reached Pramessu's villa in Pi-Rameses. Pramessu has met Hur many times and holds a grudging respect for him. The Israelite slaves are the most reliable and productive labourers in the whole project. This is, in no small part, the fruit of Hur's careful negotiations on practical matters such as working hours and living conditions. Pramessu was expecting a similar request.

'What do you want?' he asked, strutting into the room in an immaculate black wig and a precisely pleated white kilt. Moses looked at the man with a pang of nostalgia. Pramessu's entrance was the first glimpse of Egyptian nobility he had seen for many years. At one level, Moses – husband of principled and practical Zipporah – was disgusted by the wasteful opulence of Egypt. But, on another level, Moses – grandson of stern Pharaoh Horemheb – was jealous. He might have been doing Pramessu's job himself, if things had turned out differently. These thoughts distracted him. While Hur was allowing a respectful pause before answering the official's question, Moses addressed Pramessu as any prince might speak to an inferior member of the royal court.

'The Hebrew slaves,' he said in fluent Egyptian, 'have been abused long enough. You must set them . . .'

Moses became aware that his fellow Israelites were glaring at him with acute annoyance. It had been firmly agreed that Moses would say nothing. His bubble of fool's confidence popped and his demand trailed off into an indistinct mumble: '. . . se . . . se . . . set them free . . .'

Pramessu also stared at the stranger, but in a very different way. He was startled by the incongruity of a Hebrew slave with an aristocratic accent. He was not at all sure how to respond. He glanced at the other Israelites and noted their irritation at Moses. Emboldened by that, Pramessu let out a loud and slightly forced laugh.

'Very good, man!' he mocked. 'Yes, why don't I set you all free?' He became viciously serious.

'Who would make all the bricks if I did? I'll tell you who. *We* would. And, while we were muddying our hands, you would take over Egypt like you did before.'

He took up his position behind a table covered with sheets of papyrus. He raised his chin, puffed out his chest and declared, 'Never again will foreigners rule Egypt!'

There was an uneasy silence. Hur gave a nervous laugh, and said, 'My friend is joking, your Eminence.'

Pramessu stared uneasily at Moses.

Hur continued, 'We have not come to demand our freedom. We have come to beg one small concession, the importance of which even Pharaoh himself could not deny.' He had won Pramessu's attention. 'Your Eminence, you enjoy the annual festivals in honour of Isis and Osiris.'

The official bowed slightly at the mention of the deities of Egypt.

'In all the years that we have served the kings of Egypt, we have never been allowed to observe any festival to the God of *our* ancestors. The Lord, the God of the Hebrews, has met with us and commanded us to take a three day journey into the desert to offer sacrifices.' Hur paused and then added, 'We beg your leave to go.'

Pramessu let out a single snort of laughter. 'You know your quotas, Hur. If you can stockpile three days' worth of bricks to maintain the building work in your absence, then you may go.'

Abihu responded. 'Your servants are already working at

maximum capacity, your Eminence. What you demand is not possible.'

Pramessu's reply was quick, 'Then what *you* demand is not possible.'

Hur was not so easily deterred. He began to recite a long list of *impossible* concessions that he had successfully wrung out of Pramessu in the past. All the while, he studied the official's eyes, waiting for a sign that he was ready to concede. I studied the man too. His life is devoted to the completion of two new cities for Pharaoh. If they are finished on time he will become a very powerful man in Egypt. If he fails he will be lucky to smuggle his family into exile.

Maphrael interrupted my studies. 'Oriel, time for a little Heavenly intervention, I think,' he announced. Our Boss had given Moses instructions for three different signs to demonstrate that his request came with Heaven's authority.

'Jeshaphael,' I said, 'what do you know about this Pramessu? Which sign should we use?'

'The hand,' he replied confidently. 'Pramessu has a sister who suffers with leprosy. He frequently prays that the rest of the family will be spared the humiliations of the disease.'

I spoke the suggestion into Moses' mind. He did not respond. I tried again, but with no more success.

'Let me have a go,' Maphrael suggested.

'No,' I replied firmly.

I turned to Hushael, Moses' guardian. 'What do you suggest?'

He looked intently at Moses, while Hur continued to probe Pramessu's defences. Hushael replied. 'Tell Aaron.'

I nodded to Ahoshal, Aaron's Angel guardian. He whispered into Aaron's mind and Aaron, in turn, whispered into Moses' ear. Pramessu noticed this and glanced suspiciously at Moses. While Hur was still speaking in his carefully measured way, Moses raised his right hand and extended it towards the Egyptian. He then drew it towards his body and slipped it under his cloak. By the time he had done this, everyone in the room was watching him and Hur had stopped talking. Moses calmly withdrew the hand. It was white with leprosy, pitted and scarred. Moses extended the hand towards Pramessu a second time. The Egyptian backed away, sweating with fear. Moses stepped forward. Pramessu retreated. Moses stood with his arm extended, searching for something suitable to say. Everyone in the room, except for

Aaron, was gripped with terror. An experienced Angel guardian would have helped his charge to find the appropriate words, but Hushael, apparently ignorant of Moses' need, was busy studying the leprous hand. I took the offending limb and returned it to Moses' cloak.

Pramessu watched, not daring to breathe for fear that he might become infected with the dreaded disease. Moses withdrew the hand a second time. It was completely restored. He looked up at Pramessu with a smile – the first smile I have seen on the man's face since discovering him among his sheep in Sinai. The smile had a distinct resemblance to my Boss's.

Hur grabbed his opportunity. 'We need to discuss this matter with Pharaoh,' he informed Pramessu in an uncompromising tone. The official was quick to agree. He did not wish to spend a moment longer in the company of Moses.

Thebes, capital of Egypt

The journey south to the royal city of Thebes required considerable preparation. The Israelites had to pool their meagre resources to provide adequate supplies and money for their four representatives. I travelled with Moses, Aaron, Hur and Abihu, but sent Jeshaphael and Maphrael ahead to conduct a thorough survey of Pharaoh's mind.

As the humans made their way up the long stretch of the lower Nile towards Moses' birthplace, I prompted him to remember his cousin Rameses, King of Egypt. I uncovered painful memories. Throughout his childhood, Moses was uncomfortably aware that he was different. Everyone in the family knew that he was a Habiru slave by birth. His Egyptian mother had loved him and doted on him when he was young but, when she married and had children of her own, Moses soon learned that, though she was still fond of him, he was second best. Moses was educated in Pharaoh's court alongside Rameses and numerous other cousins, but he was always pushed to the edge – the butt of their jokes, never fully part of the royal fun and games. He remembers Rameses as a chubby, bossy boy who loved being the centre of attention, which – being the Crown prince – he always was. During his traumatic teenage years, Moses had harboured many fantasies concerning his older cousin. He wanted to be Rameses. He dreamt of being Rameses' chief advisor. At times he even considered murdering the spoilt royal brat.

There was nothing in these memories that appeared to be much use to me. I left Moses and interrogated Hushael.

'In all the years that Moses and Rameses lived and learned together,' I said, 'there must have been some times when they worked constructively with each other.'

Hushael said nothing and drifted away from our group to ransack the distant corners of his Angelic mind. For two entire days, while we continued to travel at the tediously slow pace of humans, Hushael did not speak. Then, without warning, he slipped alongside me and said, 'There was a duck.'

'What on Earth is a duck?' I asked.

Hushael gave me a look that expressed, *You – an Archangel – and you don't know what a duck is?* All he said, though, was, 'A duck is an aquatic bird that humans domesticate for its eggs and its meat.'

I waited for Hushael to tell me more about what this creature had to do with Moses and Rameses, but he wandered off again. I returned to Moses' memories to search for the duck.

In late childhood, Rameses had found an orphaned infant duck and taken it home to rear by hand. He had let Moses into the secret of this illicit pet and the two of them had spent a few months working together to gather and prepare suitable food for the tiny creature. These were happy days for Moses – he was both wanted and needed – but the duck was soon old enough to fend for itself and Rameses no longer required his cousin's help. Rameses returned to his usual cronies and showed off the animal, claiming that he had saved it from certain death all on his own. Whenever Moses tried to get near the bird, to stroke it as he had done before, Rameses pushed him away, reminding him that he and the duck had a lot in common: they had both been abandoned in the bulrushes!

*   *   *

When the Israelite delegation arrived in Thebes, even though armed with papers from Pramessu, they had to wait many days before they were summoned to appear before King Rameses. When the summons came, it was for Moses alone. This caused a great argument. Hur and Abihu refused to trust Moses on his own, especially after his unfortunate outburst in front of

Pramessu. Aaron's old resentments concerning his younger brother returned in force. Moses took no part in the argument, mostly because his power of speech had dried up completely at the prospect of facing Rameses again. The Egyptian officials, for their part, refused to do anything but unquestioningly follow Pharaoh's instructions. However, when they realised that Moses appeared unable to talk, they returned to their king and asked for permission for Aaron to accompany Moses.

At last the two brothers were escorted into the presence of the most powerful man in Egypt. As we made our way through successive chambers made from flat, denuded rock, Jeshaphael and Maphrael briefed me about Rameses. He remembers Moses from earlier years but has few significant memories of him. He remembers Moses' sudden disappearance following an incident, the details of which his father never told him. I asked if he remembered the duck. Maphrael quickly checked Rameses' memories and informed me that, according to Rameses, he brought up the duck on his own.

We were ushered into a large hall, filled with stone columns. It took some time for the humans to wind their way round the labyrinth of pillars and come face to face with the king. I looked at the fat-faced, cheerful man. He was holding a creature, a bird.

'Is that the duck?' I asked Hushael.

After a slightly despairing look, he said, 'That is *a* duck.'

When the pharaoh heard his subjects approaching, he carefully put the animal on the floor, stroked it and watched it waddle out of sight. Moses and Aaron were introduced as representatives of the Habiru slaves responsible for brick production in the new cities. Rameses glanced briefly at Aaron, recognised him as an Israelite and then turned his attention to Moses.

Egyptians – for reasons I cannot begin to understand – routinely scrape away the hair from their faces and from the sides of their heads. All slaves in Egypt are obliged to do the same. Moses, however, has a full head and face of tangled, straggly, slightly greying hair. Rameses peered into the face he remembered from his youth. He recognised Moses more quickly than he expected.

'So,' he said with the steady voice of a man accustomed to power, 'you came back.'

Moses wanted to reply, but could not form a word.

Rameses saw the fear and confusion in his eyes and added, 'You have not been missed.'

41

Moses fidgeted uncomfortably.

The king turned to Aaron. 'What do you want, boy?'

'This is what the God of Israel says,' Aaron announced clearly, *'Let my People go, so they can hold a festival to me in the desert.'*

Rameses looked slowly from Aaron to Moses and back to Aaron. His mind and his spirit were closed tight. There was not the slightest indication that he would agree to the request.

'I think we will need another slice of Heavenly intervention,' Maphrael observed.

'It wouldn't work,' Jeshaphael responded, calmly but confidently. Maphrael and I both looked at him enquiringly. 'I have run simulations of all three of Moses' signs through Rameses' mind. None of them would impress him.'

I turned to Maphrael. 'Any suggestions?'

'Oriel, if I may speak?' Jeshaphael's voice came from the other side of me. I turned to him. 'I have studied this human's mind in detail. He is not responding in his usual way. Characteristically, he would have slapped Moses on the back and made a joke about his hair. After that he would have taken a friendly approach to the request, subtly manipulating it to suit his own ends. This harsh silence is not usual. I suspect that the Opposition are working against us.'

The Opposition are those Angels who have broken away from the service of our Creator and gathered into an untidy confederation serving their own ends in and around the Universe. Archangel Michael is fully employed in the task of fighting this rebellion and much of my energy is employed in tidying up the mess that they leave behind them, especially on Earth.

'No, it's not the Opposition,' I told Jeshaphael. 'I need to go and speak with our Boss about this one.' My two assistants looked at me with equal surprise. 'You two stay here,' I instructed them, 'but do not intervene in any way, whatever happens.'

Before I left, I looked for Hushael. He was watching a spider as it constructed its snare between two of the stone pillars. 'For Heaven's sake, Hushael,' I rounded on him, 'look after Moses.'

In Heaven

On returning home, I went straight to my Boss's office, thankful that I did not have to work my way up through any tiresome bureaucracy. The cause of Pharaoh's resistance had been standing directly behind him. The rulers of Earth's nations do not have Angel guardians, they have Seraphs. Seraphs are the Angelic patrons of the nation they serve. They do not come under my authority, but report directly to my Boss. Egypt's Seraph, Shlyphantel, was purposefully resisting my work.

My Boss looked up at me.

'What's going on?' I demanded, acutely aware that I was being rude, but equally aware that I had been out of my depth when trying to manage the meeting between Moses and Rameses.

My Boss knew the cause of my frustration. 'Shlyphantel has hardened Rameses' heart against Moses,' he said. 'That is why he declined Moses' request without a second thought.'

'Why?' I asked bluntly.

'Because I asked him to.'

This made absolutely no sense. Why should my Boss be resisting his own plan?

'This is a much bigger story than you imagine, Oriel,' he said. 'You will have to trust me.'

'When will I get to see this bigger picture?' I asked.

'In time.'

'But I am not *in time*,' I appealed. 'I am here with you.'

'You are indeed, Oriel,' my Boss smiled, resisting my irritation. 'But this particular story will unfold within Earth's time.'

I went right back to the beginning of my instructions and tried to understand something of what was happening. 'You have instructed Moses to ask Pharaoh to release the Israelite slaves,' I said, looking to my Boss for confirmation that this was correct. He nodded.

'But you have hardened Pharaoh's heart to resist Moses' request.'

He nodded again, his face serious. I considered my next comment with great care before I said it.

'You have asked me to assist Moses against Rameses and you have instructed this Seraph, Shlyphantel, to help Rameses resist Moses.'

'That is correct.'

'But I don't want to fight against you,' I declared, 'I want to work with you, to serve you in everything you do.'

'I know you do, Oriel.'

I knew that, to my Boss, this all made perfect sense, but Angels do not see the Universe as he does. I felt myself to be faced with an unassailable barricade which, to my Boss, was no more than a line drawn on the ground.

He explained. 'Rameses' heart is not hard to the very centre, Oriel. With your help, Moses must chip away at that hardness until it has been removed.'

'I will do that,' I said, still not quite understanding.

'It will not be easy,' my Boss informed me.

I stopped in my office to consider all these things before returning to Earth. Gabriel, noticing that my door was open, appeared in the doorway.

'How's it going?' he asked

I was trying to grasp more truths than my Angel mind could manage. I looked up, baffled, but said nothing.

'That well!' Gabriel responded playfully – and vanished.

Back in Thebes

When I rejoined Moses and Aaron, they were reporting on their meeting to Hur and Abihu. It had not gone well. Rameses had refused to acknowledge that the Israelites had a god, and accused them of laziness. He had dismissed the two men, telling them to wait for his instructions on the matter.

Later that day, the four Israelites were sitting solemnly by the edge of the River Nile when a representative from the king delivered a copy of his instructions to the slave drivers and Israelite foremen. Moses was the only one who could read the Egyptian hieroglyphs.

'*The Israelite slaves are no longer to be provided with straw for making bricks,*' he read to his companions. '*With immediate effect, they must gather the straw themselves. The quota of bricks is to remain the same; no drop in production will be tolerated. These people are lazy. Make them work harder.*' Moses laid down the parchment. There was a numb silence.

'That is impossible,' Abihu said. Hur nodded in bewildered agreement.

Moses stood up, walked a distance along the river bank and stopped near to where Hushael was peering intently into the water. Aaron stayed with Hur and Abihu as they worked through the implications of the pharaoh's order. Human conversation can be tedious and I will not record it here. Their conclusion was that they will need a large team of straw collectors to scatter all over Egypt gathering stubble. But for every man and woman they take from the brickworks, they will fall further short of their quotas. Equally, for every child or young person they take from their fields and flocks, they will fall further short of essential rations. The people will become hungry and their work rate will drop. For every day that brick production falls short, the foremen themselves will receive a severe beating.

'We will have to negotiate with Pharaoh,' Hur concluded. He told Aaron to wait with Moses until he and Abihu returned. The two men walked very reluctantly towards the royal palace, clutching the papyrus scroll.

'Why are you treating us like this?' Hur demanded when he was finally taken into the presence of the king. 'If your servants are given no straw and are told to make the same number of bricks, they will fail. We, the foremen, will be blamed and beaten – but these matters are beyond our control.'

Rameses asked, 'Why do you want to travel into the desert to worship a god who has already been defeated by the great gods of Egypt?'

The two foremen had no answer to this. They were politicians, not priests.

Rameses jumped at their weakness. 'Lazy!' he shouted. 'You are lazy. I know you Israelites. You are not a religious people; you have never shown any interest in worship before. If you had, I might have believed you.'

Hur attempted to speak up, but was not allowed the chance. The king continued, 'All you want is an excuse to stop working. But I have cities to build, stores to gather, battles to win. Get back to work. You will be given no straw and your quotas remain the same.'

He picked up his pet duck and placed it on his lap.

Maphrael looked across to me and asked, 'What do we do now?'

'Wait,' I replied.

Rameses' voice came like an echo.

'Wait!' he ordered the two Israelites. 'Wait right there until I come back.'

Goshen

Moses' return journey was not a happy one. Hur, Abihu and Aaron were furious with him. 'God damn you, Moses,' Abihu had yelled when he finally emerged from Pharaoh's palace, 'you have got right up Pharaoh's nose and given him an excuse to kill us all.'

Moses was furious too – with my Boss – but he didn't dare admit it. He sank back into the depression in which I first found him. He and Hushael, between them, did not utter a single word in all the days that the Israelite delegation trudged back to Goshen.

The reason why Rameses had asked Hur and Abihu to wait was so that he could draw up a second papyrus order. This was exclusively for Moses. Moses read the scroll quietly and refused to share its contents with his fellow travellers, even Aaron.

It read: *By order of Rameses II, Pharaoh of Egypt, I grant to this man, Moses the Israelite, free passage throughout Egypt, freedom from all forced labour and immunity from any punishment, except at my personal command.* It was sealed with the king's own cartouche. During the course of the journey, Moses spent many hours staring at this scroll, trying to understand what his cousin was planning to do. I shared Moses' uncertainty but reached no more conclusions than he did.

The four travellers met an angry reception when they arrived in Goshen. Pharaoh's new orders had sped north by chariot and the beatings had already begun. The only people who had any sympathy for Moses and Aaron were their sister Miriam and Zipporah. It was quickly agreed that Aaron would have to return to work. Zipporah had already taken the place of five Israelite nurses and was caring for the youngest children. The nurses were now collecting straw. The family were less sure about what to do with Moses. Throughout their discussions, he said nothing of the small papyrus scroll that was tucked into the pocket in his cloak. Being too tired to resolve the matter that night, they agreed to reconsider the Moses issue in the morning.

In the desert

In the morning, however, Moses was gone. It was my idea. He was still angry at my Boss and I knew that, until he expressed that anger, he was unlikely to emerge from the darkness of his own mind. I also knew that if he stayed in Goshen, he would have hidden from his trauma in some mindless human task, just as he had hidden among his father-in-law's sheep for so many years.

I left Jeshaphael and Maphrael in Goshen. 'What should we do?' they both asked.

'Something useful,' I replied.

The barren emptiness of the desert suited the state of Moses' mind. He walked without purpose, randomly heading for the highest outcrop of rock he could see. He climbed to the top and sat down. I watched as his thoughts drifted like storm clouds. I summoned Hushael, who was busy digging in a small patch of sandy soil.

'Hushael,' I said sternly, 'we must get this man praying.'

'How do we do that?' he asked.

I wished that I had brought Jeshaphael and Maphrael with me. Not sure what to suggest, my thoughts went to the one thing I knew Hushael was good at.

'Sing for him,' I suggested.

'What should I sing?'

'I don't know,' I said lamely. 'Something appropriate.'

'I don't know an . . .'

'Well, make something up,' I bellowed in frustration.

The Angel was silent for a long time and finally said, 'Archangel Raphael is the one who composes our music.'

'So?' My irritation was rising rapidly. 'Go and get him.'

This was an unorthodox suggestion, but Hushael did not question it. He went, leaving me wondering what the musical Archangel would make of such a request.

'Oriel, my dear old thing!' the composer of Heaven's music exclaimed in greeting. 'What a pleasure it is to come and minister to you with a little music.'

'We need to get this man praying,' I explained, pointing to the barely-shining form of Moses.

'How right you are,' Raphael observed.

'I thought that, as Hushael is a singer, a suitable song might be the most appropriate medicine.'

'Something for one unaccompanied voice,' Raphael mused aloud. 'Hmm! Not exactly what I like to think of as music, but I do believe I have just the thing that you need.'

This was encouraging.

Raphael launched into a song made of the slowest, though strangely poignant, music I have ever heard an Angel sing.

'*When Israel was in Egypt land,*' he sang. '*Let my People go. Oppressed so hard they could not stand . . .*'

And then he did something that Heaven's music never does: he repeated himself: '*Let my People go.*'

I applauded his unique performance. 'Where did you get that from?'

'It is the fruit of a suggestion from your new assistant, Maphrael,' he told me. 'Maphrael reminded me that many of our Boss's creatures also produce a music of their own kind. He challenged me to write some music in the human style. There is more.'

Concentrating hard to pitch the bare human notes, Raphael repeated the previous line: '*Let my People go,*' and burst into a refrain. '*Go down, Moses, way down in Egypt land. Tell old Pharaoh to let my People go.*'

I cheered loudly. I had witnessed a side of my talented colleague that I had never seen before. The song fitted my need wonderfully and it was so slow I was sure even Hushael would be able to manage it. I left Raphael patiently teaching his humanesque tune to the bewildered Hushael, suggesting that they conduct their rehearsal next to Moses so the music could begin to have its effect.

Moses was staring into the thick gloom of his own mind. Gradually that darkness was matched by that of the desert itself as Sinai spun away from the light and warmth of Earth's Sun. Hushael was singing alone while Raphael corrected him from time to time on the narrow definitions of human notation. Then, suddenly, our unremarkable outcrop of lifeless rock was flooded with Heavenly light. Archangels Gabriel and Michael had arrived, accompanied by a small group of Michael's Angel warriors.

'What's he droning on about?' Gabriel enquired.

'Ignore them, Hushael, my dear,' Raphael urged. 'You are doing exceptionally well. Do not stop.'

I ignored Gabriel's question too. 'I hope you haven't only come to criticise,' I said pointedly.

'We are expecting a message,' Gabriel explained.

'What are *they* here for?' I indicated Michael and his troops.

'Routine security.'

'Routine?' I asked incredulously. Such high level security is far from routine.

'The Boss said you would ask,' Gabriel observed with a chuckle.

'All to do with the bigger picture, I suppose,' I said.

'There's no point interrogating me,' Gabriel said quickly. 'I'm just the messenger. And there's certainly no point asking Michael, because he won't tell you.'

At that moment, a faint glow of light flickered in Moses' spirit. He looked up at the stars and shouted angrily, 'Why did I bother?'

'He's praying!' I exclaimed.

'We're in business,' Gabriel said, opening the folder that contained our Boss's reply.

'God!' Moses shouted, 'whoever you are . . . Ever since I went to . . .'

Here he faltered. His anger was turning to conversation, and conversation unsettled him.

'To . . . to Pharaoh with your message, everything has g . . . got worse. Wh . . . what are you doing?'

He paused and his anger returned. 'You haven't rescued anyone!'

'Spirited little fellow, isn't he?' Gabriel said to me. He then went over to Moses. Raphael and Hushael moved away.

'Moses!' Gabriel called, reading our Boss's words, *'I know what I am doing. I appeared to Abraham, I appeared to Isaac, and to Jacob. I made a promise to them, to give them the land of Canaan. I will keep my promise. Tell the Israelites that I am about to take them away from their slavery, that I will adopt them as my own People. Then they will know that I am their God.'*

My Boss's words reverberated round Moses' small mind. There was no doubt that on this occasion he had heard Gabriel's voice. Gabriel bounded across to me with a beaming smile on his face.

'Come on, Oriel, let's go.'

'Go where?'

'Back to Goshen, of course. Moses has to pass the message on to the Israelites. And after that, I have another couple for him.' Gabriel enthusiastically waved a sealed message. He then put it carefully away, turned round and shouted, 'Michael! We're off.'

For all Gabriel's activity, Moses had not moved at all. He had barely blinked. He stared up at the light of the blazing stars and considered my Boss's clear confirmation of his task. Raphael and Hushael were lost in conversation. Hushael was trying in vain to interest Raphael in something he had seen burrowing into the desert sand. Michael and his security forces were intently scanning the horizon for any hint of Opposition presence.

Gabriel's enthusiasm was not cooled.

'Oriel, for Heaven's sake, get your man moving! Let's bring a little life to this dull party of yours.'

I thanked Raphael for his assistance and asked Hushael to rouse Moses. While Hushael did that at his usual sloth-like pace, I joined Archangel Michael.

'Michael, is there anything you can tell me that would be useful as we move this plan forwards?'

He did not take his eyes off the patch of horizon he had allocated to himself. His reply was simple and clear: 'No.'

Goshen

Moses' announcement to the Israelite leaders was even less successful than my question to Michael. They would not even listen to him. Hur refused to arrange a meeting, explaining pointedly that, since the straw deliveries had been suspended, there was no time for idle fantasies.

'Either do something useful, or get out of our way,' he told Moses.

That was the cue for Gabriel to deliver his second message: *'Moses, go back to King Rameses and tell him to let the Israelites go.'*

Moses was quick to reply. 'Why should Rameses listen to me? The Israelites didn't.'

Gabriel opened his final message: *'Rameses is afraid of you, Moses. I have seen to that. I have also hardened his heart against you so that he will not listen to you. But he will let my People go and he will know that I am the God of Israel. Moses, tell Aaron what I have told you and he will tell Pharaoh.'*

Even Aaron took some persuading. He was reluctant to leave Pithom, knowing that his absence from the clay pit would make life harder for his fellow countrymen. It was Miriam who persuaded him to go.

Thebes

Moses' personal passport from Pharaoh worked wonders. The first time he used it was as he and Aaron were leaving Goshen. An

Egyptian slave driver spotted what looked to him like a foreigner absconding with a Habiru slave and challenged Moses at the point of a sword. Moses was startled by the speed and violence of the challenge and could only say, 'I . . . I . . . I . . .' He then held up one hand to urge the Egyptian to be patient and with his other hand produced the small papyrus that was rolled up in his pocket. The slave driver, on reading the scroll, swiftly put away his sword and looked at Moses in a respectful manner that had been entirely missing before. He returned the scroll as something of immense value and was somewhat startled at the careless way that Moses stuffed it back into his pocket. When Moses and Aaron made to continue on their journey, the man was still standing in their way and asked, rather dreamily, 'Who *are* you?'

Moses was not at all sure how to reply, and could only repeat his previous answer: 'I . . . I . . . I . . .'

Aaron came to the rescue: 'He is a messenger from the Most High God.'

At this, the slave driver was totally awe-struck and stepped aside, bowing deeply. That would have been the end of the encounter apart from some freethinking from Maphrael. Somehow he managed to loosen up Moses' knotted tongue and get him to say, 'The Hebrews are a chosen People in the eyes of my God. You must not mistreat them; you must not beat their leaders. If you do, the consequences on Egypt will be terrible.'

'I understand,' the terrified slave driver muttered.

Then Maphrael, completely ignoring my irate glare, added through Moses, 'Be sure to tell this to all your people.'

I was furious. As the two Israelite emissaries continued on their way, I insisted that Maphrael make it quite clear to Moses that, though everything he had said was true, it had not been an authorised message from his God. While the apology was being duly delivered, Jeshaphael said to me, 'You have to stop Maphrael from doing things like that, Oriel.'

I agreed with Jeshaphael – but did not wish to inflame the Angel's dislike for his unorthodox colleague.

'Maphrael's enthusiasm is entirely motivated by his devotion to our Boss,' I asserted. 'And, for that reason, I am prepared to risk the occasional accident.'

Jeshaphael said nothing for some time and then remarked, reflectively, 'It will work though.'

'What do you mean?' I demanded.

'Maphrael's little scheme,' he said. 'That Egyptian set off up the road with a clear vocation to instruct his fellow Egyptians that they must honour and respect the Israelites as a race especially favoured by Amen-Re.'

'But that's nonsense!' I responded. 'Amen-Re is a phoney.'

Jeshaphael looked at me intently. 'It isn't nonsense to the Egyptians.'

* * *

When they arrived at Rameses' ancestral capital, Moses' scroll worked with such remarkable efficiency that he and Aaron were ushered into the king's audience chamber in the middle of a meeting of counsellors. I immediately recognised the fear that my Boss has caused in Rameses' mind with regard to Moses. Whatever plan it was that the pharaoh was unfolding to his chief advisors, he stopped in mid-sentence when his wild-looking cousin stepped into sight.

'I knew you would be back, Moses. What do you want?'

Moses looked to his older brother and nodded.

'Let the Israelites leave this country,' Aaron demanded.

Rameses did not take his eyes off Moses. He is accustomed to conducting business through interpreters. 'I need proof, Moses,' he demanded. 'I cannot release an entire race of slaves simply because someone asks me. Show me that this god of yours still has some power – then I will consider your request.'

Moses handed Aaron his old shepherd's staff, whispering to him as he did.

Aaron announced, 'Here is your proof,' and threw the staff to the floor. It did not clatter to the ground with the sound of wood hitting stone; instead it hissed and slithered across the chamber, past the kneeling counsellors, raised its head high and stared directly at the pharaoh, its tongue flickering. Normally a creature like a snake would be almost invisible to my Angelic eye, but this was no ordinary snake. It looked with the eyes of its Creator as it issued its wordless challenge to the ruler of Egypt.

The counsellors were frozen with fear, but the Seraph behind Pharaoh's throne reinforced the king's resolve. Rameses was less afraid of the snake than he was of Moses. This was magic. He had seen plenty of magic; he had been brought up to believe that pharaohs are magical people. The king clapped his hands and ordered an attendant to call the court magicians.

While he waited, he turned his round face towards Moses and said coolly, 'I am not impressed by your snake, cousin.'

The court magicians arrived like lapdogs, each attached to an Opposition spirit. Some men were followed by more than one spirit; some spirits were controlling more than one man. But there was no doubt where these men got their magic from. The group were led by a particularly powerful spirit. This was one of Egypt's so-called gods. The spirit cast a quick glance in my direction, wondering why an Archangel had arrived in his playground.

'Who's that?' I whispered to Jeshaphael.

'Likes to be called Osiris,' he informed me.

Rameses welcomed the sorcerers and showed them the living snake that had sprung from Moses' staff. He ordered his magicians to perform the same trick. Each went about his business in a different way: some making extravagant gestures; others chanting long strings of nonsensical words; one of them mixing powdered chemicals, causing flashes and bangs.

None of this had any meaning, other than serving the combined vanities of both self-important magi and Opposition spirits. I could sense Maphrael growing impatient beside me.

'If you do or say anything without my permission, Maphrael,' I growled, 'you will be back in the choir, at least until the end of this Universe.'

Sure enough, the Opposition spirits, entertained by the posturing antics of their pet humans, began to transform assorted sticks and wands into snake-like forms. Soon the floor was a mass of writhing multicoloured snakes. Although the Opposition spirits were able to mimic the shape and movement of snakes, only Moses' was truly alive. When the last stick had been transformed, Archangel Michael arrived. The Opposition spirits looked up at Heaven's Warrior-Angel with the same paralysed terror that had earlier struck Pharaoh's counsellors. They may have wondered why I was there. They knew why Michael was there.

Michael gave one simple order to Moses' snake and it turned on those conjured up by the magicians. One by one, Moses' snake ate the others until every one of them was consumed. Its task completed, Moses' snake slid back to its master, straightened itself into a line and turned back into a shepherd's staff.

Rameses was thoughtful. Moses reached down and picked up his staff.

'Le . . . le . . . let us go, Ra . . . Rameses,' he blinked.

'Sticks and snakes are child's play, Moses,' the king replied, urged on by the Seraph behind him. 'You will have to do better than that.'

The Opposition spirits looked mournfully on, anticipating that they had just witnessed their last moments on Earth. Michael charged at them, shouting, 'Worship is due to our Creator and to no one else!'

The spirits scattered like crows from a field of wheat, leaving behind them fifteen bewildered and staffless magi.

'Aren't you taking them away?' I asked Michael, surprised that he had not cornered and captured his quarry.

'No,' he said.

'Why not?'

'Orders,' he replied unhelpfully. He handed me a sealed message for Moses and departed.

The next day

After his challenge to Moses, Rameses simply ignored the two men and returned his attention to the dumbfounded counsellors. Eventually Moses and Aaron wandered off through the pillared hall, nobly resisting the temptation to deliver a hefty kick to Pharaoh's pampered duck. They returned to the same location on the bank of the Nile that they had visited after their previous eviction from the palace.

As the two men walked, Hushael, noting a dreary gloom descending on Moses' spirit, sang Raphael's song: *When Israel was in Egypt land, let my People go . . .*

The song worked. It established for Moses a single small reference point in the otherwise featureless night of his psyche, reassuring him that my Boss is true to his promises. Moses stared across the forbidding liquid that seeps down the Nile valley, his mind fixed on this distant assurance. It did not, however, work on Aaron. Aaron was irritated that Moses had attempted to speak for himself, doubly so because he had made such a mess of it. He sharply informed his younger brother that he would return to Pithom if Moses insisted on interfering. I delivered the message that Michael had given me.

Rameses does not intend to give in, the message read. *Join him tomor-*

row morning when he comes down to the river to wash, and take your shep-
herd's staff with you. Say to Rameses, The God of the Hebrews says: Let my
People go. Then hold out your staff and hit it against the water of the Nile.
The water will be changed into blood. Fish will die, the river will stink and
the people of Egypt will not be able to drink its water. Moses accepted the
instructions and passed them on to Aaron.

At the bottom of my Boss's message there was an additional
note addressed to me. It read, *Oriel, will you please start work on the*
above.

The shocked gapes from both Jeshaphael and Maphrael
matched my own response to this order. Water is something that
we do our Angel best to avoid when we visit Earth, and we were
being asked to transform an entire river of the revolting stuff
into a substance that is quite alien to Angelic life. None of us
spoke, though the same word dominated each of our minds:
how?

Thanks to Moses' little scroll, he and Aaron were given free
lodgings in Thebes. (No Egyptian would dare to charge a man
who carries the king's personal endorsement.) Jeshaphael,
Maphrael and I had just one night to find a way of making the
River Nile flow with blood.

'It can't be done,' Maphrael sighed with resignation.

'Of course it can,' Jeshaphael snapped.

The two Angels glared at one another until I added, 'Jeshaphael
is right. Our Boss has asked us to do it. There are probably numerous ways.' We each scanned our minds for the smallest foothold
that might help us to scale the mountain before us.

'Where do we start?' I muttered, half to myself.

'Not here,' was Jeshaphael's firm reply. Maphrael and I both
looked at him. 'We are unlikely to achieve this within a few human
hours,' he told us. 'We need to go outside Earth's time.'

'Let's meet in my office,' I suggested. Jeshaphael and Maphrael
went ahead while I looked for Hushael to tell him what we were
doing. I found him stooping over the slow-moving water of the
great river. 'You should be careful there, Angel,' I said to him.
'That stuff's dangerous.'

His only response was a mild grunt. I explained that I was
leaving and would return in the morning. I received a second,
slightly louder, grunt.

'I'm off, then,' I said to the quiet Angel.

'Take this,' Hushael said softly. He gave me a single drop of water. Ordinarily, I would have shaken the stuff off me immediately, but it was a gift, so I accepted it with as much grace as I could muster.

I arrived at my office as my Boss was stepping out of the room, having just spoken to my two assistants.

'What do you have there, Oriel?' he enquired.

'Hushael gave it to me,' I explained.

My Boss looked carefully at the tiny droplet. A smile spread over his face. 'You do not want to lose that,' he said, and left.

The three of us sat around my desk staring at the pearl of river water. If this was our foothold, none of us could fit even a toe onto it.

'There's nothing to be gained from simply staring at this stuff,' Jeshaphael announced. He went to fetch a detailed analysis of blood so we could better understand the end product of our task. I invited Gabriel to join us.

'Do you have permission to bring that in here?' he asked as soon as he identified the object of our studies.

'Our Boss seemed to think it was a good idea,' Maphrael responded.

Jeshaphael returned. 'Which type do you want? There are at least 23 varieties of blood among humans alone. After that, every single species of mammal has a different variation on the theme. Then there is fish blood, reptile blood, insect blood, spider blood . . .'

'We get the idea,' Maphrael asserted, afraid that Jeshaphael's catalogue would include every living creature on the planet. There was an uneasy silence.

'Our Boss didn't specify a particular type,' I said. 'So perhaps we can assume that it doesn't matter.'

'Which is the simplest then?' Maphrael was quick to ask.

Before Jeshaphael had a chance to consult his long list of bloods, Gabriel said, 'It needs to be something that the Egyptians would recognise as blood.'

'The clue we need is in there,' I stated, drawing everyone's attention back to Hushael's drop of water.

Jeshaphael continued to study the information before him. 'It's mostly made of water,' he informed us. He added, 'The coloration is caused by an oxygenated form of a complex iron molecule.' He carried on reading.

'Could we manufacture enough of this iron thingy,' Maphrael said, 'to turn the river red?'

'That would not make it into blood,' Jeshaphael corrected him, 'It would only *look* like blood.'

Maphrael began to get excited for the first time since our return to Heaven. 'But the Egyptians would *see* it as blood.'

'I'm not sure that would kill the fish though.' Jeshaphael was quick to burst Maphrael's bubble.

A new voice joined our conversation. 'What an absolutely splendid little specimen, my dears!' It was Raphael.

'It's only a drop of water,' Maphrael muttered.

'Not at all, Maphrael, my dear friend,' the Archangel enthused. 'It has tiny little creatures in it. Where did you get it from?'

'Hushael gave it to me,' I said.

'Well that will be why, my old thing,' Raphael glowed. 'The tinier and humbler the creature, the more Hushael is fascinated by it.'

All five of us peered intently at the water.

'Hushael hasn't given you a worthless blob of water, Oriel,' Raphael continued. 'He has given you a carefully selected collection of wonderful little creatures.' He leaned over my desk to examine the droplet at closer quarters. 'Look at the little darlings!' he exclaimed. 'They're bright red.'

At that last word, the nature of the silence in my office changed instantly. The despondent gloom vanished and was replaced by expectant hope. Jeshaphael delicately removed one of the small red creatures and took it away for closer inspection. Everyone else looked at Raphael, still wearing an enthralled smile.

'What is it?' he asked, when he realised that three sets of Angel eyes were fixed on him.

'How did *you* know that?' Archangel Gabriel demanded. The nature of Raphael's smile changed. Gabriel's question was a fair one. Raphael's dealings with planet Earth – indeed with the Universe as a whole – are minimal.

'I asked our Boss where you were, my dear,' he said to Gabriel. 'He told me you were struggling to notice some delightfully miniature plants. He *did* say what they are called . . .'

'Algae,' Jeshaphael proclaimed, striding into the room with a small container filled with red liquid. 'They are a form of aquatic, single-celled plant which plays an important part in the river's ecosystem. Their population can explode in certain circumstances. When that occurs, the algae poison the water with byproducts from their metabolism.'

'Did you understand a word of what you just said?' Maphrael enquired rudely.

'Of course.'

'So all we have to do,' I intervened quickly, 'is to replicate the necessary environmental factors and these little fellows . . .'

'Plants,' Jeshaphael corrected me.

'. . . plants,' I continued, '. . . will reproduce dramatically, turn the Nile red, poison the fish and make the water undrinkable.'

'All that is true,' Jeshaphael said purposefully, 'but you will not have turned the water of the River Nile into blood. And that is what our Boss *specifically* said.'

Maphrael and I both turned to Gabriel in the hope that he might help by defining our Boss's expectations.

'I must be going,' he excused himself, and went, taking Raphael with him. Just the three of us were left.

'Our Boss instructed us to turn the river into blood,' Jeshaphael asserted. 'That, therefore, is what we must do.'

'Our Boss did not instruct us to turn the river into blood,' Maphrael responded. 'He informed Moses that the river would be turned into blood and he asked us to arrange the effect. What matters is that the river *appears* to be blood, not that it *is* blood.' He paused briefly. 'Face it, Jesh, you told us how many different kinds of blood there are. Our Boss did not specify a particular type because it does not matter.'

'My name is Jeshaphael,' the Angel replied icily.

'Angels!' I said, stopping the squabble. 'Our Boss clearly stated that the river water would be turned to blood. He also affirmed the usefulness of the droplet that Hushael gave me, and inspired Raphael to look at the algae. This must, at least, be part of our solution. Jeshaphael, tell us what we have to do to provide the correct conditions for the algae to grow.'

* * *

While Jeshaphael and Maphrael attempted to cultivate billions of the tiny red algae, I visited our Boss.

'I don't understand,' I said. 'You have instructed us to make blood and encouraged us to grow algae.'

'That, Oriel,' he said, 'is because I never ask you to do something that you cannot do.'

'So you want us to infest the river with algae?'

'Yes.'

'And the Egyptians will see the red algae and think it is blood?'
'No.'
'I don't understand.'
He smiled.

* * *

When we returned to Earth, Maphrael and Jeshaphael went directly to the river, accompanied by a small army of delivery Angels carrying the algae which Jeshaphael had grown under optimal conditions in Heaven. I accompanied Moses and Aaron on their morning walk to the king's bathing place – the very place where the infant Moses had been discovered among the bulrushes. We found Rameses in the water, playing with his duck, while numerous officials watched from the bank, laughing obediently at their ruler's antics.

'Cousin,' he chimed, 'have you come to join me? This bathing stage is reserved for the royal family, but you qualify.' Then he dropped his cheerful tone of voice and added, 'Or does this place remind you that you do not really belong here?'

'Le . . . le . . . le . . . let my People go,' Moses stuttered. Aaron glared at him.

'First show me some more of your god's magic,' Rameses insisted, climbing out of the river.

Moses handed his staff to Aaron with an apologetic grimace and then removed his long Midianite cloak. Retrieving the staff, he strode out into the river, guided by Maphrael, who knew the precise location of every container of cultured red algae. Moses took hold of the lower end of the staff and whacked it down onto the water with full force. One of the containers burst, and the tiny red plants quickly spread across the river. Rameses watched with untroubled interest and sent an official to fetch his sorcerers. But, while Pharoah waited, the water of the great river began to turn a thick, dark red. It was far more blood-like than I had expected.

Hushael was following developments carefully.

'What's happening?' I asked him.

'Our Boss has done something to the algae,' he explained.

'What?'

He didn't reply. We both stared in silent wonder as the faint lifelight of the primitive plants grew richer, brighter and deeper. The algae themselves were being transformed; the river was indeed flowing with blood. By the time the sorcerers arrived, there were already dead fish floating on the surface of the river and, judging by the reaction of the humans, the smell had grown from noticeable to unpleasant.

Rameses demanded that the sorcerers also turn some water into blood. They had to dig into the river bank to find places where the water was still clear. That achieved, and with the help of their Opposition spirits, the magi each managed to redden some clear water without too obviously using dyes or powders. As before, none of them managed to produce something that was actually *alive*.

'*Moses tries hard but is not as capable as his fellow pupils*,' Rameses said tauntingly, accompanied by the laughter of his officials. 'Sound familiar, cousin?'

The king's chubby face glowed with self-satisfaction. Moses experienced a stab of emotional pain at the unwelcome return of childhood memories. His tongue lay paralysed inside his mouth. He turned and walked away, leaving Aaron to deliver the rest of my Boss's message to the king.

A week later

The people of Thebes have had a miserable week. Their river is poisoned. Wherever they fetch or store water, it has become infected by the red algae. And wherever the algae grow, some of the tiny plants transform into smooth dimpled cells of living blood. Every day they have been forced to dig new wells – but it's never long before these, too, become unusable.

The Egyptians are thirsty and exhausted, but their king – who does not want for clean water, thanks to the industry of his servants – is not inclined to concede. On the contrary, he is furious at Moses and determined to get revenge. The simplest path to that revenge is to absolutely refuse Moses' request.

Jeshaphael has been carefully monitoring Pharaoh's reactions and reporting to me.

'What next?' Maphrael asked as we pondered the discouraging news.

'I have no idea,' I confessed, 'but our Boss implied that this could go on for some time.'

'What about the ordinary Egyptians?' Maphrael exclaimed. 'Do they have to suffer for their leader's stubbornness?'

A good question. I returned to Heaven and put it to my Boss.

'Human leadership offers many privileges, Oriel,' he informed me. 'It also demands many responsibilities. A wise and selfless ruler is a blessing to his people; a selfish one is a curse.'

'How long will the water be poisoned?' I asked.

'Not long,' my Boss replied. 'The algae is returning to its usual state and the water is teeming with tadpoles which are feasting on it as well as enjoying the complete absence of the fish that usually eat them.'

'Oh! Good!' I said.

'No,' the Creator of All corrected me, 'not for Rameses. Tadpoles develop very quickly when there is abundant food. Any day now, they will become froglets and will leave the water in search of frog food.'

I really did not have any idea what a tadpole or a frog was, so I said nothing.

My Boss spoke again. 'Moses needs to warn Rameses.'

'I'll see to it.'

Before returning to Earth, I picked up some information about these creatures to show my colleagues. We all took an instant dislike to them, except – of course – Hushael, who carefully pored over every minute detail of the amphibious reptiles and then wandered down to the river to study the real thing. I left Jeshaphael and Maphrael to contemplate an invasion of these cold and watery hunters and delivered my Boss's instructions to Moses.

When Moses arrived, Rameses was dealing with a delegation of his wives who were demanding a larger water ration for their children. Nefertiry, the chief wife, was courageously outspoken.

'I do not believe that you would consider an old feud with that tramp Moses to be more important than your own children's welfare.'

She had more to say but her husband noticed the arrival of the selfsame tramp and held up his hand, demanding silence. Nefertiry turned, saw Moses and stomped off. The other wives followed. Rameses gave a frustrated sigh and Aaron capitalised on the moment.

'Our God demands that you let his People go,' he stated.

The king looked wearily at Moses. 'Nag, nag, nag,' he part said and part sang. 'You would make a good wife, Moses.'

'If you refuse to let them go,' Aaron continued, 'the God of the Hebrews will inundate your country with frogs.'

'Frogs,' the king repeated, unimpressed. 'Is that the best you can do?' He stared, tired, at Moses for a few seconds. Then, with forced frivolity, he sat up straight, threw out his arms and shouted, 'Well, bring on the frogs!'

Moses tried to respond. 'W . . . w . . . w . . .'

'We will,' Aaron said firmly.

The two Israelites strode towards the river, closely followed by three representatives of Pharaoh's personal bodyguard. Aaron, smarting because Rameses had not looked at him at any stage, rounded on Moses for interfering yet again. I fetched Jeshaphael and Maphrael.

'Frog time,' I announced.

I was not surprised to find Hushael bent low over the river. Aaron held his brother's staff above the smooth liquid. Nothing happened. The guards chattered with mild amusement. Aaron looked enquiringly at Moses, who told him to be patient. Still nothing happened.

'It looks as though we are supposed to be doing something,' I suggested to my team.

'I am not going any nearer to that water,' Maphrael stated categorically.

I understood exactly how he felt, but could not tolerate even a hint of rebellion.

'You will if I order you to,' I insisted.

'I'll do it,' Hushael offered in little more than a faint mumble. He lowered himself so that his Angelic form was just touching the water.

'No further than that, Hushael,' I said hurriedly. 'It's dangerous.'

I have no idea what he did, but one small watery creature hopped from the river onto the bank. I would not have noticed it but for the entertained pointing of the guards. Then another came, followed by another. Soon there was a modest army of the slimy animals. One jumped onto a guard's foot and he was quick to brush it off but, while he was seeing to that foot, three more frogs clambered up onto his other. Next moment, all three guards were hopping and yelping, trying in vain to stamp out the amphibious advance.

Moses and Aaron walked along the bank towards a series of irrigation canals. Moses allowed Aaron to carry his staff all day. Every time Aaron held it over some water, Hushael did his stuff. By early evening every home in the area was inundated by the miniature reptiles.

<hr/>

One orbit of Earth's Moon later

The following morning, Rameses summoned Moses and Aaron to meet him in the palace garden. They arrived to find the court sorcerers already assembled with their ragtag band of Opposition spirits. Those were not the only spirits present. Lucifer, the leader of the Opposition, had joined Osiris. He had forced a rebel Cherub to lay across the surface of Pharaoh's duck pond. The tortured spirit was howling in distress as the water stung his spiritual form, but Lucifer demanded that he remain there.

Rameses arrived, clutching his duck to his chest. The hapless bird obviously sensed the menace hanging over its pond and was flapping frantically. The king eventually released the creature and it waddled quickly away.

'Maybe the Israelites should try something similar,' Maphrael whispered to me.

'What do you mean,' I asked.

'The duck caused Rameses so much trouble that he let it go,' Maphrael explained.

'Look into it,' I whispered in return. 'But I only want *suggestions*, Maphrael. Any action will need our Boss's approval.'

Rameses addressed his guests, explaining that he had instructed the Egyptian sorcerers to perform the same magic that Moses claimed to be the work of his God. The Egyptian magi stood around the edge of the pond, holding each other's hands in a ring. They began to chant – and the words they chanted chilled my being. What these foolish men believed to be an ancient incantation was, in fact, a hymn of praise to Lucifer. The leader of the Opposition stood in the middle of the magic circle with an ugly smile across his distorted face. He was loving it! It was for this that he first abandoned my Boss's service. He didn't want to be a servant to his Creator; he wanted to be a master.

When Lucifer had had his fill of the sorcerers' worship, he pulled the saturated Cherub from the pond, throwing him aside. Immediately, an assortment of frogs emerged from the water.

These were bigger than last week's batch. Rameses was trium-phant and rewarded his magi for their excellent work.

'Those are our frogs,' Maphrael claimed angrily.

Lucifer leered at him.

'They are our Boss's frogs,' Jeshaphael stated precisely, simul-taneously deflating both Maphrael and Lucifer.

'Maphrael,' I said. 'Make sure that as many of those frogs as possible plague Rameses at every moment of his day.'

* * *

In these following weeks, more and more froglets have emerged from Egypt's waterways. Having set their webbed feet on dry land, they have grown rapidly. Each day Maphrael has herded a battalion of the jumpy beings into the king's throne room and even onto the throne. Rameses has been obliged to detail two slaves to the spe-cific task of picking frogs off his person. Each night, Maphrael has directed his newly-acquired frogherding skills towards Pharaoh's bed. Last week, much to Maphrael's delight, Nefertiry informed the monarch that none of the royal wives were prepared to sleep with their husband again until he had resolved the frog problem. Rameses commissioned his magicians to ward off the frogs – but the Opposition spirits refused to touch the watery beasts. The magi tried appealing directly to Lucifer. They stood around their king's bed and chanted Lucifer's praise, but Rameses dismissed them shortly after midnight, yelling, 'I would rather listen to the frogs' chorus! Go away and plague someone else.'

Yesterday, the king's resolve broke. Tired, lonely and irritated, he called for Moses.

'Pray to your god,' he pleaded. 'Get him to take away these cursed creatures.'

Moses looked at his cousin and said nothing; neither did Aaron. Rameses knew exactly what Moses was waiting for and reluctantly made his concession.

'When your god has removed every frog from the land of Egypt, I will let your people go to offer sacrifices in the desert.'

Maphrael and I leapt into the air and cheered loudly. Hushael allowed himself a satisfied smile. Jeshaphael gave a barely percepti-ble nod. Moses' face remained stern. He whispered his reply to Aaron. Aaron spoke out. 'We leave you the honour, your majesty, of naming the specific time when you wish the frogs to be removed.'

'What's he doing?' I asked my colleagues.

'Showing off?' Maphrael suggested.

'You shouldn't judge others by your own standards, Maphrael,' Jeshaphael reprimanded.

When Moses and Aaron returned to their lodgings, Jeshaphael, Maphrael and I went home to Heaven. I invited my Archangel colleagues to my office for a modest celebration. Each of us retold the story in our own way and Raphael treated us to a rendition of his Moses song. It was a rare treat to have the Leader of Heaven's Worship sing a solo. His voice is exquisite. Our Boss appeared in the doorway to enjoy the performance, and when it had been suitably appreciated, he asked me, 'What are you doing, Oriel?'

'We're celebrating,' I explained, suddenly aware that our behaviour might have been inappropriate. 'Rameses has agreed to let your people go.'

'I know,' our Boss said softly. 'But is it wise to celebrate until the task has been completed?' With that he left.

Our celebrations were severely deflated. The first to speak was Archangel Michael.

'What have you *not* done?' he asked.

Jeshaphael, Maphrael and I were thoughtful. Eventually I realised what we had left undone.

'We have to kill off the frogs,' I announced.

There was a revolted silence.

'How many are there?' Gabriel enquired.

'Approximately 32,274,000,' Jeshaphael told us.

'Have you really counted them?' Maphrael exclaimed in disbelief.

'I said *approximately*.'

None of us relished the prospect of murdering millions of frogs so we agreed to work together to share the distasteful task. Michael volunteered a squadron of his troops. We descended to Earth as the light of the Sun first reached the region of Egypt. We needed to synchronise our slaughter with the time set by Pharaoh for Moses to pray. I looked for Hushael and found him just where I expected – near the river, studying the fine detail of our Boss's Creation.

'What have you found?' I asked.

'It's dead,' he said, not exactly answering my question.

'What is?'

'This frog.'

I saw that the Angel was studying two different creatures: a dead frog and a minuscule thing with six tiny legs and transparent wings. I waited for Hushael to enlighten me in his own time. He did.

'It has poisoned itself,' Hushael finally informed me. 'All the while it lived in the water,' he explained, 'it only ate the red algae. After it came onto the land, it only ate insects like this. And this insect *also* spent its larval phase in the water and *also* fed exclusively on the algae.'

The Angel looked mournfully at the dead frog and released the insect. I was not enormously interested in Hushael's nature lesson but tried to take in as much as I could.

'What does that mean for us?' I asked.

'The frogs will die.'

'Good,' I said cheerily. Then I remembered all the Angels who were waiting for my order to kill thirty two million frogs. 'Well,' I modified my response, 'not quite so good.' Hushael was not interested in my problems. He recaptured the same insect and considered it closely.

'Oh, no!' I suddenly exclaimed. 'Not good at all.'

I raced back to my Angelic Death squad.

'You know our Boss said that we had not finished our job?' Those in the know nodded. 'I am sorry to have to tell you that the unfinished business is not the frogs.'

'What is it then?' demanded an irritated Michael.

Michael frightens even me when he is angry.

'I don't know,' I said.

Back in Heaven

'I expect you are greatly relieved to be excused from your killing spree, Oriel,' my Boss said as I entered his room. I smiled rather coyly. 'It is not good for Angels to kill their fellow creatures,' he continued, and then added, 'though there are occasions when it is necessary.'

I reluctantly considered the idea of being commanded to destroy more important creatures than frogs, then I turned my mind to more immediate matters.

'Master,' I asked, 'if Pharaoh has agreed to release your people and the frogs have poisoned themselves, what part of our task is not completed?'

'Rameses is not ready to give way to Moses. He is toying with him. You must understand, Oriel, that in all of Rameses' short life, no one has ever stood against him and won – not even his father. He will not allow Moses to defeat him so easily.'

'What will you do next?' I asked.

'Another plague.'

'What of?'

'Gnats.'

'Gnats?' I had never heard of such creatures.

'Hushael introduced you to one this morning. Did you like it?' A beaming smile spread over my Boss's face. I have seen a similar smile when he has met with the whole of Angeldom in the Great Gathering Place of Angels.

Distracted by happy memories of Angelic gatherings, I was not sure what he had asked me. 'I'm sorry,' I mumbled, 'I was . . .'

'Did you like the gnat, Oriel?'

'I . . . er . . . it was very small.'

I was puzzled to discover that my Boss seemed to gain as much pleasure from one gnat as he did from meeting the entire host of loyal Angels.

I changed the subject: 'Won't the gnats die of poisoning just like the frogs did?'

'No,' my Boss informed me. 'Their food does not come from the river.'

'What do gnats feed on?' I enquired.

'Blood.'

I find the whole idea of eating other animals very distasteful, but there is something especially revolting about one creature consuming another's blood.

'I will go and organise some gnats for you,' I told my Boss.

'This time, Oriel,' he said gently, 'talk to Hushael first.' Then he added, 'His appointment as Moses' guardian was not an accident, you know.'

'But I appointed Hushael in the misguided belief that Moses would . . .'

My words faded into silence before my Boss's beaming smile.

* * *

I headed for Earth and asked Hushael what we would need to do to arrange a plague of gnats. He was lost in thought for three Earth days before he replied. He barely moved from the river bank where he intently watched the diminutive insects.

While Hushael was thinking about gnats, the Egyptians were still preoccupied with frogs – dead frogs. They had dead frogs in their beds, in their ovens and in their cooking pots. Every day there were more lifeless amphibians to clear away. The frogs were gathered into great stinking heaps – too watery to burn, to big to bury. Ordinary Egyptians wondered to themselves whether it had been better when the animals were alive. But that had been awful too.

Rameses' nose was not troubled by the mounds of rancid frogs. He had slaves to sweep away the carcasses and to waft sweet-smelling incense around his palace. He put on a special party for his many children to celebrate the end of the plague. He would not have to release his Israelite brick-makers.

Eventually, Jeshaphael informed me that Hushael had found the answer to my question. As I approached the river bank, Hushael turned to me, looked straight into my eyes and said, 'Nothing.'

I stared at Moses' guardian, startled and perplexed. 'What exactly was the question?' I asked.

Hushael did not answer. With a mildly exasperated look, he turned away from me and began to sing quietly to Moses, who was sliding back into depression since hearing of Pharaoh's change of mind.

With help from Maphrael and Jeshaphael, I worked out the precise question that I had asked Hushael, to which he had replied, 'Nothing.' I had asked him what we needed to do to arrange a plague of gnats. Later we succeeded in getting him to explain that the bloodsucking insects had been emerging from the river in plague proportions for some while, only to be eaten by the frogs. However, since the demise of the frogs, the glut of gnats had become apparent.

With the gnat supply assured, I returned to Heaven to collect our next set of instructions. My Boss asked me to send Hushael to see him.

Two days later

Hushael was terrified by the prospect of a face-to-face meeting with his Creator. 'I won't know what to say,' he kept repeating.

Maphrael and Jeshaphael each gave the anxious Angel completely conflicting advice, which only frightened him even more.

'Be yourself,' I urged Hushael as I sent him Heavenwards. 'That is how our Boss has made you.'

I took the opportunity of Hushael's absence to conduct a thorough review of the state of Moses' mind. I compared it with Aaron's. Where Aaron's thoughts are ordered and structured, Moses' are a mess. Aaron sets time aside every day to speak with our Boss: in the morning, at midday and before he goes to sleep. Moses' practice of prayer is no more than occasional haphazard mumblings, bumblings and grumblings. I arranged with Aaron's guardian, Ahoshal, that Aaron would invite his brother to join him in his regular prayers.

I tried to understand the reasons for Moses' mental chaos. He grew up within the strict protocols of the Egyptian royal household, but it seems that this ancient regime required obedience but little self-discipline. When Moses left Egypt, all mental splints were lost. Only the practical love of Zipporah has kept him from drowning in the stormy ocean of his inner chaos. As I observed the fluctuating tides and swells within Moses' mind, I came to a simple conclusion: he needs his wife. I discussed this with my colleagues and we resolved that we must get him back to Goshen.

While we waited for Hushael's return, I was confined to Moses and Aaron's lodgings, where Moses did little more than sleep and stare blankly out of the window. I sent Maphrael to keep a careful eye on the pharaoh, and asked Jeshaphael to compile a detailed report about Opposition activities in and around Egypt. Hushael's absence was much longer than I would have expected for an interview with my Boss.

It was Ahoshal who first located Hushael.

'He is behind the palace with his face inside a vast pile of dead frogs,' Aaron's guardian informed me. 'I asked him what he was doing but he did not reply. I think he has been there for some while.'

I summoned Jeshaphael and Maphrael, and we went to investigate.

'You probably cannot see them,' Hushael told us, 'but there are some faint life forms feeding on the corpses of these frogs.'

'You're quite right,' Maphrael muttered. 'We can't see them.'

'What are these things,' Jeshaphael enquired, 'that are even faint to you?'

'They are not yet fully formed,' Hushael began to explain. Then he stopped and looked intently at Earth's Sun as it appeared to fall towards the horizon. 'I must go and fetch Moses,' he announced.

I tried to extract from Hushael some information about his discussion with our Boss but, as I looked into his Angelic mind, he was self-consciously repeating a set of instructions that made little sense to me. Hushael led Moses and Aaron towards the open ground between Rameses' palace and the river, repeatedly glancing at the Sun as he went. At Hushael's bidding, Moses stopped some way from the palace gates and sent Aaron inside to fetch Pharaoh. Rameses strode out impatiently.

'The frogs may have gone, Moses,' the king declared, 'but the Israelites are going nowhere. They have responded magnificently to their new working conditions. They meet their quotas every day and the slaves who used to gather the straw for them are now directly employed in the building work.'

Moses did not attempt to say a word.

'You have done me a favour, cousin,' Rameses beamed. 'I should thank you.'

Moses scowled darkly and handed his staff to Aaron. The Sun had now disappeared around the curvature of Earth. Aaron grasped the sturdy stick in both hands and whacked it hard on the ground with a sideways motion. He repeated this action several times, stirring up a large cloud of dust. Rameses shouted to him to stop being so stupid, but Aaron continued to whip up the dust. Hushael, meanwhile, headed for the river.

'What's he up to now?' Maphrael demanded.

'Have you noticed,' Jeshaphael said quietly, 'that Hushael has not given either of them a single word to say?'

'Typical!' snorted Maphrael.

'He's bringing the gnats,' I announced.

Hushael was driving a vast swarm of the tiny insects in the direction of Aaron's dust cloud. When he rejoined the humans, Aaron stopped beating the ground and, as the dirt settled back in its place – apart from a thin covering all over Pharaoh's robes – it left in the air a hovering mist of small, flying insects which quickly settled themselves on the exposed skin of the humans to extract a meal of fresh blood. The king and his attendants began to slap themselves frantically and Moses, in true Hushael style, walked away without saying a single word. Rameses ran back to his palace but was unable to outpace the bloodsucking swarm. Everyone, from Queen Nefertiry to the palace cats, was jumping around in a vain attempt to rid themselves of the gnats. Maphrael laughed, Jeshaphael watched carefully, and Hushael silently wandered back to his heap of dead frogs.

The next day

During the night I watched over Moses to cover for Hushael's continued absence. Jeshaphael and Maphrael pestered me about their absent colleague.

'I just don't believe Hushael is able to cope with the complexity of life on Earth,' Jeshaphael informed me. 'He has become obsessive and that is worrying in any creature. It was evident today that Moses is being affected by his guardian's malaise. I think you should replace him, Oriel.'

I turned to Maphrael, certain that he would also have an opinion on the matter.

'He's a nutter!'

I did not reply and my silence prompted Maphrael to add, 'Don't you go all silent on us too, Ori.'

'My name, Maphrael, is Oriel,' I replied testily.

'And I, Oriel, am called Maff.'

Jeshaphael joined in. 'Your name, Angel, is given to you by your Creator and . . .'

'Thank you, Jeshaphael,' I said firmly, looking sternly at both Angels. 'If your concern is genuinely for Hushael, then you must remember that our Boss is happy to trust this work to him. But if – as I suspect – your concern is simply that a junior Angel has been given a task that you thought to be your own, then be a little more gracious.'

There was a satisfying silence that was ended by Maphrael muttering, 'He's still a nutter.'

* * *

Later in the morning, I sent Maphrael to check on Hushael.

'How is he?' I asked when he returned.

'Still face down in a pile of dead frogs.'

'And the gnats?'

71

'Everywhere . . . except that, when Rameses called his sorcerers to the palace garden and commanded them to turn dirt into gnats, they couldn't. Lucifer was furious, even more so when the oldest of the old tricksters announced solemnly, "This is the work of God!"'

I asked Maphrael to watch over Moses and visited the Palace to speak with Egypt's Seraph, Shlyphantel. The news was not encouraging. Rameses is determined to complete the building of his new cities quickly so he can use them as a base for a military attack on Canaan. With the Israelite slaves producing good quality bricks more efficiently than ever before, he has no intention of letting them go, gnats or no gnats.

Next I visited the heap of rotting frog carcasses behind the palace to catch up on the progress of Hushael's work. With immense concentration I managed to see what he was looking at: a motionless smudge of life, several times larger than a gnat.

'What is it?' I asked.

He replied slowly, 'What matters is what it *will* be.'

'And what *will* it be?' I continued, struggling to be interested in such a minor life form.

'A fly.'

A few days later

Last night, Hushael walked into Moses' room while the man was lying in a sleepless stupor on his bed. Hushael said to me, 'The flies will be ready in two days. Please inform Gabriel.' Before I could say a word, he had gone.

I passed on the message and Heaven's Chief Messenger arrived with Moses' next set of instructions. I listened impatiently while Gabriel updated me on the idle gossip of Heaven.

When he had finished, I asked, 'And now, could you kindly tell me what is going on here in Egypt? I have been stuck in this place looking after Moses while Hushael has been burrowing into a mountain of rotting frog flesh.'

At that moment, Maphrael arrived. Gabriel greeted him cheerfully, 'Good to see you, Maff.'

Maphrael cast me a slightly smug look before saying to Gabriel, 'Is something going to happen at last?'

'That's why I'm here.'

'So what's happening with the dead frogs? We can't get Hushi away from them.'

'It's really very simple,' Gabriel claimed. 'Flies lay their eggs on dead animals so that the grubs can feed on the rotting flesh.'

Maphrael and I looked at each other with an expression of shared disgust.

'The more plentiful the supply of rotting meat, the more grubs will mature into adult flies.'

'And millions of dead frogs will produce billions of flies?' Maphrael asked.

'Exactly,' Gabriel affirmed. 'And, as a bonus, they will dispose of the frog carcasses in the process.'

I looked at my Archangel colleague suspiciously. 'How do you know all this?' I asked.

He evaded my question.

'If you will excuse me, I have a message to deliver.'

Moses was somewhere between sleep and wakefulness, murmuring incoherently to our Boss, venting his frustration at the apparent failure of his mission.

'It's always good to catch them praying,' Gabriel whispered.

'You call that prayer?' I replied.

'A great deal of human communication is incomprehensible,' Gabriel announced. 'Have you ever watched them kissing?'

Gabriel delivered his message directly into Moses' turbulent mind. Immediately, Moses sat upright and went to wake up his older brother. Gabriel bade us farewell. The two humans dressed and set off for Pharaoh's palace, Moses briefing Aaron as they went. There seems to be an uneasy truce between the brothers. Moses has been more careful to keep his mouth shut in public and Aaron is more accepting of his subserviant role.

They intercepted Rameses as he was making his way to the river to soothe his gnat-agitated skin in the cool water. The king attempted to ignore them but Aaron and Moses paced along beside him, delivering their message whether he wanted to hear it or not.

Aaron said clearly, 'This is what our Lord says: *Let my People go, so they can worship me. If you do not, I will send swarms of flies.*'

Rameses said nothing as he strode on towards the river. Moses spoke quietly to Aaron who then drew close to the king to deliver the second part of the message.

'It will be very different where the Israelites live. There will be no swarms there. Then you will see who is the true God in Egypt.'

This last comment goaded Rameses who has been brought up to believe that he himself is descended from the gods.

'When will this happen?' he snapped, looking – as he always did – at Moses, not Aaron.

Moses stopped walking, forcing Rameses to do the same. When the whole entourage ground to a halt, Moses looked at the king and stuttered, 'T . . . tomorrow.'

Four days after

When I heard that Goshen would be spared the next plague, I decided it was time to get Moses back to his wife – at least for a while. He responded readily to the suggestion and within a human hour we were all making our way steadily northwards along the course of the River Nile. Half way through the fourth day, two chariots from Pharaoh's household caught up with us and demanded that Moses and Aaron return to Thebes immediately because the king had a deal to offer them. While the two Hebrews sped back towards the city of the pharaohs, I cautioned Moses that he should not be too hopeful about this development. My warning was not necessary. Moses was so angry at being kept away from his family that he was not inclined to accept anything from Rameses other than complete freedom for the whole Israelite People.

Pharaoh's palace was humming like a giant bee hive when Moses and Aaron swept through its gates early the next morning. There were thick swarms of flies in every part of the building and servants were running in all directions, wafting incense and smashing the red-eyed insects against whatever they happened to settle on. The king's residence was spattered with a crunchy black carpet of dead flies. However, for every fly that died, at least two more emerged, fresh and full of energy, from the declining piles of frog meat behind the palace.

'Go and do your sacrifices,' Rameses commanded Moses. 'But you must do them here in Egypt.'

Moses looked sternly at his powerful cousin.

'No d . . . deal,' he spluttered.

Aaron took over. 'We must take a three-day journey into the desert. That is what our God has commanded.'

All the while, black flies were humming and buzzing around Pharaoh and his attendants. There were flies crawling in his hair and face, among his clothes, everywhere. Servants pathetically tried to whisk them away, but their efforts were pointless, and they, too, had their own swarms to deal with. Rameses was only focusing on the flies that crawled into his eyes, nose and mouth. Beyond the many-pillared audience hall, the palace was ringing with the shouts of angry people and the wails of tired children.

All the while, Shlyphantel was hardening Rameses' resolve against Moses – as he had been ordered to do – but that resolve was buckling under the stress of this third invasion.

'I *will* let you go,' Rameses conceded, 'but only on condition that you do not go far; *one* day's journey – no more. After that, the Israelites must return to the brickworks. Now pray to your god for me.'

Moses was not convinced. 'I will p . . . pray for you,' he said. 'The f . . . f . . . flies will be gone tomorrow.' He looked straight into the king's eyes, his anger against Rameses stronger than it has ever been.

'D . . . don't . . .' He struggled to get the word out and spat in Pharaoh's face as he did.

'D . . . don't change your mind.' He turned his back on the defeated monarch and walked out, followed by his aggravated older brother. When they reached the clear air and sunlight beyond the palace gate, Moses fell on his face in the dust, begging my Boss to end the suffering of Egypt. When his prayer had been poured out, the former prince and shepherd hauled himself to his feet and set off once again along the river, towards the place where his wife and children are caught up in the suffering of Israel.

Three days on

That night a powerful wind swept into Egypt from the Great Desert to the west. Hushael explained that this would quickly drive away the last of the flies. The following day, the two brothers were once again overtaken by Egyptian chariots. The news was no less than Moses expected: *Pharaoh has reconsidered the matter.*

Being advised that there is no way of guaranteeing that the Hebrew slaves will return to their duties once their festival is over, for the good of all Egypt, they are denied leave to stop their work even for one day.

Moses glanced south at the dust thrown up by the retreating chariots, then he looked longingly to the north, anxious for the welfare of his family. He uttered a blunt prayer: 'Now what?'

Maphrael, Jeshaphael, Ahoshal and I all looked towards Hushael.

'What now?' I asked.

'There is one more plague,' the quiet Angel answered.

'What will it be?' I asked.

'Disease,' Hushael replied with his usual brevity.

'Do we have to do anything?' Maphrael asked.

'The gnats have already done the work.'

We looked at Hushael, waiting for him to explain. For once he did: 'The livestock in Egypt have been bitten so many times by so many gnats that all the blood-borne diseases that were present in the herds and flocks have been spread to every single animal. The incubation period for the first diseases ends the day after tomorrow.'

'Will they die?' Jeshaphael enquired.

'They will.'

'What about the humans?' I asked.

'They will not get the diseases.'

'How come?' Maphrael pressed.

Hushael did not reply. I looked into his thoughts; he didn't know how. I turned to Moses, who was staring out across the river. He seemed resigned to his circumstances. Then I realised something remarkable: he had overheard our conversation. Somehow, in the confusion of his mind, Moses had picked up the basic details of what Hushael said.

'Come on,' he said to Aaron, 'back to Thebes.'

They re-entered the palace the following afternoon. Moses was no longer angry, but very tired. He walked in on a meeting of Pharaoh and his advisers. Without waiting for any indication that Rameses was listening, he nodded to Aaron to deliver his message: '*If you do not let my People go, our Lord will bring a plague on your livestock. Your horses, donkeys, camels, cattle, sheep and goats will all die. But none of this will happen among the Israelites.*'

Rameses studied Moses intensely, struggling to maintain his resolve. He feared that Moses had already gained the upper hand in their private duel, and he did not look forward to the reaction of his wives when they learned that their children would have to go without meat, and would have to travel by foot rather than horseback or chariot. But he also considered the urgency of his building programme and the need to comprehensively defeat the troublesome tribes of Canaan. He needed to regain the initiative. Shlyphantel whispered defiance into Rameses' mind.

'Come back here at this time tomorrow,' Rameses ordered Moses.

* * *

Moses and Aaron returned the next day, as commanded. They sat watching the palace for some time before they entered it. They knew that the plague had struck because no horses, camels or donkeys entered or left the palace grounds all afternoon. The communication network by which Rameses rules his nation has been crippled. During the morning, the brothers had walked through riverside pastures populated by dying cattle. They had witnessed the distress of ordinary Egyptians at this latest trauma. Moses' anger had risen. He knows the intimate mutual dependence between herdsman and herd. He understands the financial calamity that this will bring to Egyptian families. Fathers will not be able to feed their children. Mothers will not be able to clothe them. I expected him to blame my Boss, but he did not. He now knows the God of the Israelites as a God of purpose and action. This was Rameses' fault. The pharaoh has had every chance to back down, but he is still an arrogant fool. Moses' concern for his own family has also increased. Cruel slave drivers would be driven to greater cruelty. The disease-free flocks of the Israelites would be plundered by hungry Egyptians. He is all the more anxious to return to Goshen.

Rameses was sombre but defiant.

'Your god hit Egypt hard today, Moses.'

I was relieved to hear that the king now recognised who he was up against.

'You said this disease would not affect the flocks of the Hebrews.' Moses did not respond. 'I want proof, Moses. You will ride with my officials to Goshen to investigate your claim.'

'What w . . . w . . . will we ride?' Moses asked sullenly. 'Your horses are d . . . d . . .'

'The chariots will be pulled by slaves,' the king interrupted savagely. 'I would have used Hebrew slaves but I need them to make bricks. You will have to settle for Africans.'

Goshen

Moses and Aaron were hurried north to Goshen by Pharaoh's representatives. All along the busy Nile road fresh slaves were ordered from their different duties and forced to pull the five chariots for gruelling miles. For Aaron, it was a first ever experience of driving a chariot – not that it required much driving with a team of humans pulling it along. Moses is an experienced charioteer. He remembered his youth; he beat Rameses in more than one chariot race. As he stood behind his team of wretched slaves, his mood was brighter than it has been for a considerable while. He sensed he was beating Rameses once again. That made him feel good. More importantly, he was going to see his beloved Zipporah.

The Israelite slaves were startled to see two of their number rumble into the Hebrew settlement riding in Egyptian chariots. Abihu, one of the Israelite leaders, running out to see what was causing such excitement, quickly ushered Moses and Aaron into his shack.

There was much news to exchange. The Israelites had heard about the livestock plague that was afflicting the Egyptians. They had been forced to introduce a day and night watch on all their flocks to prevent desperate Egyptians from stealing their animals. Aaron was eager to learn how the Hebrew community could staff such an operation while meeting an increased brick quota and also gathering their own straw. The answer was that Hur has organised the entire community into a three-phase continuous shift pattern. Adults and older children each work for eight hours at the brickworks, immediately followed by eight hours of community work. (This includes: looking after Israelite children; security operations; well-being of the flocks and herds; cooking; gathering firewood; local straw collection.) The final eight-hour shift is for eating and sleeping. The brickworks are now in constant production. In addition to these responsibilities, every adult now spends one week in four travelling further afield to collect straw. These straw collection teams take with them all children who are old enough to travel but too young for brick making.

'No wonder the king is feeling pleased with himself,' Aaron observed. He explained to Abihu that Rameses was now refusing to let the Israelites go because he cannot afford to lose such efficient workers.

'We have forgotten about all that escape nonsense,' Abihu said, sharply.

A moment later, Hur, the chief representative of the Hebrew slaves, pushed open the door to the shack. He was clearly displeased at Moses' return. The very first thing he said was: 'I don't want to hear any talk about religious festivals. Do you understand?'

Aaron, abetted by numerous stuttering attempts from Moses, tried to tell the two men about the remarkable things that their God has done against the Egyptians. Hur admitted that he had heard of problems with frogs and insects, but refused to accept that they were anything other than 'natural disasters'.

'You have already set our production back for today by riding in here behind a team of slaves,' he warned. 'I must caution you both to say nothing whatsoever about miracles, gods or escapes for as long as you are here. If you do, we will be forced to deal with you ourselves. And,' he added menacingly to Moses, 'your charter of safe conduct from the king has no value *here*.'

Moses stared darkly at the man. Hur had not finished.

'We are working at absolute maximum capacity. We cannot afford for you two to go upsetting the Egyptians again.'

Moses was shocked and angry. He knew that the God of the Hebrews was working powerfully towards their freedom. He found it hard to believe that the Hebrews themselves could be so dull to what was being done for them. He didn't attempt to speak. He stood up and walked out of Abihu's shack, not stopping to hear Hur calling after him: 'I'm warning you. I'm warning you, Moses.'

Moses marched through the Hebrew settlement, pursued by Aaron. Aaron understood Hur's warning. The Israelite community could not cope with any more misfortune; they are quite capable of murdering their own saviour. As Aaron's slavery-ravaged body was catching up with the better maintained form of Moses, a young man came charging down the lane towards them, closely followed by a furious Angel guardian. On seeing me, the Angel's distress was doubled by a wave of intense shame.

'He's turned thief!' the despairing Angel called.

'Stop him!' I quickly instructed Moses.

Moses deftly flicked out the bottom of his shepherd's staff and caught the thief's ankles as he sped past. The young man tripped and tumbled across the dirt, scattering and destroying an armful of fresh eggs. At that moment, a woman came running round the corner, pursuing the thief and shouting after him. It was Zipporah.

Moses stretched out the curved end of his staff and hooked it round the neck of the egg-splattered villain as he was getting to his feet.

'What's your name?' he growled.

'Joshua, sir,' replied the captive.

'Moses!' Zipporah exclaimed and flung her arms around her husband's neck.

What followed was much hugging and crying through which Moses never lost his hold on the thief. He achieved this by twisting his staff so that its curved point pressed up into the man's chin.

'What should I do with this lost sheep?' he asked his wife when the initial greetings and explanations were completed.

'Let him go,' she said in a defeated tone. 'It happens most days. The eggs are already lost.'

Moses looked at his wife with concern. She had lost her spark and her fight. I had noticed the same. 'If it's all the same to you,' he mumbled to himself (I observed that he didn't stutter when talking to Zipporah), 'I will bring him home. I haven't finished with this young man yet.'

They set off, Moses maintaining his extended grip on the young thief's throat.

'It's exhaustion and hunger, Oriel,' Joshua's Angel guardian explained as we followed the little group further into the Hebrew settlement. 'Joshua has been doing double shifts in the clay pits for the past month to cover for his father who is sick. He had intended to ask Zipporah for the eggs but, when he found the shack empty and the eggs there in a basket, he stupidly grabbed them and ran. I tried to stop him, honestly I did, Oriel, but . . .'

'It's all right, Angel,' I soothed. 'You don't have to justify your human's behaviour to me.'

'Miriam's on straw collecting,' Zipporah explained, when they entered the shack. 'She'll be back in three days.' Then, without pausing, 'Moses, what are you doing with Joshua?' She had just noticed how her husband was dragging the young man along like a miscreant sheep.

'He's hungry,' Moses declared. 'He needs feeding.'

'You'll have to feed him yourself,' Zipporah said. 'I'm due at the brickworks.'

'*What!*' bellowed Moses. 'I thought you were helping with the children.'

'That all changed with the new quotas,' the educated Midianite woman replied. 'Everyone who is remotely capable is included in the shift system. I have to go.'

'But I've only just arrived,' Moses floundered. 'I haven't seen you for months. Stay!' Panic and desperation were rising through his body; his limbs felt numb. 'Can't you be a bit late?'

'If I'm at all late, we'll fall behind with the quota,' Zipporah explained dispassionately. 'The Egyptians have had all kinds of problems lately; they don't need much excuse to be utterly brutal.'

She was rushing round her small home, tidying things up as she talked.

'Ruth, one of my team, was beaten last month and died two days later. We've only just replaced her.' Zipporah was now at the door. 'If you are staying here, you will have to work. I'm sorry, my love – I'll be back tonight.'

She set off down the lane towards the brickworks. Moses ran out after her. 'Where are the boys?' he shouted.

'With Miriam.'

Moses watched his wife disappear, the harsh reality of his People's plight weighing him down like a bellyful of lead. He walked back into Miriam's shack with his head bowed and his soul aching. By the time he raised the wooden latch to the door, he had trebled his resolve to liberate his fellow Israelites.

'Right, Joshua,' he said firmly, pulling up a stool right in front of the exhausted young man. 'I need some answers.'

Moses interrogated Joshua for the rest of the day, extracting from him meticulous detail about the lives and routines of the Hebrew slaves, as well as the abuses and insults of their Egyptian masters. It soon became clear that petty crime is rife in the Israelite community. With so little time to spare and with so many homes predictably empty, it's all too easy for people to help themselves to their neighbours' food and possessions.

Meanwhile, I sent Jeshaphael and Maphrael to gather supporting information from various Angel guardians. I restricted my own researches to Moses himself. A change has come over him since arriving in Pithom. His spirit has grown brighter and stronger. This surprised me, considering his disastrous reunion with Zipporah. At one point, as he was firing yet another carefully worded question at Joshua, I realised again that he was not stuttering.

Aaron had ransacked his sister's home to provide himself, Moses and Joshua with a meagre meal, and was busy pressing the egg thief for information about the spiritual welfare of his people. Joshua's reply backed up what I was hearing from Jeshaphael: the Israelites have largely given up worshipping my Boss and many of them have taken to making offerings to the Egyptian deities. It appears that Hur has encouraged this practice in the hope that the Hebrews might ingratiate themselves with local Egyptian families.

'Who, among the Israelites,' Aaron asked through a mouthful of stale bread, 'is still faithful to the God of Abraham and Isaac?'

'There is a small group of us,' Joshua explained, 'who still talk about the old stories. But we have to be careful. Hur has banned all talk of worshipping God for fear of upsetting the Egyptians.'

'Who is the leader of this group?' Moses demanded.

'Jephunneh,' Joshua replied.

Moses glanced at Aaron to see if he knew the man. Aaron turned to Joshua.

'The toolmaker?'

'Yes. He has a workshop in the brickyard. He mends broken tools. Whenever someone snaps something, I offer to take it there. I say it's because I run faster. Jephunneh tells us the old stories while he does the repair. At the moment, he is telling me how Abraham found a suitable wife for . . .'

'Could he make weapons?' Moses interrupted.

'What?' Joshua asked, surprised by the question.

'Swords and spears,' Moses persisted. 'Does Jephunneh have the wherewithal to make them and conceal them?'

'I suppose so, but there's no way we could take on the Egyptians and . . .'

'God will deal with the Egyptians.'

There was a hint of Archangel Michael in Moses' sudden confidence.

'When we get out into the desert,' he whispered to Joshua, leaning forward on his stool, 'we will need to defend ourselves against the desert tribes. They won't sit and watch us take over their valuable grazing sites. We will need fighters, Joshua. Men who trust God.'

Joshua stared back blankly. Moses was trained in the brutal art of warfare as a child and had employed those skills on more than one occasion to defend his father-in-law's sheep. These memories flooded his mind as he studied the dumbfounded young man in front of him. Before today, Moses had understood his task to be about handling Rameses and little more. Now the realisation was growing on him that the Israelites are ill-prepared for freedom. They know nothing about the desert. Their herding skills were learned on the lush, well-watered plains of the Nile delta; their water is delivered every morning by other slaves; they are defended by the Egyptian soldiers who guard their settlement.

I sent Ahoshal to fetch Archangel Michael. If Moses is going to found an army, I want him to have the best advice that Heaven can provide. Inside his mind, Moses was already forming a training scheme for his new militia, but I did not want him to do that until Michael arrived. I directed his thoughts back to Jephunneh.

'I need to meet this toolmaker,' Moses declared. 'Can you take me to him?'

'He lives at the workshop,' Joshua explained. 'He has to be on call for all shifts. It would be safest for us to go there at midnight, during the shift change.'

'We will do that,' Moses resolved.

'The problem is, I need to be at work. If I am late, they'll *all* be beaten.'

Moses' mind flashed back to Zipporah's hurried departure.

'Is that usual?' he asked anxiously.

'Standard practice,' Joshua said flatly.

A fresh wave of horror swept over Moses. Regular beatings for all, his own wife and children in forced labour. These images tumbled around his mind. Suddenly I realised the cause of Moses' new confidence. Yesterday he had seen himself as no more than the unfortunate messenger, reluctantly doing a job for a god he knows next to nothing about. Today, his mission has become personal.

Aaron had been quietly clearing away after their meal. The talk of weapons and warfare had disturbed him. He wanted no part in such things and judged that Moses was allowing himself to get carried away by dim fantasies from his extraordinary childhood.

'I'll do Joshua's shift then,' he announced.

Moses stared at his brother with as much surprise as I did. Aaron's mind was quite serene. I studied it intently, searching for an explanation. It wasn't hard to find. My Boss had spoken into Aaron's thoughts. I had not heard it, neither had Hushael or Phaliel, Joshua's guardian, but the effect was unmistakable.

The next day

Later that Earth day my musings were interrupted by the sound of approaching laughter. Moses, Aaron and Joshua were all asleep. Three Archangels and two Angels burst into Miriam's shack, scattering the interior darkness.

'Oriel,' Gabriel announced cheerfully, bubbling with amusement, 'we decided to come and see you.' He and Maphrael exchanged conspiratorial glances.

'And what is so funny?' I asked, feeling uncomfortably an outsider to the mirth of Heaven.

'Raphael is stuck,' Gabriel explained.

I looked at the Leader of Heaven's Worship, who was quietly enduring the gibes of his colleagues.

'I am having a little trouble with my song,' he admitted. 'I had only succeeded in constructing half of a verse when Maphrael sought to assist me.'

I turned to Maphrael.

'All Raphy had was . . .' (Raphael gave a gracious bow at the abuse of his name): '*No more shall they in bondage toil. Let my People go.*'

Maphrael has a clear, rich singing voice, though no match for Raphael's.

He continued, 'And I suggested: *We'll whip that Pharaoh with his flail . . .*'

Maphrael's rendition was joined by the raucous singing of Gabriel and Ahoshal singing along with the repeated line: '*Let my People go*'.

I returned my attention to the long-patient Raphael.

'Human music is harder to master than I had expected,' he confessed graciously.

'You surprise me,' I said. 'I would have thought that you, of all Angels, would . . .'

'It would be akin to an eagle imitating a slug.'

84

All eyes turned immediately to Hushael.

'Thank you, Hushael.' Raphael gave another gentle bow. 'I am delighted to discover that *one* Angel understands these things.'

While the others looked enquiringly at Hushael, Phaliel roused Joshua from his slumbers. The young man woke Moses and Aaron, and they each ate a hunk of old bread. Then we set off towards the brickworks, leaving Aaron to make his own way to Joshua's team of brick moulders. Joshua took us to Jephunneh's workshop and I briefed Michael on my reasons for calling him.

Jephunneh is a brightly shining human whose spirit dines richly on the stories of Abraham and his family. He welcomed young Joshua and the stranger, and closed his door on the darkness of the night. He greeted Moses enthusiastically.

Joshua brought Jephunneh up to date on Moses' meetings with Rameses, and the connection between those encounters and the successive troubles experienced by the Egyptians. Jephunneh, who meets with a broad cross-section of both the Israelite and Egyptian communities in the course of his work, had already worked out some of these things for himself.

Meanwhile, Archangel Michael sifted though Moses' knowledge and experience of human warfare, highlighting those memories that will be most useful to the Israelites. When Joshua had finished explaining the background to Moses' visit, the prince-cum-shepherd-cum-prophet was prepared.

'The Egyptians do not only beat and abuse our People, Jephunneh,' Moses said, 'they also protect them.' The toolmaker listened attentively. 'Slaves cannot be trusted with weapons, so it is the Egyptians who defend your flocks and your women against raids by Midianite tribes. However, when we leave Egypt – and we *will* leave Egypt; God has promised it – we will have to protect ourselves. We will need battle axes and spears, and we will need men who know how to use them.'

'I have an Egyptian axe here,' Jephunneh offered. 'I repaired it the day it came in, but I told the Egyptians that it's not ready yet, if you understand me.' He produced the axe from under his workbench.

'We will need hundreds of them,' Moses said, holding out a hand for the weapon. 'And we will need lighter, shorter ones.'

Jephunneh observed, 'I'll be hard pushed to get hold of the materials.'

'The spears will also need to be short and light,' Moses insisted. 'They will be held in inexperienced hands.'

'Spears are not such a problem,' the toolmaker assured him. 'They don't need so much metal. But who's going to teach the young men to use these weapons?'

'Joshua.'

'Me?' Joshua was astounded. 'I'm more of a . . .'

'God will be with you, Joshua,' said Moses, repeating what he himself had only recently learned.

Just two thoughts dominated Joshua's mind: pain and death. The very thought of fighting in a real battle terrified him. I glanced at the Leader of Heaven's Armies.

'I'll sort him out,' he said gruffly.

'Shame, though,' said Gabriel reflectively. 'He would have made an excellent prophet.'

Joshua questioned Moses. 'How do you expect me to train an army while moulding bricks all day?'

'Pick your men carefully,' Moses instructed him. 'Choose young men you trust. Encourage them to break into fights with each other when they are working. If they fight with determination, the Egyptians will assume it's just a squabble and will leave you to it. Jephunneh, can you make them tools which will give them a feel for the length and weight of the real weapons?'

The toolmaker nodded thoughtfully. Moses returned his attention to Joshua.

'You may get a few painful bruises, but bruises make excellent teachers.' He was remembering his own first childhood bouts with wooden weapons.

'Won't we break a lot of tools if we fight with them?' Joshua asked.

'I hope so,' Moses replied with a rare smile. For the first time since leaving Sinai, he was on familiar ground. 'Then you will have to bring them here for Jephunneh to repair. You can try out the real weapons while you wait.'

'The Egyptians will get suspicious,' Joshua suggested.

Moses was tempted to become impatient with the young man's excuses, but I reminded him of his own poor performance when he was first recruited by my Boss. He stepped towards Jephunneh's workbench, taking a firm grip of the battle axe. He swept the axe effortlessly up through the air and then plunged it down onto a length of timber. The wood sprang up from the bench, sliced cleanly into two pieces, and clattered to the floor. The battle axe remained where it was, deeply embedded in the workbench.

Joshua and Jephunneh stared at Moses, startled. Archangel Michael grunted, 'Not bad.'

Moses surveyed his handiwork and muttered, 'It's funny how you never lose it. It's skill, you know, not strength.'

In the silence of admiration that followed, Raphael quietly sang the line of his song. *'No more shall they in bondage toil. Let my People go.'* At that point he stopped singing and said, 'I think I know what the next line should be.'

There was a knock at the door. Quickly Jephunneh took his position behind the bench and pretended to be working on the embedded axe. A clay-caked Israelite walked in, carrying a long shovel with a broken shaft. It was Jephunneh's son.

'What have you done now, Caleb?' the toolmaker asked.

'Eliab was grinding on about how there's no use looking to our own God for help,' the young man explained. 'He said we should look to the gods of the Egyptians. I took a swipe at him with my shovel.'

'So I see,' observed the toolmaker solemnly. He smiled. 'Caleb, do you know Joshua? He needs your help.'

*   *   *

My Archangel colleagues returned to Heaven and Joshua went home for some much needed sleep. When Moses, Hushael and I returned to Miriam's shack, Zipporah was there. Before her husband managed to say a word, she silenced him, pointing to a neat row of six small children asleep on the floor. She was crouched on a low stool, mending a Hebrew tunic made from different coloured strips of woven cloth.

'I can't stop,' she explained apologetically. 'I have to get this lot finished before the morning shift change.'

Moses looked down at the children and sighed. 'How often to they get to see their own parents?'

'It depends on the shifts,' Zipporah replied without expression. 'Most children see at least one parent for some part of each day.'

The two adults sat in solemn silence for a while, each busy with their own thoughts. Moses was forging more plans for Joshua's army. Zipporah was suppressing all the questions she longed to ask her husband.

'I am more concerned for the parents,' she said casually.

'What do you mean?'

'Most couples rarely get to see each other.'

'Are you talking about us?' Moses asked defensively.

'No, I'm used to you being away,' Zipporah said distantly. 'I mean the Israelite parents. They work different shifts so they can look after their own children when they're not at the works. So they only ever see each other for a hurried handover at the shift change.'

'I would have thought that was a blessing for some couples,' Moses suggested, rubbing his sword arm, which had become sore from its earlier exertion.

'Light a fire under the oven will you, love?' Zipporah asked. When Moses was snapping small pieces of wood into the fireplace, his wife added, 'Soon we will be raising a generation of children who have no idea who their actual fathers are.'

Moses stopped his work. 'Is it that bad?'

'With Hur's shift system, no one is quite sure who is meant to be in which bed when.'

She folded a finished garment, stood up, stretched, checked the children, and settled down to the next tunic.

'There is talk of him introducing a nine-hour pattern so that the shifts rotate in and out of the daylight hours.'

I quietly observed this domestic scene, while Hushael followed a moth as it flitted through the night air. Outside Miriam's shack the muted misery of routine oppression drifted down the lanes and alleys of the Hebrew settlement. At the morning shift change, the children were collected by assorted parents and carers, as were the mended clothes by their owners. Shortly after, Aaron returned, dirty and exhausted. The three humans were soon asleep.

*　*　*

They were woken in the early afternoon by the sound of thumping hooves and rumbling wheels. There was urgent banging at the door and impatient Egyptian voices. Pharaoh's officials had returned to collect Moses and Aaron, having equipped their chariots with a muddled combination of ponies and donkeys commandeered from the Israelites. Moses was allowed no opportunity to say farewell to his wife. The officials were in a hurry; they had bad news for their king. They literally dragged Moses from the shack, pushing Zipporah away. Zipporah's subdued calm from the previous night abandoned her. She screamed and cried, directing her ire at Moses for allowing himself to be treated like that. Moses stood impassively in his chariot, refusing to accept the guilt Zipporah was heaping on him. It was for love of his wife that he was returning to Thebes – to take on Rameses and defeat him.

In Heaven

I left Hushael and Ahoshal to look after their charges on the southward journey. I collected Jeshaphael and Maphrael, and returned to my own home. Moses' confrontation with Rameses would almost certainly involve another plague. I needed to know what was next.

'How are we doing?' I asked my Boss, having gone straight to his office.

'We are doing very well, Oriel,' he replied with a quiet smile.

'There is something I don't fully understand,' I said to the Creator of All.

His smile broadened.

'Is there anything that you do – fully – understand?'

I should have abandoned my enquiry at this comment but didn't.

'Why must there be such widespread suffering in Egypt before the Israelites can go free?'

'Rameses is still refusing to release Abraham's children from their work,' he said carefully. 'You know that, Oriel.'

I did know that.

'Every time Pharaoh looks likely to give in,' I said to my Boss, 'Egypt's Seraph – on your instructions – turns his thoughts against the Hebrews again.'

'That is true.'

'Why?'

My Boss's expression suddenly became extremely serious.

'One other Archangel began to question my wisdom regarding the affairs of men and women, Oriel. His name is Lucifer.'

My Angelic being went cold, and I quickly stepped back from

questioning my Boss's judgement. He looked intently into my eyes. Gradually, his smile returned, warming my spirit with its blaze. I felt foolish and ashamed, and tried to account for my unsuitable enquiry.

'The question came from Moses and Aaron,' I muttered. 'I just thought I would take this opportunity to . . .' My excuse faded like a burnt out star.

'Moses and Aaron are not Angels,' my Boss stated. He continued to study me and I endured his gaze uneasily. When my Boss looks into the soul of his creatures, there is nothing that he does not see.

'Humans are smaller and weaker and darker than Angels, Oriel,' he said. 'Their lives appear, to you, like the brief flash of a meteorite. But you must not underestimate them.'

Shame burned inside me. Angels generally consider human beings to be an inferior race and – from what we see of them – they are. But, as my Boss held me in his unflinching gaze, I learned that he sees things very differently.

'You came here for your instructions,' he said in a lighter tone, releasing me from the intense beam of his scrutiny.

'I assumed there would be another plague for Egypt,' I said.

'You assumed correctly.'

Love and forgiveness were pouring from my Creator's ageless eyes.

'What's next?' I asked.

'Staphylococcus Aureus.'

'Sta . . . what?'

A divine hand extended towards me. Nestled in its brightness was the tiniest spot of dark matter. It was far smaller than a gnat, or even than the red algae that had colonised the waters of the Nile, yet somehow this speck of Earthly stuff was alive – a truly miniscule scrap of life. I could only have noticed such life when it was held in the very hand that created it.

'What does it do?'

'Far more than you would imagine, Oriel.'

I remembered our earlier conversation and readily accepted that even this microscopic being could have more purpose in the plans of its Creator than I dared to consider.

'What will it do to the Egyptians?' I asked more carefully.

My care was rewarded with another divine smile.

'You will see,' he said. 'There is a consignment of these bacteria waiting in your office, along with instructions for their deployment.'

I asked no more – content simply to follow instructions.

* * *

I returned to my office to find it filled with thousands of small faintly-shining packages of Staphylococcus Aureus.

'What does this lot do?' Maphrael asked.

'There are some instructions somewhere,' I told him.

Jeshaphael picked up a note and read it. '*Apply to the inner layers of the skin three times a day until symptoms begin and once daily thereafter.*'

'Does it say anything else?' I asked.

'*For external use only. Do not apply to women or children. May be used on animals.*'

'We have work to do,' I informed my team. 'Come on.'

Thebes

We were in Thebes two days ahead of Moses and Aaron. On the first night, Jeshaphael and Maphrael assembled all the Angel guardians of Egypt in the courtyard of Pharaoh's palace. I arranged for Michael's army to be on temporary watch for Opposition activity because Lucifer was bound to show interest in such an unusual gathering.

I was not surprised to discover that there was precisely one package of bacteria for every Angel present. Jeshaphael dutifully explained to the Heavenly Host what they must do with the little creatures, instructing those with adult male humans to treat their own charges, and those with female or immature humans to use their packages on the few animals that survived the previous plague.

Just as the Angels were departing, Maphrael chimed in mischievously, 'Pay special attention to their buttocks.' A shimmer of amusement rippled across the assembly.

'Wait a moment, Angels,' I called, and turned sharply to Maphrael. 'What do you mean?' I demanded. 'Do you know something about these bacteria that you haven't told me?'

Jeshaphael was glaring at Maphrael even more darkly than usual.

'No!' Maphrael replied, less troubled than he should have been after causing an Archangel's displeasure.

'Whatever unpleasant effect this stuff has – and, let's face it, it's going to be unpleasant – they're not going to want to sit on it, are they?'

Several thousand Angels waited on the outcome of our discussion. Keen to get Moses and his People out of Egypt as soon as possible, I instructed them, 'You *may* pay special attention to their . . .' I paused for the briefest of moments.

'Bottoms!' Maphrael completed my sentence for me. I glared at him.

'I don't know why you put up with him,' Jeshaphael muttered privately, as the guardians of Egypt dispersed.

I looked into the eyes of the cautious Angel and decided to follow Hushael's example. I said nothing.

Two days later

When Moses expertly steered his chariot into the royal city, he had already received his instructions from Gabriel. Aaron was some way behind, weaving his way down the track, preoccupied by old resentments fermenting in his mind.

Ahoshal came straight up to me and said, 'I can't do anything with him, Oriel. Moses has been racing against Pharaoh's officials and Aaron was left behind. He has been spitting self-pitying obscenities at every bump in the road.'

As the returning Egyptian officials swept into Pharaoh's palace by the back gate, Moses squeezed past them with a triumphant cheer, his chariot on only one wheel. They disembarked and waited for Aaron, who trundled in cautiously. Moses helped Aaron down from the chariot, reassuring him that his technique had improved during the journey. Aaron was so relieved to have completed the journey that he gave his brother a weak smile; it carried the beginnings of forgiveness. As the two Israelites crossed the yard, they paused to collect handfuls of soot from the large furnace where the palace's waste is burned. The Egyptians looked quizzically at their blackened fists, but said nothing. Like many Egyptians, they have acquired a fearful respect for the solidly-built Israelite in the Midianite cloak.

Beneath the superficial exhilaration of his chariot race, Moses was still boiling with indignation at the way his wife and his fellow Israelites were being treated by the Egyptian authorities. It was not the dark, selfish rage that Aaron was nursing, but the bright, selfless wrath that pours from my Boss whenever his love is wounded. Moses is marching to war against his cousin – and it is a holy war.

Rameses' usually round, cheeky face was hollow and grey. The report from his envoys was no less than he had expected: the disease that had decimated the famous herds of Egypt had not touched the flocks of Israel. The king looked defiantly at Moses. Moses looked back with blazing eyes. Rameses was determined not to be defeated. Moses, more than ever, was resolved to win.

Pharaoh's guardian, Egypt's Seraph Shlyphantel, whispered into the king's mind: 'You must stand up for your people, Rameses. If the king is weak, Egypt is weak. Will you let the land of your fathers be ruled by outsiders again?'

I watched as the compassion in Pharaoh's mind cooled and froze. With icy resolve, he shouldered the weight of his family's history, remembering the instructions of his father, King Seti: 'Make Egypt great again.' Rameses stared forbiddingly at Moses.

Moses stared back. Rameses was distracted by a glimpse of Moses' sooty hands. He looked down at them and then back to his cousin's face. Moses wanted to speak. He wanted to say all the things that he had thought of on his journey back up the Nile. But he didn't dare. He was afraid that his stammer would return and, anyway, nothing needed to be said. He raised his hands swiftly and threw the soot into the air, clapping the remaining dirt off his fingers. Aaron followed suit. A fine cloud of black dust dispersed and settled over the king, his officials and his furniture. Moses continued to clap his hands until the last of the soot was gone. Then he threw a look of pure fury at his adversary and turned to leave.

'What now, Moses?' Rameses shouted after him. 'What does this mean?' Moses strode on, too angry to speak. The picture of his wife, being pushed back through Miriam's doorway, dominated his mind.

'I deserve an explanation,' Rameses yelled.

No you don't, Moses thought. Aaron broke into a trot to keep up with him.

'Tell me, Moses!' thundered the king.

While this order was still rebounding off the stone walls of the palace, Moses was lost to view. Rameses' pet duck was standing beside its owner, a thin coating of black soot over its back. The king spun round and kicked the hapless creature.

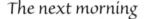

The next morning

Maphrael arrived at Moses' room, and said, 'Oriel, you must come and see this.' His eyes were sparkling with Angelic mischief. He led me to Rameses' palace where the king of Egypt was eating breakfast with his chief wife, Nefertiry, and their children.

'Look!' Maphrael urged, pointing at Rameses and his eldest son, Crown Prince Amenhirkopshef.

Both men were perched on stools at ungainly angles, wincing with discomfort every time they moved. This was causing great amusement among the younger children who couldn't resist the temptation to point and giggle. Amenhirkopshef stood up to escape the mockery of his siblings but his father admonished him.

'Hirkop,' he said sternly, 'a king must bear discomfort with dignity. You must be above such matters; you are descended from the gods.'

Amenhirkopshef returned cautiously to his stool, suppressing a howl of pain as swollen flesh encountered hard wood. Laughter pealed around the room and it did not only come from the children. With just two exceptions, all the Angels present were tumbling around in unsuppressed hilarity. Only Shlyphantel and I maintained our composure – Shlyphantel in respect for the suffering of the king, I in respect for the suffering of Egypt.

A week later

Moses has so far made no approach to Pharaoh and was not expecting to be approached. He saw plenty of evidence of the bacterium's work in the distress of the Egyptians who were lodging in the same building. All the men were covered with large, pus-filled boils. The more they scratched the sores, the more the infection spread. The only men in the whole of Egypt who were spared were Moses, Aaron and the Israelite slaves. News of these notable exceptions spread, and ordinary Egyptians began to take notice of the powerful God of the Hebrew slaves.

Two nights ago, Archangel Gabriel arrived with new instructions for Moses. 'I see that Staphylo-whatever-it-is has been doing its work,' he commented. 'Maff tells me that the palace magicians have had an extra dose of it on their feet. Hopping mad they are!'

I could not share in his entertainment. Since my last discussion with my Boss, I have found myself deeply troubled by the suffering of the humans around me.

'Has Hushael worked it all out yet?' Gabriel asked, not bothered by my failure to respond.

'Yes,' I said, 'the boils are a reaction to infection deep in their skin.'

'Good old Hushael,' Gabriel beamed. 'Where is he now? Got his face up close to some Egyptian's . . .'

'Do you have a message to deliver?' I asked pointedly.

'Yes,' said Heaven's Chief Messenger, waving a folder. 'Moses has to visit Rameses first thing in the morning.' He turned and spoke our Boss's words into Moses' sleeping mind. That done, Gabriel handed me a small note from my Boss.

'This is the next plague,' he explained.

I opened the note. There was only one word: HAIL.

'I can't do weather,' I said urgently to Gabriel. 'None of us can.'

'Do you think he doesn't know that?' my Archangel colleague replied.

I stared at the note, wondering what, if anything, I was expected to do. Gabriel said, 'Thought you might like to know: Raphael's making progress with his song.'

'Why is he bothering?' I asked. 'Moses doesn't need it any longer. Ahoshal and Aaron have had him praying regularly for weeks.'

'He says he has an idea what he might do with it when it's finished.'

'What?'

'I didn't ask.' Gabriel left again.

I summoned Hushael, Jeshaphael and Maphrael. I informed Hushael that Moses had received his next message for Pharaoh, and showed my Boss's note to the other two.

'We don't do weather,' Jeshaphael said anxiously.

'That's what I said.'

'We could try,' Maphrael insisted. 'What *is* hail?'

'Hard frozen rain,' Jeshaphael explained impatiently.

'That would be easy enough,' Maphrael said. 'We could whiz up to the Arctic, pick up a big lump of ice, break it into bits and then throw them down on Egypt from the sky.'

'I suspect there is rather more to it than that,' Jeshaphael responded.

'Angels,' I intervened, 'our Boss does not ask any of us to do what we cannot do. As he has not asked us to *do* the hail, we can surely assume that he does not expect us to.'

* * *

Back at the palace, Moses insisted on meeting with the king in the presence of all his advisors. Rameses sat with practised dignity on his elevated throne; beside him Amenhirkopshef struggled to emulate his father. Below the pharaoh and Crown prince stood various advisors and magi. I could not help but notice how the magicians were shuffling uncomfortably from one foot to another. Maphrael smiled smugly when he saw me looking in their direction. I have no doubt that it was his idea.

Moses spoke to Rameses at length, and there was no hint of his stutter. He controlled his passion with the same mastery that Rameses was applying to his posture.

'This is what the Lord, the God of the Hebrews, says,' Moses stated. '*Let my People go, so that they can worship me. If you do not, I will send more plagues against you, until you know that there is no other god in all this Earth.*'

The palace officials looked anxiously at one another, but Rameses preserved his same dignified expression.

Moses continued, 'My God could wipe you off the face of the earth, Rameses, but he has spared you. Why do you still set yourself against his People?'

The thoughts of Pharaoh's advisers were not difficult to read. *Let them go*, each man was screaming within the privacy of his thoughts. Shlyphantel whispered into the king's mind, 'Who is the most powerful man in Egypt? Rameses or Moses?'

Moses delivered the rest of his message: '*At this time tomorrow, the God of Israel will send the worst hailstorm that has ever fallen on Egypt. Give orders now for all livestock to be brought in from the fields, because the hail will fall on every man, woman and animal that is not brought into shelter. And many will die.*'

96

After their customary mutual stare, Moses walked out through the pillared hall. Those of the royal household who have learned to respect Moses sent urgent messages to their families, warning them to bring their animals into shelter. There were others, though, who mistook the king's impassivity for disdain and did nothing.

* * *

This morning, Gabriel came again, looking more serious than on his previous visit. Clearly he was in some awe of the message he was about to deliver. He waited until Moses was fully awake and quietly uttering the morning prayers his brother has taught him, and then delivered our Boss's words: *'Moses, I, the God of Abraham, give you authority over the weather in Egypt. When you say, It will hail, it will hail. When you say, The hail must stop, it will. If you call up thick clouds to block out the light of the Sun, they will come. You are my servant.'*

Jeshaphael, Maphrael, Ahoshal and I listened in dumbfounded silence.

'He can do weather!' Maphrael said in disbelief. My mind went back to the conversation I had had with my Boss about the importance of humans. He was giving Moses an authority that has never been entrusted to any Angel. No wonder Gabriel was rather quiet.

Moses stood up and pulled around him the thick cloak that Zipporah had woven as a wedding gift. He grasped his staff and strode out into the grey Egyptian dawn. A few people were already out and about, some busy herding their cattle towards their homes.

Moses stretched his staff up towards the sky and quietly ordered: 'Let it hail.' There was not a scrap of uncertainty in his mind. This man who had once abandoned all belief in religion now knows that there is a God. He also knows that what the God of his People says, happens.

At that moment, a surge of electricity leapt between the clouds and the ground. Light flashed across the sky, sending a shock-wave roaring through the landscape. Every man, woman and child looked up as large round droplets of ice began to fall from the clouds, pounding into the dry earth. People howled in pain, cattle stampeded, birds hid in the trees and crops of ripening barley and flowering flax were flattened. Moses did not stay to watch. He pulled his cloak over his head and walked back to his room. His neighbours were rushing around, securing shutters and doors. Moses sat on his bed, and prayed that his family would be kept safe from the storm.

***

Next

It was two days before a messenger from Pharaoh arrived at the lodgings, riding a chariot with a hastily erected wooden roof to keep out the persistent hail. Moses and Aaron climbed aboard and were driven to the palace as fast as the mud-drenched roads would allow.

Rameses was clearly shaken by the severity and length of the storm. His people had already lost most of their livestock; now their ripening crops were destroyed. He was mindful of his father's instruction that his life was bound up with the lives of his people; if he flourished, they flourished; if they died, he would die.

'This time I have wronged your god,' Rameses said to Moses.

Only this time! Moses thought contemptuously. It was not enough.

'Your god is right,' Rameses continued. 'I and my people are in the wrong.'

Moses did not respond.

'Pray to him,' the king implored. 'We have had enough thunder and hail. I will let your People go. You do not have to stay any longer.'

Maphrael nudged me in celebration – but Moses was unmoved. I studied Rameses' mind. His words were genuine. He meant them. I looked into Moses' mind. He has known Rameses since childhood. His judgement was that there would be many false dawns before the sun finally shone.

'When I get out of the city,' Moses told the humbled king, 'I will spread out my hands in prayer and the hail will stop. Then you will know that this world belongs to God.'

A slight hint of a pale smile appeared on the king's face. Moses wiped the smile away.

'I know you don't fear God, Rameses,' he declared.

The two men stared at each other. All the fear was in Pharaoh's eyes.

As Moses and Aaron left the palace I gave instructions to my small team. 'Maphrael, I want you to keep a careful watch on Pharaoh and his advisers. Jeshaphael?'

98

'Yes, Oriel?'

'I would like to see a complete inventory of all the sufferings the Egyptian humans have experienced as a direct or indirect result of these plagues. I will be in my office.'

In Heaven

In the safety of my office, I distracted myself with some of the routine affairs of Heaven: rotas, training programmes, news from across the Universe and beyond. Maphrael was the first to report. As anticipated by Moses, Rameses' contrition had vanished with the hailstorm. Indeed, he is now considering a further increase in the Israelites' brick quota, simply as a means of hitting back at his cousin. This information concerned me. I sent Maphrael to Pithom to look for a way of easing the stresses on the Hebrew workforce.

When Jeshaphael arrived he was carrying several folders filled with information.

'I have brought you the prayer logs,' he announced. He held up several thin files. 'Here are all the prayers for help and mercy the Egyptian people have petitioned to their own deities.' He put those files down and picked up a single sheet of data. 'These are the only prayers currently being directed at Rameses' supposedly divine self. And this,' he heaved up the largest of all the folders, 'is a record of all the prayers that have been directed by the Egyptians specifically at the God of the Israelites, our Boss.'

I took the file and browsed through it. Recorded in graphic detail were the woes of the Egyptian people – those who do not have stone palaces to protect them or talented slaves to meet their demands. My spirit was greatly darkened by the scale of the suffering.

Jeshaphael loomed over me as I read.

'Yes?' I enquired.

'What would you like me to do now, Oriel?'

I looked down at the daunting catalogue of disaster.

'I don't know, Jeshaphael. I really don't know.'

Not until I had read every single prayer for deliverance that has been uttered in Egypt did I put the files down. At the back of the largest file I found a small, separate section. These were the prayers for deliverance that have been prayed by the Israelites. There were worryingly few. Hur has obviously succeeded in wiping all thought of escape from the minds of his fellow Hebrews.

I went to see my Boss.

I stood before my Creator in silence. On my previous visit I had expressed my concerns and been corrected. This time I said nothing. My Boss was grave. He knew my thoughts. He knew what I had been reading. He knew, in minute detail, the content of every one of those prayers, whether or not they had been addressed to him.

'Speak to me, Oriel,' he coaxed gently.

My silence was pointless, so I expressed the question that was echoing through my entire Archangelic being.

'Why?'

My Boss looked at me steadily and waited – not waiting for the right words with which to answer my question. He was waiting until I was ready to hear his reply.

'There is a pattern, Oriel,' he said quietly, 'that is carved into the history of my People. It runs through every bruise and insult that they have suffered. What you have seen is part of this pattern.'

The silence resumed. I briefly wondered why I had not noticed this pattern in my Boss's work in humanity. Then my thoughts returned to the plight of Egypt.

'Will it end?'

'It will.'

'Will it end well?' I extended my enquiry as far as I dared.

A profound sadness clouded my Boss's face and I sensed that I had asked the one question he least desired to answer. He looked at me, his face an ocean of sorrow.

'That I cannot tell you,' he said quietly. Without another word, my Boss handed me my instructions for the next chapter in Egypt's misery.

* * *

'Not more insects!' Jeshaphael exclaimed despairingly.

'Big ones this time,' Maphrael added.

'Perhaps this is another job for Hushael,' I suggested.

'I don't know why you bother with us,' Jeshaphael complained. 'Moses handles the weather, Hushael looks after the animals. All we get are little scraps that any Angel could manage.'

'Jeshaphael,' I said firmly, 'our Boss knows what he is doing. If he says I need a team, I need a team.'

I received a sulky look in reply.

'Go and fetch me a locust. Bring it to Moses' lodgings.'

Eastern Persia

Hushael informed us that millions of locusts would not simply appear of their own accord. We would have to fetch them all.

'What do you mean by that?' Maphrael asked.

Jeshaphael joined the conversation. 'Find several million locusts? Just like that?'

Hushael said nothing.

'Hushael?' Maphrael enquired insistently, 'I noticed that you said we will have to find the locusts. Can't you do it for us?'

'No.'

Despite much pleading and numerous offers of an exchange of duties, Hushael insisted that his place is with Moses.

'It could be fun, Jesh,' Maphrael said. 'You were complaining that there's nothing for us to do.'

Hushael agreed to prepare us for our mission, which appeared more daunting the more we considered it. He introduced us to various species of locust and educated us, in fine detail, in the biology, ethology and ecology of these dull creatures. When our lesson was over, the three of us travelled east into Persia in search of large numbers of the brown insects.

Maphrael was the first to spot a small swarm tucking into a field of ripe wheat at the edge of a lifeless desert. We watched as an anxious peasant farmer ran through his meagre crop, banging two pieces of wood together in a desperate attempt to save his livelihood. The locusts rose into the air on their long wings and resumed their meal in a nearby tree. The farmer sat below the tree and watched the swarm nervously. I was pleased to consider that we would be helping this man as well as Moses when we removed the pests from his land.

Jeshaphael, Maphrael and I took our positions around the tree. On my signal, we disturbed the air with a series of high pitched clicks. It worked. The locusts abandoned the tree, flew upwards and scattered in all directions. The farmer, who had heard and seen nothing of the three Angels around him, cheered at the departure of the pests.

I shouted, 'Quick! Catch them.'

The farmer's Angel guardian watched as we shot off in different directions, pursuing the locusts. When we returned to the tree, Maphrael had five of the creatures, Jeshaphael was very carefully holding just one, and I had captured three, but sadly had crushed them all to death.

'May I enquire,' the peasant's Angel guardian said with unveiled amusement, 'what you think you are doing?'

I explained.

The Angel said, 'Quite a challenge.'

He was rewarded with three disgruntled glares.

'Can you help us?' I pleaded.

'Humans have two ways of herding animals,' the Angel replied. 'They either lead them from the front or chase them from behind.'

'Which is easier?' Maphrael asked.

'With only three of you,' the Angel said, 'your only option is to *lead* the locusts. To do that you will have to win their trust and establish yourselves in the role of chief locust for the swarm. However, to be quite honest, I am not sure that locusts are capable of such trust.'

'What if there were more than three of us?' I suggested, exploring the second option.

'In theory,' the Angel said, 'if you formed a long enough line, you could beat the locusts forwards, ahead of you, all the way to Egypt.'

I was anxious to get started and decided to employ whatever resources were necessary.

'If I wanted to cause instant devastation in Egypt,' I asked the Angel, 'how long a line of beaters would I need?'

'I really don't know.'

'No Angel knows,' I responded with some exasperation. 'But you know more about these ugly insects than I do. Make a guess. How long?'

'A thousand miles?'

My mind spun. The dimensions of the physical Universe are something of a mystery to me. I had no idea how many Angels it would require to form such a line.

'Jeshaphael,' I commanded, 'go to Heaven and bring down

every Angel you can find who has some experience of Earth and is not involved in an essential activity.'

'What do you rank as *essential*?' he asked.

'Worshipping our Boss, and . . . bring me the rest.'

'What about the army?'

The thought of asking Archangel Michael to donate his highly trained troops for locust herding duties did not appeal to me.

'Leave the army,' I instructed. 'Maphrael, you and I must get some practice at chasing these ghastly creatures.'

While Jeshaphael visited Heaven, Maphrael and I located the reassembled swarm and pursued it across the Persian plain. Maphrael appeared to be thoroughly enjoying himself. I found the activity utterly tedious. As Earth slowly spun on its tilted axis, we were joined by a dazzling assortment of Angels sent by Jeshaphael. Our team of Angelic locust-herds soon grew into a small army, but our progress was frustratingly slow.

Angels, being spiritual creatures, only see the spiritual attributes of our Boss's creations. Locusts are not well equipped spiritually. An average Angel has to concentrate fairly hard in order to see a human being; the majority of Jeshaphael's recruits were completely blind to the locusts. In order to save time – as humans see it – we revisited the same swarm of locusts on the same Earth day, again and again, until my locust-herds had become proficient in their unusual task. And, over and over again, I endured the relentless complaints of frustrated Angels. Eventually, I conceded my limitations and called on the services of Archangel Michael to instil some discipline into my eco-army. He arrived reluctantly from the brickworks of Pithom, where he had been training Joshua's militia. He brought with him those of Heaven's warriors who could be spared.

'Oriel,' he asked, 'are you quite sure that you have understood your orders correctly?'

'I am.'

'Well, let's get this rabble organised.'

Michael's presence made a huge difference. There is not an Angel in Heaven who does not respond with instant obedience to Archangel Michael. He soon had my long line of Angelic locust-herds marching in order.

The only Angel deriving pleasure from the whole exercise was Maphrael. He somehow discovered a way of forming a locust swarm into different shapes. He started with a perfect sphere; the next time he whipped them into a tall tower; then an Egyptian pyramid. Since then he has refined his skills considerably. A short while ago he shaped his herd into a passable resemblance of Rameses.

Michael insists that both he and I must work alongside our fellow Angels. So I find myself in the longest line of Angels ever to have crossed Earth in peacetime. Our task is to gather the scattered locust populations of Persia into a single mega-swarm and drive them into Egypt. Maphrael – to give credit where credit's due – had one very helpful idea: that we sweep the locusts up into the air and then push the air westwards rather than the locusts themselves. Being flying insects, they are carried along in the air current.

'Wouldn't that involve making weather?' Jeshaphael asked critically when Maphrael first made the suggestion.

Maphrael was undeterred. 'This is to making weather, Jesh, what your singing is to making music.'

'Maphrael!' Michael thundered. 'You have work to do.'

After all this moving back and forth in time, tomorrow will be our first genuine tomorrow for a great many days. I will be relieved to move off this one wretched day and begin our progress towards Egypt.

On the edge of Egypt

It has taken several weeks to get here. Each morning we have stirred up our long wave of insects. Each morning, as I have looked along that voracious line of invertebrate life, the monotonous bank of dark, fluttering creatures has been broken by Maphrael's latest living sculpture. Recently, he has been trying to perfect a technique that makes his giant Rameses look as though it is walking. Nothing has entertained our Angels more than to see part of the locust-pharaoh's body suddenly explode when Maphrael loses control of his swarm.

During our trek, I soon discovered what such a vast number of locusts can eat. I insisted that we steer our swarm around human habitations to prevent our work from bringing destruction to every community we pass through. I also ensured that Maphrael was never in a part of the line that could be seen by humans, in case they mistook his giant walking pharaoh for one of their deities.

Now we are just one day's sweep from Egypt, and the locusts are hungry. They will devour every green plant they find, especially the wheat. The wheat crops of the Nile valley survived the hail because the plants were still young. Indeed, the extra watering greatly enhanced the year's harvest prospects. This wheat – a year's supply of bread for all Egypt – is about to be devoured.

* * *

I visited Heaven to inform my Boss that we were ready.

'Does this *have* to happen?' I asked, little doubting his answer.

He passed me a folder containing his next message for Moses: *I have hardened the king's heart and the hearts of his officials,* it read, *so that I can perform these miraculous signs among them. One day you will tell your children and your grandchildren how I dealt harshly with the Egyptians and how I performed these signs among them. Then they will know that I am the Lord.*

The words seemed cruel, even arrogant. Then I looked into the eyes of pure selfless love in front of me. I re-read the message and looked again at my Boss. I knew that there must be thorough good and undiluted justice in his plan, but I could not see it. When I looked at my Boss, I knew that I trusted him. When I looked at the warning that Moses will be asked to deliver, I was daunted by the scale of the destruction my Angels and I are about to cause.

My Boss allowed me to struggle. He willed me to grasp a greater understanding of his plan for humanity. I could see the lines of destruction and suffering that scar human history, but I could not make out any pattern. In the end I simply looked into my Creator's eyes. Only there did any of this appear to make sense.

'Oriel,' he said, his quiet voice restraining unimaginable power, 'I never do anything to my creatures that I am not prepared to go through myself.'

I would have stayed at that moment for eternity. From that privileged vantage point, I could see deep into the story of the human race. I glimpsed the tragedy of their selfishness and the enormity of their Maker's love. I saw things that made the pale obedience of Angels look little more than so much Staphylococcus Aureus in the face of my Boss's great adventure of

Creation. However, it was not mine to stay there. I am only an Archangel.

'Please hand the message to Gabriel,' my Boss said.

* * *

Now back at the dry and dusty eastern edge of Egypt, all I can see are thousands and thousands of hungry brown locusts, settled on sand and rock, ready to pounce. I would like to be with Moses as he visits the royal palace today. I would like to see into Rameses' troubled mind and hear his officials beg him to spare Egypt by letting the Israelite slaves go. But Michael insists that a commander's place is among his troops, sharing the discomfort and uncertainty of battle. My place, today, is among the locusts. We are waiting for a signal from Hushael for our invasion to begin.

The Sea of Reeds

At Hushael's signal, 70 legions of Angels rose and swept the locusts into the air. We spread out our Angelic forms, joining ourselves once again into a kind of giant net, and pushed the locusts and the air together towards Egypt. I looked across to Maphrael's place in the line. Above the uniform dark wave of hungry insects, in the script of Angels, he had written a message for Rameses, made entirely from flying locusts. It read, *Let my People go.*

When we came to the first Egyptian settlements, the locusts descended on the wheat fields like an all-consuming carpet. They devoured the entire crop, and we moved on. Our thin line stretched the entire length of Rameses' kingdom, from the Mediterranean in the north to Nubia in the south. Egypt would be stripped bare.

Michael had carefully positioned me in the section of the line that would sweep into Thebes itself. As soon as Rameses saw the advancing swarm, he sent for Moses.

I waited in the palace while locusts nibbled at every green leaf on the eastern bank of the great river. Rameses was terrified, overwhelmed by the scale of the disaster. He knew that Egypt would never recover if the swarm crossed the Nile and devastated the wheat crop on the western bank. He waited for Moses at the entrance of his palace, striding anxiously between two colossal stone statues of himself. These proud symbols of Pharaoh's power looked unimpressive – veiled by a heaving mass of insects.

'I have offended you and your god,' Rameses wailed when he saw Moses approaching. 'Forgive me once more.' The king gripped Moses' hand in desperation, aware that every yard the locusts advanced was costing his nation millions of gold coins. 'Pray to your god to take this deadly plague away.'

There was a time when the brash confidence of Rameses overwhelmed Moses. Not so now. Moses' steady faith eclipsed the idle glimmer of Pharaoh's royal power.

'I will pray.'

Rameses loosened his grip on his cousin and Moses returned to his lodgings. Only when he got there did he pray and only when Moses prayed did Michael send out the command, 'About turn!'

As one, seventy thousand Angels leapt to the western edge of the swarm, reformed their chain and herded the locusts back out towards the desert.

'What are we going to do with them?' I called to Michael.

'Destroy them,' he said.

'Are we allowed to?'

'Yes.'

'How do you propose to do it?' I asked.

'In the sea.'

A troubled silence seeped along the line of Angels. The sea – indeed any large body of water – is a terror to all Angelkind. Angels have, at times, been damaged beyond all usefulness by the thin fluid that clings to Earth's surface. Where we possibly can, we avoid it. There was no doubt in my mind that this would be an efficient way to destroy the swarm, but I wondered what the cost might be in lost Angels.

We crossed the devastated plain of eastern Egypt, carefully closing in on the swarm, gathering it together into a tight circle. Michael guided us towards a broad inland lake. Here the fatal trap closed around the locusts, and the mammoth swarm was forced onto the Sea of Reeds while the line of Angels formed a ring around the shore. We maintained our locust-proof fence around the lake until every single insect had fallen, exhausted, into the water and drowned.

I looked at the seventy thousand grim-faced Angels who witnessed the massacre. I saw in their eyes a fear similar to the one that had gripped Rameses as he watched the advancing swarm.

The Sea of Reeds could swallow up seventy thousand Angels just as easily as it devoured those locusts – without a ripple. When the last lingering locust had vanished into the murky depths, we quickly backed away from the liquid terror.

I cannot write for the other Angels, but my own eternal spirit was distinctly disturbed by our close encounter with the Sea of Reeds. Even Maphrael's noisy bravado has given way to a queasy silence.

Thebes

Returning to Thebes, Maphrael and I went straight to the palace. Rameses was distraught. With the help of his son and his officials, he was assessing the scale of the calamity that had visited Egypt since the return of Moses. They concluded that the damage is temporary. The fields will produce a new harvest next year, the remaining cattle will breed and the herds be restocked. Just as the boils healed up without leaving lasting scars, Egypt will recover from these traumas.

'They will be quickly forgotten, when better times return,' one of the older advisers told the king. 'Egypt does not remember its troubles; only its triumphs.'

There was another concern in Rameses' mind. The quickest way to regain Egypt's lost wealth would be to conquer the troublesome tribes of Canaan. To do that, he will need to move north to his new capital, Avaris, and finish building the store cities, Pi-Rameses and Pithom. For that, the brick making expertise of the Hebrew slaves will be essential. Rameses saw no alternative but to ride out the storm of my Boss's anger. He looked at his son, Crown Prince Amenhirkopshef, and renewed his commitment to restore Egypt to its former glory, so he can pass the kingdom on to his heir, strong and secure. In all these discussions, Egypt's Seraph, Shlyphantel, encouraged the king in his quest for power – as instructed.

Maphrael and I met up with Jeshaphael and Hushael at Moses' lodgings.

'I gather from a former colleague in the Prayer Department that Pharaoh has reneged on his promise again,' Jeshaphael said.

'Yes,' I responded distractedly.

'What's next?' Jeshaphael asked.

'I don't know.'

'How about a stampede of all the elephants in Africa?' Maphrael suggested.

'What good would that do?' Jeshaphael demanded disapprovingly.

'It's not intended to do good,' Maphrael replied.

'If you hadn't noticed, Maphrael,' Jeshaphael proceeded with irritation, 'these plagues have targeted the health and wealth of the Egyptian people. We are not in the business of wanton destruction.'

I was not entirely sure that I agreed with Jeshaphael, but I silenced my two assistants before their argument went any further.

Gabriel arrived. 'Good day, comrades. Did you enjoy playing with the locusts?'

'No.'

'No.'

'Yes.' That was Maphrael.

'Never mind. The next plague will be rather easier for you.'

'Is it elephants?' Maphrael asked enthusiastically.

'No, Maff,' Gabriel replied. 'It's more weather.'

'Moses!' Gabriel recalled Moses from his anxious imaginings about the welfare of his wife and children: *Stretch out your hand towards the sky and order darkness to spread over Egypt – deep darkness that can be felt.*

Gabriel turned to me. 'I have no idea what that last bit is supposed to mean, but the Boss assured me that Moses would understand.'

Gabriel led Moses out of the building to the struggling remnants of the local market. Watched by a few intrigued Egyptians, Moses held his hands up towards the sky and muttered a simple prayer. Jeshaphael, Maphrael and I watched in wonder as dark clouds responded to the man's command. They gathered in large numbers in the skies over the Nile valley. People looked anxiously around them as midday brightness turned swiftly to twilight. Stall holders packed away their goods, as if it were evening. The Egyptians were too troubled by the eerie darkness to take any notice of the hairy foreigner who was praying in their market square. By mid-afternoon it was as dark as night. This darkness made little difference to us Angels – our sight does not rely on created light – but for the humans it was profoundly unsettling.

The people of Egypt have been repeatedly battered by our plagues. They have no crops in their fields or livestock in their pastures. Now they are cowering in their homes, unable to do anything but wait and hope for the return of Earth's Sun.

In the gloomy depths of the royal palace, the physical darkness was dissipated by rows of burning lamps. But the air was heavy with moisture, dampening the spirits of the whole household. Pharaoh's children soon tired of the novelty of day-long night and vocally expressed their boredom to their distracted mothers.

There were soon greater concerns being discussed in Rameses' council chamber. The council was joined by Khaemwaset, the king's most favoured son, who is High Priest in the temple of the Egyptian sun god, Amen-Re. This darkness – which had already lasted for three days – was, according to Khaemwaset, an omen foretelling the destruction of the gods of Egypt. When the prince-priest heard that it had been caused by the prayers of just one man – an Israelite – he went cold with terror.

'There can be only one meaning to this,' the prince declared. 'The God of the Hebrews is overpowering the gods of Egypt. This could be the end of the new kingdom. Egypt will be ruled, once again, by Canaanites.'

Khaemwaset looked directly into his father's exhausted eyes and said, 'Whatever this Moses has demanded as an appeasement for his god, you must do it.'

Rameses was facing defeat for the first time in his life, and was doing so in the presence of his full council, and the company of his two best-loved sons. He lowered his gaze while he considered the prospect of capitulating to Moses. Moses had been a joke among the princes of Egypt when they were children – the one who had been easiest to ignore or bully. To lose to Moses would be utter humiliation.

The Opposition spirits who have set themselves up as the gods of Egypt were nowhere to be seen. I suspected that they were consulting their own master, Lucifer. Shlyphantel, my Boss's ambassador in Egypt, continued to urge Rameses to be strong. However, the Pharaoh was won over by the dire warnings of his second son. Rameses and his family were in the process of rebuilding Egypt after centuries under the rule of foreign pharaohs. To lose the kingdom again was a greater threat than being defeated by Moses. The king dragged his head upwards, gripping firmly onto the crook and flail that symbolise his shaken power.

'Send for Moses,' he ordered, fighting his emotions to keep his voice steady.

The two princes talked together in muted tones while they waited. Rameses stared into the darkness as he prepared himself for his first taste of failure.

Moses walked into the council chamber confidently. During the days of darkness he had begun to consider the vast responsibilities that my Boss has entrusted to him and, in being trusted, his sense of self-worth has grown. He performed a small but gracious bow to the king. Rameses struggled to maintain his composure. Had it not been for the presence of Khaemwaset, he may not have succeeded.

Khaemwaset surveyed Moses with great interest. He sees this man, whom his father considers a renegade prince, as a rival priest – one who has power even to blot out the Sun. Such authority demands respect.

'Go and worship your god,' Rameses ordered. Moses said nothing. He looked into his cousin's eyes. The last time they had discussed this matter, Rameses had spoken of only the Israelite *men* going.

'Your women and children may go too,' he added quickly, to cover up the echoing silence of defeat. There his concession ground to a halt. He was not ready for unconditional surrender. There was still some fight in him. 'But you must leave your flocks and herds behind.'

Moses had anticipated as much.

'We cannot worship God without animals to sacrifice,' he stated.

'Then take what you need, but leave the rest.'

Khaemwaset tried to intervene, to advise his father against angering so dangerous a god, but Amenhirkopshef would not let him speak. My attention was drawn to the Egyptian officials. They were praying. They were not crying out to the rebellious deities of Egypt; they were praying to the God of Moses. 'Please spare us,' they implored. 'We will give you whatever you demand. We will heap our wealth on your People, the Israelites. Only, please let us be.'

Their prayers were answered by a Heavenly voice. It resonated hauntingly around the stone pillars of the palace, singing: *No more shall they in bondage toil. Let my People go. Let them come out with Egypt's spoil. Let my People go.*

Archangel Raphael!

Khaemwaset looked around. He sensed a spiritual presence and interpreted it as the arrival of the Israelite God in person. Any other Angel would have been proud to be so mistaken; Raphael sang on.

Moses, seemingly unaware of all this, calmly rejected Pharaoh's offer. 'Our livestock must go with us,' he insisted. 'Not one hoof must remain. Until we get out into the desert, we will not know which animals we will need.'

'Father,' Khaemwaset called urgently. 'Do what the man says, or we will suffer even greater humiliations.'

'Khaem!' Rameses spat back in a fierce whisper. 'Be quiet!'

Amenhirkopshef leaned towards his father's ear, urged on by Shlyphantel. 'We need to finish building the cities, father. Tell him that you will let his People go when their work is completed and, the quicker they make their bricks, the sooner they will worship their god.'

Rameses straightened up and motioned for Moses to step forward. He said coldly, 'Get out of my sight, Moses. If I ever see you again, I will have you killed.'

'So be it,' Moses replied serenely. He did not stay for their usual exchange of defiant stares. He turned immediately to leave but Gabriel arrived and stood in his way. Gabriel spoke quickly into Moses' thoughts and Moses turned round to face the king.

'This is what our Lord says,' he announced, casting a swift glance in the direction of the anxious High Priest, Khaemwaset: *I will bring one more plague on Pharaoh and Egypt. Then you will know that our God makes a distinction between Egypt and Israel.*

Rameses stared back blankly. He had already assessed the risks, and was prepared to accept them.

'These officials of yours,' Moses declared, sweeping his arm along the line of terrified councillors, 'will come crawling to me, begging us to leave.'

The royal advisers held their heads stone still, but their minds nodded in anxious agreement. Moses was silent while they squirmed under the complex etiquette of political survival. Then he stepped forwards and climbed the steps onto the throne platform, drawing closer to Rameses than court protocol allowed.

There he stood, looking down on the defeated king. Rameses did not flinch; he stared back with dull eyes.

The storm that had been brewing in Moses' mind for so many years suddenly broke: the childhood pain of discovering that he was not a real Egyptian; the repeated humiliation he had suffered at the hands of Rameses and other royal children; the desperate loneliness of decades in exile; his fury at the way his own family, as well as the Hebrew slaves, had been treated; along with all the pent-up tension of his very personal tussle with King Rameses II. These agonies bubbled up into his consciousness like molten lava. To my Angel eyes, Moses became incandescent with blazing wrath. This fire, however, did not consume him. It inspired him. He stared, wild-eyed at the king.

'When you plead with us to go – then will I leave.'

PART TWO

Heaven

Moses went to his lodgings and informed Aaron that they were returning to Pithom and that they would soon leave Egypt for good. While Moses and Aaron walked through the darkness, down the Nile Valley, Rameses also travelled north. He had resolved to move his residence to Avaris – his newly completed royal city on the edge of Pi-Rameses. From there he could oversee the building work personally, and begin preparations for his long-intended invasion of Canaan.

While accompanying Moses on the long journey, I took Jeshaphael and Maphrael on a series of visits to a variety of Egyptian homes. The first family we came to were farmers. For them, as for every Egyptian family, day and night had become indistinguishable. Just one oil lamp lit the modest, single-roomed home. The mother and father sat close to it; the mother sewing, the father sharpening his tools. Their children were lying, some asleep, some awake, on their beds. There was a heavy, stifled silence in the home. No one dared speak. The anger of the mother and the anxiety of the father were unmistakable.

We received a distinctly cool welcome from the Angel guardians of the household. They were bewildered by the havoc we had caused in Egypt, and bemused that our Boss should have ordered such distress. The family had lost all their crops; everything that had survived the hail had been consumed by the locusts. They had also lost their cattle and now owned only a single milk cow, which they had bought at a considerable price. The father had spent many hours on his knees in the darkness, planting any seeds that had a chance of producing some food before the winter. They had already eaten most of the seed grain reserved for the following year.

'These people,' the father's Angel explained, 'have never known anything but plenty. The children simply expect to be well fed. But now the oldest child, Prahotpe, has contributed his own small hoard of gold to buy food – if there is any – when the darkness ends and the market opens.'

I looked at young Prahotpe and studied his mind. He has

115

grown up suddenly and prematurely. He has given up his friends and his play in order to work: nursing sick animals, gleaning whatever is edible from the fields, distracting his younger siblings from hunger and boredom. I marvelled at how his human spirit has thrived under these stresses. There is hope yet for Egypt, I thought, if it has children like Prahotpe.

We moved on. In home after home, though the personalities changed, the story did not; the careful cultivation of wealth has given way to a struggle for survival.

I returned to Heaven and sat alone in my office, thinking deeply. The pain of Egypt lay heavily on me. I have witnessed numerous episodes of human suffering in the course of my Archangelic duties. I have witnessed disasters caused by the weather, by the instability of Earth's thin crust and by the terrible injustice of humankind's treatment of its own species. I have seen these things and not been moved (apart from some incredulity at the stupidity of *Homo Sapiens*). The suffering of Egypt, however, has been caused by me, and at the specific instruction of my Boss. And now there must be one more plague, one more trauma for Prahotpe and his fellow humans to survive. I wondered what it might be. Jeshaphael and Maphrael had quickly fallen into an argument about it. I told them to continue their disagreement elsewhere. It was in a dark mood that I eventually entered my Boss's presence.

'Oriel,' he said gently, 'you do not have to do this. You may choose.'

I stared at my Creator in amazement. This was an outstanding offer. We Angels are our Boss's servants; we are created to obey our Master. For us, the only alternative to complete obedience is irreversible rebellion with immediate consequences. Humans are different; they are given a broader choice. They are allowed to believe or not believe, to follow or not follow, to love or not love, and they are only judged at the end of their finite lives. Such freedom is not part of an Angel's lot, even an Archangel's. And yet, my Creator was offering me just such a choice.

I wondered what this final plague might involve, and wanted to find out before I made my decision. But I knew better than to ask. If he had wanted me to know, he would have told me. It was not that kind of choice he was offering me. This was a far greater matter than one particular task. By allowing me to choose, my Boss was not commanding me, but inviting me beyond Angelic obedience into the realm of love. How could I reject such an invitation?

He looked into my mind, following my thoughts, waiting with eternal patience for me to reach a decision.

'I will do it,' I declared.

There was a profound silence. When I looked again to my Boss, he handed me a file detailing the tenth and final plague. When I opened the file, my spirit froze. *EVERY FIRSTBORN SON IN EGYPT WILL DIE, FROM THE FIRSTBORN SON OF PHARAOH TO THE FIRSTBORN SONS OF HIS SLAVES, AND ALL THE FIRSTBORN CATTLE.*

I looked up at the author of this genocide order, expecting to see a difference in my Boss, to sense a coldness or a hardness I had not noticed before. What I saw in those eyes was what I always see – indescribable gentleness. I struggled to reconcile the divine generosity before me with the instructions I had just read. I remembered what he had told me at our previous meeting: *I will never do to any of my creatures what I am not prepared to go through myself.* I could not begin to imagine how that principle could apply to this.

I looked into those eyes, searching for a foothold by which I might climb the challenge before me. *Do I trust you?* I asked within my thoughts. *Yes, I have always trusted you.*

My Boss, of course, knew this. 'Oriel,' he asked deliberately, 'will you love me?'

The word *love* fluttered round my mind like a moth around a lamp. This was a question I had never been asked before. It excited me. It terrified me. All loyal Angels adore our Boss – but self-denying, freely-given love is neither asked nor expected of us. I was intoxicated by the experience, but my mind and my will were clearer than they have ever been.

'Yes,' I replied with unprecedented sincerity, 'I will love you.'

I returned to my office exhilarated, horrified and profoundly alone. I did not call for Jeshaphael and Maphrael. I read and re-read my Boss's instructions for the final plague. My mind went back to the farmer's son, Prahotpe, who had seemed such a bright hope for Egypt. It would never happen. I, Archangel Oriel, will soon be arranging Prahotpe's death.

My lonely meditations were joined by a familiar voice echoing down the corridor. Raphael was singing: *Thus saith the Lord, bold Moses said/ Let my People go/ Unless you want your firstborn dead/ Let my People go.* The words of his song made me shudder.

'How are you, my dear?' the Leader of Heaven's Worship asked as he appeared at my doorway.

I was not sure I was capable of answering, so I changed the subject.

'Raphael,' I enquired, 'what do you plan to do with that song of yours?'

'It will come in useful one day,' he replied vaguely.

It was unusual for Raphael to talk in such Earthly terms.

'One *day?*' I pressed.

'One day, my dear Oriel,' he said thoughtfully, 'another race of humans will be forced into slavery by their fellow men and women. I will teach my song to them. They will understand it.'

Raphael drifted across to my desk, read the instructions for the last plague, and drifted out again, singing as he went.

I called Jeshaphael and Maphrael and showed them the file. They seemed remarkably untroubled by it.

'How many Angels will that require?' Jeshaphael asked, matter-of-factly.

'I would like you to find out,' I answered. 'Maphrael, you work on the logistics from the Egyptian end. I need you to calculate exactly how many firstborn there will be.'

'How do you want to kill 'em?' Maphrael said breezily.

'Swiftly and painlessly,' I replied.

'Come on, Jesh,' Maphrael said. 'We have some sums to do.'

Again I was alone. I reflected on the fact that my colleagues seemed quite undisturbed by the prospect of destroying human lives. There is more to love, it would appear, than I had anticipated. I did not want to be left alone with such unmanageable thoughts and wandered into Gabriel's office.

* * *

'Cheer up, Oriel!' was Gabriel's immediate reaction to my news. 'They're all going to die, anyway. It doesn't make a great deal of difference which day it happens.'

I had hoped for a more sympathetic response.

'That's my very point, Gabriel,' I said. 'Their mortal lives are brief as it is, without being cut even shorter.'

'You think about things too much. Just carry out your instructions and be done with it.'

'Gabriel,' I asked, 'do you never give any consideration to why you do what our Boss gives you to do?'

'No,' he informed me. 'My job is to deliver, word-for-word, whatever message the Boss gives me. If I took to thinking about the messages and trying to understand them, then I would be in great danger of adding my own interpretation. That would be disastrous.'

'But you have a mind,' I insisted. 'Surely you should use it?'

'Thinking and understanding are what you and Raphael do, Oriel,' the Great Messenger told me. 'Michael and I just do what we are told.'

'You have opinions though, don't you?'

'Of course. I'm an Archangel. But I keep them out of my work. How are you going to kill all those Egyptians, then, Oriel?'

* * *

'By far the easiest way to do it,' Maphrael explained when he and Jeshaphael found me in Gabriel's office, 'would be for each Angel guardian to dispatch his own human.'

'No!' I said quickly. 'That would go against everything the Guardian Scheme exists for.'

'That was about the response I got from the guardians I spoke to.'

'There are countless alternatives,' Jeshaphael added pointedly. 'You remember Staphylococcus Aureus?' I nodded. 'There are various similar creatures that are capable of actually killing a human. There are also even smaller beings that can do much the same. The trouble is that they are rather unreliable and can be easily passed on to other humans.'

'We need a method that is quick, reliable and safe to use,' I insisted.

'One suggestion that sounded interesting was to use the Destroying Angel,' piped up Maphrael.

'We do not have a *Destroying Angel*,' I said sharply.

He looked at me with amused impatience and explained, 'It's a species of mushroom, Oriel.'

'What's a *mushroom*?'

'A sort of plant but it's not actually a plant.'

'Go on.' I was encouraged.

'If you feed it to a human,' Maff went on, 'they get terrible stomach pains for a few hours, then they feel better.' He paused and smiled. 'And then they die.'

'I don't want pain.'

'I didn't say it was a *good* idea,' Maphrael defended himself. 'I said it was an interesting one.'

119

Jeshaphael rescued me. 'We have the figures for you here,' he said, handing me a page of numbers. 'Obviously it depends on which day this is to actually happen, because of births and other deaths. The figure should be near enough for now, though.'

'Thank you, Jeshaphael,' I said, relieved to be rescued from Maphrael's mushrooms.

Gabriel joined our conversation. 'The safest thing to do would be to act directly on each human's body. That way you would have complete control over exactly who dies when.'

Jeshaphael picked up the thread. 'Quite right. But it would be very labour intensive, and we would need to know exactly how long each individual death would take.'

I found the whole conversation very disturbing. Even more disturbing was the fact that the Angels around me seemed so undisturbed.

'Doesn't all this concern you?' I asked. 'Does it mean nothing to you to destroy the life of one of our Boss's own creatures.'

'We killed the locusts,' Maphrael said.

'No, we didn't,' I corrected him. 'The water killed them. We just stood round and watched.'

'You killed three locusts,' Maphrael put in swiftly.

'That was unintentional,' I pointed out. 'What we are planning now is the deliberate extermination of our Boss's favourite creatures.'

Jeshaphael opened up a fresh strand of discussion: 'I think we will need to practise on a few humans first, like we did with the locusts.'

'What!' I asked in disbelief.

'Practise,' Jeshaphael repeated. 'Work out the best way to do it and find out how long it takes per human.'

'I can't believe I'm hearing this!' I exclaimed.

'It should be possible,' Gabriel stated dispassionately. 'I'll speak to Hanuphel. He'll probably let you have a go on some humans who are on their way out anyway.'

'Does none of this bother any of you?' I shouted at my colleagues.

'Jeshaphael's quite right, Oriel,' Gabriel said. 'If you don't practise, you won't be properly prepared when the day comes. I'll clear it with our Boss first, if that will make you happier.'

I indicated my agreement reluctantly.

* * *

Maphrael and Jeshaphael returned to my office in a much more sober state.

'It was a lot harder than I thought it would be,' said Maphrael, hesitantly.

'We tried holding onto their hearts or their lungs to stop those organs from functioning,' Jeshaphael explained, 'but it took a long time for them to die and if we didn't hold on long enough, some of them started up again when we let go.'

Both Angels had been profoundly affected by the experience. Maphrael added, 'And those were humans who were already seriously weakened by illness or age.'

'The most effective method,' Jeshaphael said, tentatively, 'was to physically mush up their brains. But it was messy – and I can't imagine many Angels wanting to do it repeatedly.'

'Why don't we get the army to do it?' Maphrael asked.

'Do *you* want to ask Michael to devote his troops to exterminating humans?' I asked.

'He helped with the locusts.'

'Not exactly,' I corrected him. 'I asked Michael to help me with the Angels, not with the locusts.'

'What about the Opposition?' Jeshaphael suggested. 'They wouldn't mind finishing off a few thousand human lives.'

'Absolutely not!' I stated. 'If the best suggestion we have is mushing brains, then we will do that. Maphrael, you go back to Egypt and prepare a project schedule. Jeshaphael, you have my authority to form a death squad of whatever size you consider appropriate. I need to find out what is happening with Moses.'

Pithom

I found Moses at Miriam's shack. His fury against Rameses was burning as brightly as when I last saw him. Its resurgence was prompted by the news that his eldest son, Gershom, has been declared old enough to work in the clay pits. My mind went back to the young Egyptian boy, Prahotpe. He is a similar age to Gershom. The traumas of Egypt have forced both boys into premature adulthood. Zipporah was busy kneading dough for the next day's bread, her once-bright spirit dulled by the unrelenting stress of slavery.

The brick quotas have been increased since Moses last saw his wife, on orders from Prince Amenhirkopshef. Hur responded with his usual creativity. Enlisting child labour was only a token. His main plan was to employ Egyptians to cook for their Israelite slaves. Having been protected from the ravages of the successive plagues, the Israelites are now, in some ways, better off than the Egyptians who live around them. Egyptian women who have no food to feed their own children are more than happy to cook meals for the Hebrews, in return for a bowlful of stew to take home at the end of the day. Egyptian men, likewise, having no cattle to herd and no crops to harvest, have offered their agricultural skills to the brick-making slaves for a small share of the produce. This has allowed for new shift patterns; the Israelites work extra hours at the brickworks, where they are fed twice a day from huge communal pots of Egyptian-style boiled meat.

Hur stormed into Miriam and Zipporah's small home. 'Get out!' he ordered Moses bluntly.

Moses looked at him with mute surprise.

'I warned you not to interfere,' Hur bellowed. 'Your meddling has achieved exactly what I predicted. Pharaoh has upped the quotas and we are now paying our own slave drivers.'

'I . . . I . . . I,' Moses struggled. The ferocity of Hur's unexpected attack brought on his stutter.

Zipporah spoke for him: 'Rameses is just one step away from admitting defeat,' she told the Israelite leader. 'Your People will soon be free to leave.'

'We don't want to leave,' Hur roared. 'We want to *live*.'

Aaron arrived, out of breath from running. Again, Hur took the initiative.

'Aaron,' he ordered. 'Take your brother away at once. Take him back to Midian – and leave him there.'

Aaron looked at his tongue-tied brother, quickly assessing the situation.

'We will not leave this place until we can take the whole Israelite People with us,' he told Hur quietly but emphatically

Aaron's calm disarmed Hur's rage. Moses' long-suffering brother sat Israel's chief spokesperson down and proceeded to give him a thorough account of their negotiations with Rameses. Aaron impressed on Hur the fact that the Israelites had been spared the ravages of the plagues which had afflicted the rest of Egypt. While Aaron explained, Hushael sang. He sang Raphael's song deep into the subtle pathways of Moses' mind. The singing gradually restored some balance to Moses' intellect and emotions. Over and again Hushael sang the simple song, while Hur quizzed Aaron about the precise timings and circumstances of the plagues. Then Gabriel arrived.

'Enjoying yourself, Oriel?' he asked carelessly. I scowled.

'I have another message for Moses,' he informed me.

Zipporah continued to push dough around her kneading trough, listening intently to Aaron as he revealed all manner of interesting details that her husband had failed to mention. Hushael wandered off, saying that he wanted to check on the Israelite flocks. Gabriel delivered our Boss's latest instructions, after which Moses rose to his feet, retrieved a small lump of bread dough that his wife had dropped on the floor, and squeezed his way round the crowded room until he was standing in front of Hur.

'Hur,' he said authoritatively, 'tell the whole Israelite community that on the tenth day of this month each family must select a young male lamb or kid from their flock. They must make sure that there will be enough meat to feed every member of their family. The animals must be prime specimens, no more than a year old. Make sure each family keeps their animal apart from the rest of their flock until I give you further instructions.'

I looked enquiringly at Gabriel, who replied with a satisfied smile, 'I don't try to understand it, Oriel. I just deliver the message.'

Hur was staring at Moses with similar incredulity. Aaron had succeeded in convincing him that the God of his forefathers was indeed working powerfully through Moses, but the Hebrew spokesman was not quite sure that he was ready to take orders from the man. Gabriel observed Hur's thoughts intently. When the Israelite leader took a breath and opened his mouth to reply, Gabriel swiftly interrupted, 'Do what he says, Hur.'

Hur closed his mouth and abandoned his complaint. 'I understand,' he said meekly. 'They are to keep these animals separate from their other flocks.'

'That is correct,' Moses replied.

'Why?'

Moses looked intently into Hur's eyes. I looked at Gabriel. As Gabriel had not considered asking our Boss that important question, I knew that he would not have furnished Moses with the answer. Hur's Angel guardian rescued the situation by reminding him that Moses was the man who had given orders to the hail and to the clouds, and they had obeyed.

'I will see that everyone complies,' he conceded.

'Come on, Oriel,' Gabriel called to me. 'You have a massacre to plan.'

Back in Heaven

Away from the tiresome restraints of Earth's narrow stream of time, Jeshaphael and Maphrael have been working hard on our preparations for the final plague. Maphrael has drawn up a detailed map of all our intended victims, which is updated daily with information about all relevant births, deaths and movements. Jeshaphael has recruited and trained a band of 147 Angels.

When I visited Jeshaphael's death squad, there was none of the usual Angelic banter among them. All these Angels will have blood on their hands. It is only their unwavering obedience to our Boss that holds them together. Not one of them is looking forward to the task ahead, not even Maphrael. The sight of the sombre Angels worried me. Heaven is a place of light and laughter. Jeshaphael's gathering felt more like an assembly of Opposition spirits.

'Our Creator wants to see you,' Jeshaphael informed me.

I looked around the room again, delving into the minds of all 147 Angels. These honest spirits are prepared to do whatever I ask – no matter how distasteful the task – as long as it is in the will of their Creator. I went to see him.

Making my way towards my Boss's door, I considered the one factor that sets me apart me from that gathering of solemnly obedient Angels. I have chosen to accept this task; they have not.

'Oriel,' my Boss greeted me, 'the final plague will occur four nights after the Israelites have selected their sheep and goats. Gabriel will deliver the instructions to Moses after his first order has been carried out.'

'May I ask what the Israelites will be required to do with these animals?'

'They will kill them.'

A shiver ran through me.

'There is a lot of killing involved in this,' I observed.

'Death, Oriel, is the tragic consequence of all rebellion within the Universe. You know this.'

Looking into those all-seeing eyes, I began to glimpse something of what I had been unable to recall previously after leaving our Boss's office: the shape and pattern to his plan for the Universe.

'What about the sheep and the goats,' I asked. 'Must they suffer the consequences of human foolishness?'

'The lamb must play its part too,' he assured me.

I couldn't see how. Though I have gained a rudimentary grasp of my Boss's greater plan, the fine detail is beyond my insight.

'Master,' I asked, moving on to the matter that was most concerning me, 'is the plan that I have worked out with Jeshaphael and Maphrael all right?'

'If you are planning to do what I asked you to do, yes.'

'But are we going about it the right way?'

He gave me a certain kind of patient look that meant, *I have just answered that question.*

'Would you have gone about it differently?' I tried again.

'My way of going about it, Oriel,' he smiled, 'is to leave it to you.'

I was hoping to feel reassured about the 147 glum Angels who were waiting for my command. Instead, the weight of responsibility lay even more heavily on me.

'Oriel,' my Boss said, 'Gabriel is waiting for you in your office. Will you please give him this?' He handed me a folder containing instructions for Moses.

I still felt uncomfortable. 'Is it right that I should ask you questions – but Gabriel does not?'

'Are your questions a rebellion against my instructions?'

'No.'

'Is Gabriel's unquestioning obedience a prelude to mutiny?'

'Of course not.'

Again he smiled. 'Gabriel is waiting for you.'

I worked on the puzzle as I returned to my office. Even Gabriel appeared to have lost some of his sparkle as I handed him our Boss's folder.

'I have just visited your death squad, Oriel,' he informed me.

'There's more death in there,' I said, watching him open the instructions concerning the lambs and kids. Heaven's Messenger studied his orders without any noticeable reaction.

'I'll come with you,' I suggested.

Egypt

We found Moses in Hur's modest home. The Israelites' *former* leader was reporting to his successor the results of the first phase of his plan. Suitable young sheep and goats have been selected and separated. Hur could not resist detailing a tedious description of how he had cleverly arranged for the message to be spread through the entire Hebrew community, in Pithom and beyond. While Moses struggled to look interested, Gabriel spoke into his vacant mind. When Hur proudly held his arms out wide and said, 'So that's how I did it. What do we do next?' Moses was ready with an answer.

'In three days' time, at twilight,' he explained, 'each family must slaughter their lamb or goat. Then they must cook it – not boiled like the Egyptians do, but roasted over a fire – and eat it with bitter herbs and bread made without yeast.' Hur took careful notes. 'They are to take the animal's blood,' Moses continued, 'and smear it on the door frames of the houses where they are eating.' Hur pulled a revolted face.

I glanced at Gabriel, who whispered, 'Don't ask me!'

Moses continued, 'Tell them that they must eat the whole animal. Anything left over should be burned in the fire.'

'What is the meaning of all this?' Hur enquired.

'On that same night,' Moses pressed on, 'God will pass through Egypt and strike down every firstborn male, both humans and cattle. He will bring down judgement on the gods of Egypt but he will pass over the homes of Israel.'

Gabriel turned to me. 'Let's go back.'

'I'll stay here for a while,' I told him.

Gabriel returned to Heaven. I wandered around Pithom for a while. In contrast to my own growing anxiety, there was a renewed brightness among the descendants of Abraham. Hur's change of heart has rekindled the People's hope. There is talk of freedom: freedom for mothers to be mothers, for shepherds to be shepherds, for children to be children. People working in the clay pits have been excitedly gossiping about Moses' dramatic confrontations with Pharaoh. I found young Gershom, Moses' son, and listened as he told his enthralled friends how his dad had physically pushed Pharaoh into the River Nile and threatened to turn him into a frog. They believed every word.

Next I returned to the home of young Prahotpe, whose short and traumatised life is only three days from its conclusion. The boy's Angel guardian greeted me, 'Why does it not encourage me to see you again, Archangel?'

'You are a questioner,' I observed, studying the Angel's mind. There was no trace of rebellion there; he simply wanted to know what was happening.

'Even if I had all the answers,' I informed the Angel, 'I would not be allowed to share them with you.'

'I know that,' he said graciously.

'Could I be alone with Prahotpe for a while?' I asked.

The boy was busy unwinding the threads from his old clothes so his mother could re-use them. I watched him closely. He is completely ignorant of his imminent fate, innocently daydreaming about restoring his family's fortunes. I considered the bold images that he was projecting across his thoughts. They were not as innocent as I had supposed. His fantasies were stained by all the usual selfishness of human greed and ambition. I longed to speak to the boy – not to warn him, but to explain; to tell him about the greater picture, about the part that his demise will play in the intricate pattern of my Boss's astounding plan. But I knew that I could not. Instead, I stayed and watched as he unravelled his soiled and worn out garment so that his mother could weave a new one.

If I could not tell him the wider truth, I thought, at least I could show him a glimpse of the Heavenly realities around him, about which he is almost totally ignorant. I began to slow my Angelic form in order to appear to the boy within the range of his dull human senses. A moment before he would have seen me, an idea leapt through my mind – an alternative to my plan, a better way of dealing with Prahotpe and all the other eldest sons of Egypt.

Heaven

I hurried back to Heaven. Jeshaphael was instructing his team in the physical make-up of the human brain, showing them exactly which part of the slushy organ to destroy. Maphrael was distributing copies of his map, impotently trying to cheer up the miserable Angels. I stood in the doorway and watched. They were too preoccupied to notice me. All I saw and heard reassured me that my revised plan was much better.

My Boss emerged from the far end of the corridor and stopped by my side. Together we observed the intense industry before us. Various Angels looked up, then returned to their solemn preparations. I looked into my Boss's eyes, hoping for some reassurance that he approved of my intentions. I did not put my request into words; nor did he express his reply. When my Boss departed, I stepped into the room and called for the attention of the assembled Angels.

'Thank you, all of you, and especially to Jeshaphael and Maphrael for their careful planning and preparation.'

There was a rumble of agreement.

'However, your services are no longer needed,' I informed them. 'You are not required to kill anyone.'

What had been grunts of agreement immediately became cheers. The cheers quickly grew into songs and then burst into the delightful blossom of Angelic dance. In an instant, the accumulated tension of our gruesome plan dissipated, and the sheer joy of Heaven was regained. There was only one Angel who was not singing and dancing: me. I quietly picked up one of Maphrael's maps and left them to it.

Egypt

I returned to Egypt at midnight on the fourteenth day of the month and headed straight for the home of Prahotpe. The boy was asleep.

In my usual form – like any Angel – I am too brilliant for human senses to register. For a few Earth minutes I stayed as I was and observed the sleeping boy. I was anxiously watched by Prahotpe's Angel guardian. Then I thinned my Angelic being down to a level at which it would stimulate Prahotpe's sleeping senses (though far stronger than the level that Gabriel employs when he delivers messages to men or women). For a brief moment young Prahotpe saw, heard, smelt, tasted and felt the intense beauty of Heaven. Then, when his fragile body could take no more, he let out a scream of pure wonder, and the light of his life went out. I did not stay to watch over his now lightless form. I looked briefly at the astounded Angel guardian beside me, and left.

I did not only leave the house. I left Earth's narrow stream of time and returned to the next house on Maphrael's map at exactly the same moment that I had arrived at Prahotpe's bedside: midnight. It was the home of Prahotpe's uncle, his father's older brother. I gave him a fatal glimpse of Heavenly light, and moved on, returning – once again – to midnight.

In this way I progressed around Egypt, home by home, eldest son by eldest son. I visited fathers, grandfathers, boys and babies, overloading their senses with a fraction of the true wonder of Heaven. At one point in this elongated midnight, my attention was distracted by an unexpected sight. I was standing at the bedside of an elderly Egyptian grandfather and caught a glimpse of the doorway of a house across the road. It looked as though someone had smeared light on the wooden door posts of the home. After gently putting out the life of the old man, I crossed the road to investigate this strange phenomenon. As I approached the shining door I could hear excited voices. Inside, three families were squashed around a fire, all dressed in travelling clothes, their sandals strapped on their feet. They were Israelite slaves. The incandescent daub on the door frame was the blood from the lamb that the family was busy eating. It was a signal to me that I should not visit my Boss's final plague on this particular home.

At that moment, the jollity of the midnight feast was interrupted by a loud scream of horror from a home behind me. That scream was quickly followed by other exclamations of grief. Wives and mothers throughout this small village were discovering their dead. The air was thick with wailing and shouting. People ran into the street carrying hastily-lit torches. What they discovered only intensified their anguish. Almost every household in the village had suffered at least one loss. Soon a deputation of traumatised Egyptians was banging on the only door in their village that was not already open: the shining door (though they could not see the shining) of the shanty home of their Israelite slaves.

The Egyptians did not knock in anger; they knocked in despair. They had seen so much in past months: their homes had been filled with frogs but the Israelites' home had not; their flesh had been bitten by gnats and covered with boils, but the skin of the Israelites had not; their cattle and crops had been destroyed by disease, hail and locusts, but the crowded little community of Hebrew slaves had been spared. When the door was opened, the distraught Egyptians begged their neighbours to leave.

'Go, join your fellow countrymen and women,' they implored. 'Go into the desert. Go and worship your God.' They offered pursefuls of gold and precious stones. 'Here, take these. Please go. Please leave us. You are free. Go. *Go!*'

The Israelites were ready. They had received Hur's message. Their possessions were packed. They picked up the dough that was already mixed for the next day's bread, and left, while I returned to the tranquility of midnight, to another Egyptian home and another first-born son. I was shaken by the intensity of the grief I had just witnessed and resolved not to be distracted again but to limit my activities to the briefest possible stretch of Earth's time.

I became more efficient in my work: arrive, appear, disappear, depart . . . over and over again. I discovered that I did not need to fully resume my Angelic brilliance to cross such a small stretch of time. Further into my lonely mission, as I arrived at yet another Egyptian home, I found Maphrael standing by the victim's bedside holding a copy of his map.

'I came to help you,' he said.

I was stunned, but I did not have time to consider. If I stayed too long in that home, at that time, I would be overtaken, for a second time, by the tidal wave of grief that I was causing.

'I don't need any help,' I said hurriedly.

'I want to help,' Maphrael insisted.

'I don't have time to argue,' I told him. 'Let me deal with this father and son first.'

I rapidly thinned my being to that condition where it caused the father of the household to sit bolt upright in bed, gasp in wonder and expire. I did the same to his eldest son, and led Maphrael out of time before the mother of the home and her other children were woken by the vocal grief of their neighbours.

'That's neat!' Maphrael exclaimed.

'It's awful,' I replied.

Although Maphrael was right in front of me, it felt as though there was an invisible barrier between us. Our spirits were separated by the indefinable fog of human suffering.

'What about the cattle and poultry, Oriel?' I heard Maphrael's voice saying. 'Aren't they supposed to be killed as well?'

'Yes, I know,' I said. 'I'll go back and do them when I have finished with the humans.'

'Isn't that a waste of effort?'

I looked at him, suddenly weary from the strain of my terrible activity. The matter of efficiency had not occurred to me. I was doing something so alien to my existence that waste of effort was a meaningless concept.

'Let me deal with the animals . . . please,' Maphrael said, invading my lonely chaos.

His offer infused me with such profound relief that I did not move. Then a trace of bitter uncertainty drifted across my mind.

'Did our Boss send you?' I asked.

'No. When I realised that you and a map had disappeared, I wondered what was happening. I rushed to the Boss's office and asked him if he had changed his mind. He laughed. Then I began to understand. I have been looking for you ever since but it was difficult to find you in such a narrow slice in time.'

I looked at my companion. 'Thank you,' I said. Then I returned to my work.

*   *   *

Gradually we worked our way down the length of the River Nile. When we came to the slave-built cities of Pithom and Pi-Rameses, the midnight streets were filled with the aroma of roasted lamb and fresh-baked bread. In every Israelite home the occupants were bright with hope that their God was about to do something wonderful.

'I don't know about you,' I said to Maphrael, 'but it doesn't feel very wonderful to me.'

The blood of lambs and goats, daubed on the door frames, signposted our way up and down newly-built streets, in and out of the homes of wealthy, slave-driving architects and master builders. Our journey finally brought us to the grandest building in the region, the new palace of Rameses II. This great edifice was also stained with blood – the blood of human slaves. That blood did not shine out to protect its occupants. It screamed for their justice.

131

Maphrael and I strode into the palace together and headed for the king's bedchamber. We stood looking down on the man whose stubborn pride had permitted such terrible suffering. Shlyphantel, the Seraph of Egypt, watched from the far side of Rameses' bed.

'He's not on the list,' Maphrael stated with unconcealed disappointment.

'His elder brother died as a young child,' Shlyphantel informed us.

'Pity.'

'Who *is* on the list, Maphrael?' I asked.

'Amenhirkopshef.'

Shlyphantel watched in silence as we crossed the palace complex to the Crown prince's apartment. On our way we encountered Rameses' pet duck – a drake, the first hatchling from its mother's first clutch of eggs. Maphrael dealt with it.

Amenhirkopshef was the last name on our itinerary. He was not asleep. He was busy entertaining one of his father's lesser wives. He died in her arms. The woman shrieked and ran naked through the palace, screaming and howling. Minutes later, the King of Egypt came face to face with the dreadful consequences of his arrogance. He was soon joined by those of his leading officials who were still alive. They were all fathers, and I had visited all their homes. Rameses was ushered through the confusion to his throne room. A succession of messengers was arriving at the palace from surrounding communities. They all brought the same news.

With the help of the Seraph, who has guided him since the death of his father, the king struggled to put aside his personal grief and deal with the distress of his nation. However, Amenhirkopshef's empty throne would not allow him to forget his own loss for more than the briefest moment. Pharaoh's favourite son arrived – Khaemwaset, the High Priest. He, too, was cold with shock. Khaemwaset stood in front of his older brother's vacant throne, his mind numbed by the terrible scenes he had just left behind in his own home.

'It is yours, Khaem,' his father said weakly. 'You are the Crown prince now.'

Khaemwaset understood the significance of his father's words and sat, very reluctantly, on his dead brother's seat. The council was assembling – or what was left of it.

'Send for Moses and Aaron,' Rameses ordered.

I was exhausted from my night's work. I longed to get away, to escape from all memory of time and place, never to see the faint spirits of broken humanity ever again, but I could not leave. My job was not yet done. Rameses had threatened to kill Moses if he ever saw him again, and his thoughts were now saturated with death. While Rameses waited for chariots to rush the new Israelite leader from his family dinner in Pithom, he had to tolerate a succession of desperate pleas from his bereaved subjects. There was only one message: *Please let the Hebrews go.* From the throne on his right, Khaemwaset repeated the same advice.

Rameses absorbed the mounting pressure of these demands. With Shlyphantel standing behind him, he maintained his royal dignity in the face of unimagined devastation until, out of the corner of his eye, he spotted a bedraggled slave carrying the limp form of a dead duck by its neck.

'Stop that woman!' the king roared. Palace guards charged after the startled slave, snatched the duck from her and delivered it to their king's lap. Rameses scooped up the creature in his arms and ran out into the palace gardens. There his emotional restraint dissolved and he sobbed uncontrollably into the white feathers of his dead pet.

His grief was not for the duck. It was for his son, and his grandson, and his trusted officials and their sons. It was for sons and fathers across Egypt and, most of all, it was for his own failure in the task he had inherited to protect the nation from the tyranny of foreign rulers. His sense of failure was complete.

Shlyphantel stood impassively behind the king, as he always did. I wondered if I should apologise to him for the devastation I had brought to his nation but, like him, I had been following orders. He noted my unease.

'Egypt will recover, Oriel,' he said stiffly. 'Egypt honours only its triumphs. It hides its failures.' I looked at the proud Seraph who has guided this powerful nation for many hundreds of orbits around Earth's Sun. He was studying me with equal intensity. 'Oriel,' he said, 'now *you* have a nation to lead.'

'What do you mean?' I asked. 'I'm an Archangel, not a Seraph.'

'The Israelites need an Angel to lead them.'

'I'm sure our Boss has someone in mind,' I said.

A messenger arrived in the courtyard and spoke to Rameses: 'Moses and Aaron have arrived, your highness.' We returned to the Throne Room.

The pharaoh washed his face before entering his palace and resuming his regal posture. The murderous fury that he had felt against Moses earlier in the night had been washed away by his tears. He sat upright on the throne and looked into the eyes of the only adversary to have comprehensively defeated him.

'Go!' he ordered coldly. 'Go tonight. Take your men, your women, your children, your sheep and your goats, and go. Leave my nation and never come back.'

Moses bowed graciously and said nothing. He and Aaron turned to leave. When the two Israelites were half way along the pillared hall, Rameses shouted after them.

'Moses!'

They stopped and turned. Pharaoh's voice was quieter: 'Moses, give me your blessing.'

I watched as Moses retraced his steps to the raised platform where the king sat.

'Oriel!' a sharp voice called to me. It was Shlyphantel. 'Oriel, stand behind your man. This is not a blessing between cousins; this is a blessing between rulers.'

I looked across to the Seraph. He was utterly serious. I moved obediently to Hushael's side behind Moses. 'What's happening?' he asked anxiously.

'I'm not sure,' I replied.

By this time Moses had already climbed the steps and was standing in front of the throne of Egypt. Rameses was standing too. Moses' mind was busy with silent prayers for another set of instructions from Gabriel.

'Where, in all this round planet, is Gabriel?' I asked nobody in particular.

'Oriel!' came Shlyphantel's sharp voice again. 'Your leader must bless mine.'

'I am not a Seraph,' I protested.

'Yours is no ordinary nation,' Shlyphantel replied.

I looked questioningly across the hall to Maphrael.

'Don't ask me,' he insisted.

I was stuck in the unrelenting stream of Earth's time and hurriedly tried to assemble some constructive thoughts. *My Boss never asks us to do things we cannot do. He always gives us the information we need.* I could see no alternative but to follow Shlyphantel's instructions.

I spoke into Moses' thoughts. 'Hold your old staff up in front

134

of you and say: *I bless you in the name of the God of Abraham, the God of Isaac and the God of Jacob.* Then kiss him on both cheeks and leave . . . slowly . . . without turning back.'

I looked anxiously to Shlyphantel hoping for affirmation. He was speaking into Rameses' mind: *When he raises his wooden staff, kneel before him. When he lowers it, rise.* I wanted the Seraph to give me a reassuring Heavenly smile. He did not. He stood sternly and formally behind his man while Moses blessed his cousin. I left with Moses.

Not long after leaving the palace, we encountered Lucifer, the leader of the Opposition, with the so-called gods of Egypt. They were accompanying a procession of grieving Egyptians to the temple of Osiris. Lucifer was thoroughly enjoying the mayhem.

'Oriel, you idiot,' he sneered, 'you've really messed things up this time.'

I knew better than to reply.

'No wonder your Boss has demoted you to Seraph.'

This second comment hurt me deeply. A flash of darkness shot through my being. Could it be true? Had I messed up? Was I being banished from Heaven to live on Earth?

* * *

I need to discuss these matters with my Boss – if he will allow it. I have asked Maphrael to stand in as Seraph for the People of Israel. (I had been thinking that he deserved some honour for helping me tonight, but now I am wondering if he will be condemned as my accomplice.) I find it hard to believe that I could have so comprehensively misunderstood my Boss's instructions. Yet the misery of Egypt suggests that it's all been a terrible mistake – even though Moses and his People have been given their freedom.

Heaven

I went directly to my Boss's office, only to find the door open and the room empty. This confirmed my worst fear. He did not wish to see me. I made my way down the corridor, passing the offices of my fellow Archangels. Only Lucifer's door was closed, as it always is. The other rooms were all open and deserted. I concluded that my colleagues must have been instructed to avoid me. I proceeded further. Not an Angel to be seen.

I was alone in Heaven. Indeed, I could no longer call it Heaven. Heaven is where my Boss and his servants live joyfully together. I could only think of one explanation for this terrifying turn of events: perhaps – like humans – I had become incapable of seeing or hearing my Boss and his spiritual creatures. I scrabbled around my mind in search of a more optimistic alternative. There was one. Maybe all of Heaven had been called to a meeting with their Boss. I hurried to the Great Gathering Place of Angels and found it to be filled with all the orders of Heaven. I entered at the very back, where the minor Cherubs stand. They did not notice me. I could hear my Boss's voice filling the assembly.

'And so,' he was saying, 'in Earth's today, a new nation is born. This is no ordinary Earthly nation. I have chosen this race of humans to be my own.'

I followed the attentive gazes of the Cherubs. My Boss was surrounded, as he always is on such occasions, by his Archangels. There were two vacant places: one where Lucifer once stood; the other was my own place.

'I have chosen this nation,' my Boss continued, 'to be a model for all humanity.'

I nudged the nearest Cherub. 'Has he said anything about me?' I asked. He ignored me; I wasn't sure that he could see me at all.

'Like all things newborn on Earth,' our Creator informed the Heavenly gathering, 'this nation must grow and mature. Today it is only an infant.' This very human image brought smiles to the faces of the Cherubs around me.

'When infant Israel reaches independence,' the King of Heaven said, 'I will entrust it to the leadership of a Seraph. Until then it will need a nurse.' A ripple of amusement spread among the Angels.

'The Angel who will wet-nurse my People is . . .'

The Angels were bubbling with excitement. They followed their Master's steady gaze as it swept along the line of Archangels, past various ranks of Angels, and settled on the mass of Cherubs at the very back of the Gathering Place. The Cherubs squealed with delight as all Heaven turned and looked at them.

My shame opened up like a bottomless chasm. The thought that a mere Cherub was being entrusted with the task in which I had failed, was more than I could bear. I left. The rowdy Angelic cheers from the Gathering Place faded into silence as I made my way into eternal exile. I stopped, and turned to take one last look at my former home. What I saw transformed my lonely misery into sheer terror. An Angel warrior was hurtling down the corridor at me. He was approaching at a speed Angels only use when in battle. I was paralysed by fear.

'Archangel Oriel,' the warrior shouted. 'You must come with me.'

I was incapable of movement. My Angelic body refused to obey the instructions my mind gave. I was imprisoned by my fear.

The Angel stopped in front of me, his face closer to mine than is normal among Angels. I was unable to look away, my eyes not responding to my instinct to hide. What I saw, directly before me, was not the blazing wrath of divine judgement but a radiant smile.

'*You're* the wet-nurse!' he grinned.

A small part of me understood what this meant. The rest was utterly confused. I numbly followed the warrior back towards the Great Gathering Place. In through the small door by which I had left, I was led down an avenue of bright smiling faces. At the end of that avenue was the smile from which all laughter flows. My Boss directed me to my usual place between Archangels Gabriel and Raphael and then turned to address the gathered Angels. Before he did, Gabriel said quietly, 'Welcome back, Destroying Angel.'

His happiness was infectious. Utterly relieved to be back where I belonged, I leaned towards him and stated categorically, 'I am *not* a mushroom.'

Pithom

Before returning to my new duties as acting Seraph, I spoke with my Boss. He reassured me that I had not failed him in any way, and insisted that I return to the exact moment in time I left Egypt.

'Back there and then, Oriel,' he told me, 'the infant Israel has not been born. Egypt's labour pains have reached their climax, but Israel's waters have not yet broken.'

This comment meant very little to me, but I noted a certain ironic amusement in his eyes.

'Waters?' I asked, shuddering at the very word.

My Boss smiled even more brightly. 'Oh, yes!' he said.

* * *

I rejoined Maphrael a fraction of an Earth second after I had left him.

'That was quick!' he commented.

'Maphrael,' I said, 'I must thank you for what you did for me tonight. If I could, I would reward you fully for stepping beyond your duties to support me, but we have much still to do.'

Maphrael, more accustomed to criticism from senior Angels than to praise, was uncharacteristically quiet. Meanwhile, Moses and Aaron were racing back to Pithom in the same chariots that had brought them to Avaris. We were following the chariots. Maphrael finally broke his silence.

'There is one thing you could do for me,' he said tentatively.

'If I can, I will,' I stated.

'Oh, you certainly *can* do it,' he said, with more than a hint of his usual mischief.

I began to regret the openness of my offer. 'What is it?' I asked cautiously.

'Call me Maff.'

'Why?'

'Because I prefer it.'

I have always considered it a profound disrespect to my Boss that any Angel should fail to use the name given to him at the moment of his creation, but I was held by my promise. I conceded.

'Yes . . . *Maff.*'

* * *

We found the sprawling Israelite settlement in some confusion. The People had finished their symbolic dinners and there was a great amount of coming and going. Families who had been released from domestic slavery by their wealthy Egyptian owners were arriving, carrying their possessions. Large numbers of Egyptians were arriving on their own initiative to urge the Hebrews to leave the country as soon as possible. They brought with them barrow-loads of rolls of cloth as well as generous amounts of gold and silver. There was a buzz of excitement. Everyone seemed to know that they were about to leave slavery, although no one had actually been told.

Hur had been trying to instil some order into the community. He repeatedly sent messengers through the streets, urging people to return to their homes and await instructions. However, no matter how often he tried to impress on his fellow Israelites that they were not necessarily free, nobody believed him. There was a reason for this. Every human messenger that Hur sent was accompanied by his or her Angel guardian and, among the Angels, Pharaoh's orders were already known. Whatever messages of caution and restraint the People heard with their ears, their spirits heard something different. Some were scuttling back and forth into the areas where the Egyptians lived, borrowing carts and barrows. The Egyptians, still in the first shock of their grief, were generous without exception. They too were the unconscious hearers of Angelic news. They knew in their spirits that the freedom of the Hebrew slaves was the only thing that would save them from the downward spiral of disaster and death.

It was not only Hebrew slaves who were celebrating their liberty. Many others had also been set free, and were clamouring to go along with the Israelites.

When Moses and Aaron's chariots rumbled into the view of this liquid mass of humanity, they were greeted as conquering heroes. Everyone – Israelites, other slaves, even Egyptians – stopped what they were doing and cheered. Even funeral processions – and we passed a good many – offered their praises to the tall Israelite in a Midianite cloak driving an Egyptian chariot. I was startled by the graciousness of these humans. So many personal hurts and griefs were laid aside. To watch bereaved Egyptian mothers embracing excited Israelite youths and wishing them well infused me with a new respect for humanity. As I rode behind Moses, I began to think that being nursemaid to this People may not be as daunting as I had assumed.

I focused my thoughts on Moses himself. There was a thrill of joy surging through his body such as he had not experienced since the days when he fed at his mother's breast. For as long as he remembers, he has always been an outsider, always been treated with suspicion. This adulation was a measure of value that Moses understood. As an Egyptian prince, he had been taught to measure the approval of the people. He knew that this outpouring of admiration was utterly genuine. Moses surveyed himself from a new perspective. He found that he believed in himself, that he valued himself, that he loved himself.

I looked to the next chariot, in which Aaron was content to ride as passenger to an experienced Egyptian charioteer. For the first time since I found him in the clay pit – indeed for the first time since the birth of his infamous younger brother – Aaron was holding no resentment against Moses. The bitter pain of slavery had produced blossom. Somewhere in the inaccessible depths of Aaron's mind, it all made sense. He remembered the story of his ancestor Levi, who had also suffered from a younger brother problem, until that brother saved his family's lives.

The news of Moses' return sped down the streets of Pithom more swiftly than his chariot. When we swept into the entrance of the Israelite settlement, Miriam and Zipporah were already there. Aaron ran to embrace his elder sister. Moses secured the horses' reins, stepped down from the chariot and walked straight past his wife and sons, directly into Hur's small house.

'We leave tonight,' Moses instructed the man who had managed the affairs of the Israelite slaves for many years. 'Send messages at once. Tell the People to assemble their families outside their homes and wait for my orders. No one is to leave the settlement until we all leave. Any family which owns sheep or goats must send one person to lead their flock. They will bring up the rear.'

Hur may have been Moses' sternest critic in the past, but he too was caught up in the ecstasy of the night. At that moment he would have done whatever Moses told him.

'I'll be in Miriam's hut,' Moses told him. 'Send me a message when everything is ready. Before that,' he added, 'I need to speak to young Joshua.'

Outside Hur's house, Moses gave more orders: to his wife, his sons, his brother and his sister.

'We must get our things packed,' he instructed and strode ahead, leaving them to follow.

I followed too, alongside the ever-supportive Zipporah. She was suppressing a storm of anger against her husband. When the door of Miriam's shack closed behind the family, she let her feelings loose.

'What do you think I've been doing since the moment you left here without even bothering to tell me where you were going? I had to ask Hur where they had taken you. For all I knew, you might have gone anywhere. And now you walk straight past us as if you didn't even know us. I got more respect tonight from the Egyptian architect than I got from you. You just took it for granted that we would be waiting for you when you returned. You just *assumed* that we would follow behind you like obedient sheep. You just *assumed* that we hadn't done anything to get ready, just because *you* weren't here to give us orders.

'If you are going to be the leader of this People, Moses, you need to do a damned sight better than that because, right now, you are making a total mess of leading your own family. Don't we matter anymore? Don't we deserve to be told what you are doing? Don't you need us now that you are everyone's hero? How do you think we feel? Do you care what we feel? Did you stop to think of us for a single moment while soaking up the adulation of everyone else? We cared for you long before they did. I didn't *have* to leave my home to come with you. I didn't *have* to become a slave while you strutted around Egypt with the *safe conduct* given to you by your precious cousin – who happens to be the same man who made your own son work as a slave in the clay pits. Did you notice any of that, Moses? Or were you too busy trying to save the world?'

There was more – a lot more. Miriam and Aaron busied themselves with irrelevant tasks and the boys played very quietly in the corner of the home. Moses gradually shrank back to the stature of an ordinary man while Zipporah vented the pain of many months of isolation and humiliation. At the end, after repeated demands to, 'Say something, then!' Moses managed a deeply contrite, 'I'm very sorry, Zipporah.' There followed a long silence during which I had second, and third, thoughts about the prospect of living with so many assorted humans while they mature into a cohesive nation.

After Zipporah had explained to her deflated husband that she had already packed everything they needed – *no thanks to Moses* – the family had nothing to do but wait and I was able to get on with my own preparations. I sent Maphrael to fetch Jeshaphael from Heaven and tell Gabriel that I did not know which road we should take once we left Egypt. I then explained to Hushael that he and I would be sharing responsibility for Moses until the Israelite nation was ready for a Seraph of its own. I suggested that he consider what he might do when that happens. The quiet Angel looked quite crestfallen, though, typically, he said nothing. This left us in an awkward silence, during which my thoughts wandered back to puzzle over my Boss's ironic smile when he had talked about Israel's 'waters' being broken.

* * *

141

When Hur's messenger arrived to tell Moses that the People were ready, I had still not heard from Gabriel, and that concerned me. Joshua arrived with the messenger. Moses drilled Joshua on having his trained troops march at the very front and very back of the Israelite column.

'Which column?' Joshua asked.

'The People are all leaving today,' Moses explained impatiently. 'I want one troop of armed men at the front and another troop at the back.'

'But the People aren't leaving in one line,' Joshua replied. 'Different groups are going different ways.'

'Don't be ridiculous,' Moses spluttered. 'They'll get lost. Whose idea is this?'

'Hur's, I expect.'

'Stay here,' Moses barked at his family. 'I will come back if I can. If not, go with the others.'

'MOSES!' bellowed Zipporah, to remind him of their earlier conversation.

'I have to sort out this mess.'

He didn't stop to shut the door behind him.

Moses surged past family after family of Hebrews loaded to capacity with possessions and provisions. They kept out of the way, somehow perceiving the fully charged thunder cloud that was sweeping by, and not wishing it to unleash its energy on them.

'HUR!' Moses boomed when he spotted his intended target. 'What's this nonsense about dividing the People?'

Hur was remarkably steadfast under the attack.

'There are too many People for us all to leave by the same road,' he asserted. 'It would take a whole day to clear the settlement and the front of the procession would be so far from the back that it would be impossible to maintain communication.'

'But if we leave in different directions, the People will be scattered. What will be *impossible* will be defending them.'

'The People will *not* be scattered,' Hur insisted, 'because they will all head towards the signal in the desert.'

'What signal?'

Moses' question surprised Hur. 'The signal that you . . . Didn't you tell me about a signal?'

'I did not.'

'Who did, then? I am absolutely sure that someone told me to tell the People to head for the signal.'

Moses glared at Hur and Hur looked urgently around him, searching for the source of his information.

'It was me,' a voice declared from behind me. The humans did not hear this admission but the Angels did. It was my Boss. I turned to him with considerable relief.

'Oriel,' he said, 'I would like to borrow Hushael, Jeshaphael and Maff.'

'Of course,' I muttered, surprised by this unexpected visit.

'I need to teach them something.'

'Is this to do with the signal that Hur was talking about?' I asked, trying to keep track of the increasingly complex progression of events.

'It is.'

'Do you really need Maphrael?' I enquired tentatively. Before my Boss's arrival, I had been experiencing a sense of rising urgency as the implications of being a Seraph began to impact on me. I did not want to be alone with such a huge responsibility.

'For now, yes,' he said calmly.

In front of me, Moses – who had sensed my Boss's admission, even though he had not actually heard it – was conceding to Hur on the matter of the departure plans. He then returned to his family.

Succoth

In Miriam's hut, Moses' family were seated on the floor around an old barrow filled with their meagre possessions. The camp had reached a state of restless quiet. Everyone knew they were leaving their life of enforced labour and there was now nothing to do but wait for the order to depart. Miriam and Aaron were sitting, each with an arm around the other, looking at the tatty wooden shack that had been their home since they were transferred from Thebes to the brickworks in Goshen. Although theirs had been a miserable existence in so many ways, it had become familiar. Their future – even though it means freedom – is uncertain. They have dreamed of this moment all their lives. But now that it has come, they are afraid. Zipporah has no such fears. She knows where she is going. Home to the desert.

Moses was talking quietly to his two sons. 'After the Lord

brings you into the land of Canaan and gives it to you, as he has promised, you must never forget this day. When your own sons ask you, "Dad, what happened?" say, "The Lord brought us out of Egypt and out of slavery with a mighty hand".'

Then Moses roused his family. He and Aaron each took a handle of their barrow. In his other hand Moses clutched his old staff. Zipporah and Miriam hoisted flat bowls of bread dough onto their shoulders. The boys each had a small sack to carry. They lumbered forwards, along a route marked by burning torches. And all along the track other families rose to their feet, picked up their belongings and started to move. Soon all the shacks were dark and deserted. No one asked where they were going; few even spoke. All that mattered was that they were leaving.

I became aware of the sound of Angels singing. Rich harmonies and countermelodies drifted through the night air towards me. Archangel Raphael had placed a small choir at each of the exits from the Hebrew settlement. They were there to celebrate the moment when the descendants of Abraham stepped out of slavery and into freedom. Their song remembered the relationship that Abraham had enjoyed with his Creator, and how he trusted my Boss's promise that he would be the father of many nations, even though both he and his wife were old and had no children. The passing Israelites could not hear Raphael's composition, but the music stirred their spirits. They too began to sing, in low chants, as they climbed the high ridge of discarded rubble which had been the boundary to their world since the day they were rounded up into the slave camp. For as long as most of them could remember, day and night, that ridge had been topped by a row of armed Egyptian guards, there to keep the Midianite tribes out and the Hebrew slaves in. Now the guard posts were abandoned.

Unhampered by the effects of Earth's feeble gravity, I reached the top of the ridge ahead of the humans and looked for the 'signal' that our Boss had promised as a gathering point for the separate lines of Israelites. I saw my Boss instantly, high in the night air, some distance away across the Egyptian plain. Maphrael and Hushael were below him on the ground, but I could not see Jeshaphael.

The first in the line of human refugees puffed their way to the top of the ridge, took one look across the nocturnal plain and exclaimed, 'What, in the name of God, is that?' They were staring

144

at the sky between the two Angels and my Boss. I looked again. The reason I had failed to notice Jeshaphael was that he had dramatically dimmed his usual Angelic brightness. He was floating in the air above his colleagues looking decidedly uncomfortable. But to the insensitive eyes of the breathless humans, he appeared as a tall column of multi-coloured light. Without exception, every Israelite seeing him let out an exclamation of sheer wonder. Those further back in the line scrambled quickly up the ridge to share the sight. Moses crouched down between his sons and whispered, 'The Lord will provide, Gershom. The Lord will provide, Eliezer.'

The flat, locust-decimated plain before us was streaked with numerous lines of excited Israelites, all making their way towards my Boss, though they could not see him. What they were seeing was Jeshaphael's pillar of living fire.

Maphrael saw me on the ridge and came to join me.

'Sorry I didn't come earlier, Oriel,' he said. 'Jeshaphael isn't very happy, and insisted that I stay.'

It occurred to me that Jeshaphael would have to be extremely unhappy to want Maphrael to stay with him, but I did not say so. My Boss called me.

'I will leave this in your care, Oriel,' he said. 'This sign of my presence must continue, day and night, until my People reach the land I promised to Abraham. Jeshaphael, Hushael and Maff know what to do.'

At that he left his specific vantage point above Jeshaphael's shining signal and disappeared, spreading his presence out across the plodding lines of the Israelite People.

'Jeshaphael,' I called, looking down, 'You are wonderful!'

'I don't feel very wonderful,' he replied. 'How long do I have to keep this down for?'

'I'm not exactly sure,' I told him, 'but it could be several orbits of their Moon.' The deliberately dimmed Angel suddenly returned to his usual condition.

'Don't do that!' I shouted urgently. 'They won't be able to see you if you get any brighter.'

Jeshaphael slowly resumed his gloomier state.

'I wish you could see the effect you are having on the Israelites,' I said. 'You are the most wonderful thing they have seen in all their short lives.' This news had the desired effect on Jeshaphael. 'I suggest that you and Hushael take it in turns. That will make it easier to sustain this signal through a long period of human time.'

145

'What about Maphrael?' Jeshaphael asked.

'There will be other challenges for him,' I replied.

Jeshaphael and Hushael agreed that they would exchange places when Earth's Sun became visible over the planet's horizon, and swap back when it disappeared again.

I stayed with my Angels and watched as the Israelites made their slow progress towards us. When the feeble brightness of the Sun crept over the barren fields, Hushael replaced Jeshaphael above our heads. I immediately sent Jeshaphael to join the Israelites, to discover for himself how magnificent a suitably dimmed Angel appeared to the Israelites' watery eyes. When he returned, he was not impressed.

'Apparently I look like a rather peculiar cloud,' he informed us glumly.

'That's not what they were seeing earlier,' I assured him. 'Hushael must be doing it differently. Look in their memories,' I suggested. 'There was nothing cloudy about what they saw last night.'

*   *   *

A deputation of Angel guardians informed me that their humans were in desperate need of rest. We agreed that they should halt their progress to eat and sleep when they reached Hushael's signal. At the very front of the Israelite advance was the leader of their novice army, Joshua. He and the young men around him were not carrying any belongings, only battle axes and short spears. I informed Joshua's guardian, Phaliel, that they could stop here. The young men rested while their fellow Israelites caught them up and now, as others begin to arrive, they are using their energy to help the tired travellers set up camp.

Etham

The People only stopped at Succoth for a few of Earth's hours. The children slept; the women baked flat loaves of unfinished bread using dough from their kneading bowls; and the men reorganised their packs and carts. Meanwhile, Moses, Hur and Joshua met with representatives of the twelve Israelite tribes to discuss what to do next. There was an argument. Moses wanted to return to Midian, to the mountain where he had spoken with my Boss. Hur wanted to head directly up the Way of Huros towards the territory which my Boss promised to Abraham's descendants. Hur's subservient awe in the presence of Moses seems to have waned. He was full of confidence after the logistical triumph of getting the Israelites out of the slave settlements so efficiently, and was eager to maintain the momentum of their activity. It would take just nine days to travel up the famous Egyptian highway to Canaan. But neither man was prepared to give way.

'We must go to the land that God promised us,' Hur asserted.

'But first,' Moses replied, 'we must worship God on the mountain where he spoke to me.'

They repeated these positions several times. Phaliel, Joshua's guardian, turned to me.

'You are Israel's Seraph, Oriel,' he said. 'You have to resolve this.'

The idea did not appeal to me. I looked hastily around, only to find myself pinned down by the expectant eyes of 17 Angels.

'Gabriel will arrive with some instructions, I'm sure,' I said uncertainly.

'I used to work with Gabriel,' Jeshaphael whispered to me, 'and I don't remember him taking endless messages to Seraphs.'

'Then I shall have to visit our Boss and speak to him,' I squirmed.

'Do you often see queues of Seraphs waiting outside our Boss's office for instructions?' Maphrael asked.

I looked plaintively at Hushael.

'Oriel,' he said, 'you expect guardians to make their own decisions, based on their knowledge of Our Creator.'

'But this is different,' I pleaded.

'Only because you are the guardian of a nation rather than an individual,' Maphrael replied, rather accusingly.

I was cornered. There were 17 Angels still waiting for me to make a decision and I knew, in the depths of my being, that my Boss was willing to trust my judgement.

'To take this many humans through territory held by other tribes is a recipe for war,' I stated. 'We need to lead them through undisputed lands until they are ready.' I looked at Hadziel, Hur's guardian. (Hur was still locked in an escalating row with Moses.) 'Hur must concede,' I told him. 'We are heading into the desert.'

Each Angel guardian attended to his respective human and drew their opinion towards that of Moses. I spoke to Moses and the matter was resolved. I recommended that Hur be given some significant responsibility to keep his mind off this defeat. Moses asked him to draw up a schedule for the journey.

Hur's plan reflected his usual ruthless efficiency. The People would travel by day and night, walking for four hours, then stopping for four hours. The leaders of the Israelite clans wanted to get as far away from Egypt as quickly as they could.

* * *

The journey from Succoth has taken us several days. We have travelled through sparsely populated farmland tended by Egyptian peasants who appear to have suffered less intensely from the plagues. Though daunted by the number of the departing slaves, they have been generous in providing food and water for little cost. The gold and jewellery acquired by the Israelites from their former neighbours has been very useful. Today we arrived at the edge of the desert, which is also the limit of Pharaoh's rule. Moses insisted that the People be allowed to rest for a few days. They are exhausted from their long walk and anxious about the barren wilderness ahead of them.

During the night, while the People were enjoying their first full night's sleep since the implementation of Hur's shift-work system, I was visited by Shlyphantel, the Seraph of Egypt. I welcomed him warmly. He stood, upright, serious and silent.

'You have cost Egypt dearly, Oriel,' he said.

I didn't know what to say. I wanted to disown all activities, and direct his criticism at my Boss, whose instructions I had been following. But I didn't get the opportunity. Gabriel arrived.

'Oriel, Shlyphantel,' he said, checking his instructions, 'the Boss wants to see you both.'

Shlyphantel bowed graciously.

'Are we allowed to leave our people?' I asked Egypt's experienced guardian.

'Only if we return to the same point in time that we leave,' he informed me.

That's what we did. In our Boss's presence, Shlyphantel was tense and uncomfortable. It surprised me. How could any being be uncomfortable in their Creator's company? For Shlyphantel, however, the cult of power and respect is normal. He stood before his Creator with the same subservient fear he has taught Rameses to expect of the Egyptians.

'Oriel,' my Boss said warmly, 'I want you to lead your People back into Egypt.'

I was startled by this instruction but did not question it. It seemed important that I should display a certain Seraphic dignity.

'Shlyphantel,' our Creator continued, 'you must harden Rameses' heart against Israel one last time.'

Shlyphantel bowed. I stared at him. A moment earlier, I had looked up to him and imitated his dignified restraint. Now he had become my enemy. I was to lead my fledgling People back into Pharaoh's clutches and the Seraph of Egypt would turn him against them.

My Boss dismissed Shlyphantel, who left expressionless, upright and proud as ever. My mind was reeling from the implications of the two brief commands.

'You have a question, Oriel,' he said, with an inviting smile.

I had thousands of questions, all jostling in my mind to be the first to be asked. All I could manage was a feeble squeak. 'Why?'

'If my People turn back,' my Boss explained, 'Rameses will conclude that they are confused, hemmed in by the desert and wandering aimlessly. Then he will come after them and try to force them back into servitude. But he will fail. Only then will he understand that he has lost his slaves for ever.'

'More deaths,' I observed sombrely.

My Boss did not reply. He looked into my eyes, and in that gaze I glimpsed, for the third time, an insight into the deeper patterns of his plan. As before, I couldn't fully understand what I saw. Also as before, the insight evaporated when I left his presence. I returned to Earth. Shlyphantel did not even turn to look as we arrived side by side; he sped back to Avaris to rekindle Rameses' hatred of Moses.

Eastern Egypt

I passed the message on to Moses, including the warning that Rameses would be coming after him. He took the news calmly.

'What has become of the depressed shepherd who had all but abandoned human life?' I asked Hushael, while Moses helped Zipporah to pack their few possessions onto the borrowed barrow. He said nothing.

I really don't understand humans. Angels remain much as they are created to be, although we can be changed – in certain ways – by our experiences. Humans, on the other hand, seem to change continually – though that may be a good thing considering that they start their lives incapable of doing just about anything for themselves.

I was pondering these things when Hushael unexpectedly said, 'He's still the same old Moses, really.' I looked enquiringly at the Angel but knew better than to expect any explanation.

Hur was less resistant to the new plan than I expected. He is afraid of the desert and was content to remain in the more fertile Egyptian borderlands. He might have reacted differently, though, if Moses had told him about the renewed threat from Pharaoh.

For a few days the People wandered fairly aimlessly around eastern Egypt. Each time they were packed up and ready to depart, I left it to Jeshaphael and Hushael to decide where to position their columns of fire or cloud. My only instruction is that we do not return to any place already visited. This is for two reasons. Firstly, because it is not in the nature of Angels to do the same thing twice, and secondly, because the People are dependent on the food they can buy from Egyptian farmers and they tend to exhaust all available supplies in one visit. The consequence of this is that we have drifted slowly southwards along the eastern fringe of the country.

Today, Archangel Gabriel arrived with a message: *Go and camp near Pi-Hahiroth, on the plain below Migdol.* I was pleased to have a clear objective but my pleasure was short-lived. Pi-Hahiroth is worryingly close to the Sea of Reeds, where we disposed of the locust plague. The plain below Migdol is directly adjacent to the seashore. This is the last place I would want to take my People. Water is dangerous enough at the best of times, but this particular body of the dreadful fluid is an unwelcome reminder of just how awesomely destructive the stuff can be. Hushael, who has no such reservations, was happy to lead the way with his pillar of thick bright cloud.

Pi-Hahiroth

Jeshaphael was much more uneasy when Earth's Sun set and it was his turn to lead the Israelites towards the designated camping ground by the water's edge. He put up a token resistance at the idea of stopping quite so close to the sea but did as he was asked. As the pale light faded, I realised that the People would not reach the shore that day and instructed Jeshaphael to stop. Only a short time after Joshua and his little army had put down their untested weapons, the darkly shining Angel called me up into the sky to join him.

'Look, Oriel,' Jeshaphael said anxiously, directing my attention towards Egypt. In the distance, across the flat and featureless landscape of the Nile Delta, I could see a large crowd of Angels, all moving in our direction. Below those Angels, though I could not see it yet, was Pharaoh's army.

'Do you think the Egyptians will be able to see your pillar of fire?' I asked Jeshaphael.

'I have not made any attempt to hide it from them,' he told me.

I called Maphrael and Hushael to view the advancing doom.

'They shouldn't be able to see Jeshaphael yet,' Maphrael suggested. 'We can only just see the Angels, and Jesh is more than a little dim at present.'

I ignored the low growl from Jeshaphael and instructed Maphrael to cross the plain and report back on the size of the approaching force. The news was not encouraging. Rameses is leading the assault himself, accompanied by his elite chariot regiment and Egypt's entire rapid reaction force of chariots and cavalry. The only encouragement was that they had halted for the night to allow troops and horses to rest.

Back at Pi-Hahiroth, the Israelites set up their camp, looking forward to a full night's sleep and completely ignorant of the calamity about to descend on them. I have decided not to alert Moses yet. Hushael's advice was that a good night's sleep is the best preparation we could offer him. I did, however, suggest that Phaliel encourage Joshua to give his little army a training session, and invited Archangel Michael to come and oversee it.

I passed the night hours in the sky above the camp, discussing the situation with my team. Michael and Phaliel joined us when Joshua and his young companions finally gave in to their need for sleep. He was not optimistic.

'They could possibly defeat an army that was half the size of their own,' he reported, 'but against Pharaoh's professional soldiers they will only be a fraction better than useless.'

'Our Boss is preparing for historic victory against Pharaoh's army,' I explained, trying to raise the spirits of the Angels around me.

'I don't doubt that, Oriel,' Michael agreed. 'What I am telling you is that you will not achieve it with Joshua's amateurs.'

'Surely our Boss will send some instructions?' Jeshaphael wondered.

'Not necessarily,' Maphrael said. 'I expect that warfare falls within a Seraph's standard duties.' He looked questioningly towards Archangel Michael and I followed his gaze.

'Maphrael is right,' the Leader of Heaven's Armies told us. Everyone looked at me.

'Hushael,' I said, 'how long will it take the Egyptians to reach us?'

There was a long silence, after which he tentatively said, 'As the crow flies, I should think . . .'

I interrupted. 'I'm not interested in crows. How long will it take?'

His reply was instant. 'One or two days.'

'Very well, Angels,' I said. 'We have until tomorrow afternoon to come up with a plan to defeat that army.'

* * *

I moved away from the Israelite camp to be alone and consider my responsibilities in the impending war. Until my recent appointment as acting Seraph, I was only a visitor to Earth's time. Time has always annoyed me, but before I could always escape it whenever I wished. Now I am confined to its narrow stream, not allowed to miss a single passing second. Tonight those seconds are passing very rapidly.

* * *

When Earth rolled into view of the Sun, Jeshaphael left his fire duty and joined me. I was staring across the Sea of Reeds.

'What are you doing here, of all places?' he demanded.

'Wondering,' I replied. 'Wondering why our Boss instructed me to bring the People here.'

'They will be hemmed in,' Jeshaphael observed. 'Pharaoh's army will spread out and surround them on three sides with their backs to the sea. They'll be slaughtered.'

A chill swept through my spirit at the memory of the silent efficiency with which the Sea of Reeds had consumed a billion locusts.

152

'Total and utter madness,' Jeshaphael muttered.

'Jeshaphael!' I gasped. 'Do you dare to insult our Creator?'

The Angel shrank in embarrassment, drifting away from me without a further word.

I considered my options afresh. I have received only one instruction, and that is to lead the Israelites to the open pasture beside the sea. This is all I have to work with.

Between Migdol and the water's edge

Moses was inclined to allow the People a gentle start to their day, knowing that they have only a short distance to travel. I persuaded him to move them on at a faster pace. I wanted to get to the location my Boss has specified as early as possible. While the Israelites patiently packed up their bedding and ate what food they had left, I waited anxiously for a visit from Gabriel. He didn't come.

When we reached the grazing land on the western shore of the Sea of Reeds, I gathered my team around Hushael, who had settled his pillar of cloud uncomfortably close to the water's edge.

'If you have any suggestions at all, I want to hear them.'

'We could stand all the guardians in a wall around the camp,' Maphrael suggested, 'and when the Egyptians approach, dim our spirits to a fatal brightness and destroy the lot of them.'

'I've done that before,' I pointed out.

'Or,' Maphrael continued excitedly, 'dim ourselves down further than that so we only burn out their eyes. Then we could divert the army away from their course, drive them all into the sea and drown them.'

The mention of the sea caused a shudder in my inner being.

'Or,' Maphrael began again, his imagination gaining momentum (I recalled that it was for this very quality that I chose him), 'perhaps our original plan for the firstborn was not wasted after all. We could mince their brains while they are asleep.'

Jeshaphael, meanwhile, was sulking, as he had been ever since his rash outburst this morning.

'Keep it up, Maphrael,' I said. 'So far, I like the blinding option best.'

'Oriel!' Maphrael reprimanded me, 'I thought we had an agreement.'

'Ah, yes ... I'm sorry ... Maff.'

'Oh, please,' Jeshaphael interjected, disgusted. 'Surely you haven't agreed to call him that!' Then he added, 'I can't imagine Shlyphantel abbreviating an Angel's name. Can you?'

Jeshaphael used this as an opportunity to move away from the shore – something he had been longing to do since we arrived. He left behind him an awkward silence, which Hushael ended.

'Whatever we do,' he suggested, 'it must involve this water.'

'I wish that was not the case,' I reflected, 'but I think you are right, Hushael.'

Time was sweeping us onwards. I needed to make a decision and start working on it.

'Ma ... Ma ... *Maff*,' I said. 'Get started on your blinding plan. Find out how many Angels feel confident about accurately reaching the precise level of dimness we will need. Hushael and I will continue to ponder this great mire of water that our Boss has directed us to.'

* * *

Midway through the Sun's apparent descent in the western sky, the pattern of activity among the humans below me suddenly changed. They had spotted the Egyptian army. An assortment of Israelites ran through the camp, shouting, 'The Egyptians are coming!' Everyone stopped what they were doing. Mothers rounded up their children, fathers rounded up their possessions. Fires were stamped out and weapons grabbed. Many people joined the headlong rush towards the front of the camp where Moses and his family were innocently relaxing together.

Panic swept the community as the details of the Egyptian advance passed from person to person. In my limited experience of human communication I am aware that such messages tend to become exaggerated through repetition. There is, however, little scope for exaggeration when the content of the message is *certain Death*. What did change was the state of people's minds as they advanced on Moses. Fear distilled into anger, and that anger was focused on one man. The People's entire response to the brutal might of the Egyptian army was directed at Moses. In some part of their consciousness, they knew they could not defeat the Egyptians, so they picked an easier target. I stood beside Moses as, armed only with his familiar wooden staff, he stepped forward to meet the enraged mob.

It would be tedious to record all that was said to Moses in that encounter. Over a thousand terrified humans all had something to say, and they shouted it at the same time. I didn't attempt to hear their actual words, I looked instead into their failing spirits. There was very little to see. On the day that the Israelites processed, singing, out of their slave slum in Pithom, their spirits were bright with renewed trust in their God. They glowed with fresh hope in the promises he made to them through their ancestors. On that road to freedom, they encouraged and helped one another: carrying their neighbour's luggage; caring for their friends' children. On that day, they reflected something of the One who had called them and freed them – a spiritual nation in promising infancy.

Surveying the screaming mob now confronting Moses, I could see none of these Heavenly qualities. They had no faith in the God who had so powerfully kept his promises, and they had no concern for their fellow Israelites. There was just one reference point in the frightening chaos around them, and that was Moses. If he failed them – they feared – they would be totally lost; and it looked very much as though Moses had failed them.

Moses was overwhelmed by this turn of events. Out of the inarticulate roar of abuse pouring from the People, a few phrases deposited their poison in his mind.

'Were there not enough graves in Egypt?'

'Did you bring us here to die?'

'You are Pharaoh's spy.'

'Didn't we tell you to leave us alone?'

'We were better off as slaves!'

Moses did not know how to respond. He was almost as lost as the people screaming at him. He too had only one point of reference in the advancing tide of destruction: the God who had got him into this mess.

I spoke urgently into his mind. 'Don't let them frighten you, Moses. Stand firm. God will rescue you. After today, you will never see these Egyptians again.'

I was saying these things as much to myself as to Moses, quickly realising that the calmer I was, the calmer he became. One thing was absolutely clear to me: these people are not capable of securing their own deliverance. They are an ungovernable rabble. Whatever form my Boss's victory might take, it will be the work of Heaven and not of human hands. Once I had fully grasped this fact, I was able to support Moses more effectively.

'All you need to do is remain calm,' I told him. 'We will sort this out for you.'

Moses stood still and upright. The Israelites continued to howl at him. I was amazed at the length of time that they managed to keep up their torrent of abuse. I urged the Angel guardians of Israel to moderate their charges' fear, but the great majority of the humans were beyond Angelic influence. Jeshaphael abandoned his sulk and kept me informed about the advance of Pharaoh's army. He and Maphrael estimated that they would arrive at about the time that the Sun set.

'If Hushael moves round behind the People,' Maphrael suggested, 'and spreads his cloudiness over the ground, that should accelerate the darkness around the Egyptians and might well force them to postpone their attack until the morning.'

'Do it,' I ordered.

'What should I do?' asked the newly-helpful Jeshaphael.

'Go with Hushael,' I instructed. 'When the light of the Sun is no longer reaching us, shine your fire onto these People. Make it more beautiful than ever. They need to know that we are with them.'

When Hushael's tall pillar of shining cloud rose up from the water's edge and flattened itself out above their heads, the panic-stricken Israelites went quiet. They turned their backs on Moses to watch as Hushael darkened himself further to form a barricade of thick cloud separating them from the approaching chariots and horses. As Earth's Sun sank behind that Angelic screen and none of its yellow light managed to shine through, the People's anger began to dissipate. It was with a certain embarrassed shame that they turned their faces back to Moses.

At that moment, Archangel Gabriel arrived: *Tell the People to prepare to move on. Then raise your staff over the sea. The water will divide, and the People will walk through the middle of the sea on dry ground.*

Moses listened attentively to these thoughts as they emerged into his mind. *The Egyptians will chase after you, but they will never make it the other side. Then all Egypt will know that I am God.*

Moses stood still, reviewing these instructions carefully. The People were now totally quiet, mostly due to the influence of their guardians. I attracted Gabriel's attention.

'What should I do?' I asked.

'Simple,' he said with an amused smile. 'Sort out the sea.'

* * *

'Hushael, Jeshaphael, Maff,' I called out across the Israelite camp. 'Come with me! We're stepping out of time right now.'

'We can't leave the People, Oriel,' Hushael called back. 'At present, I am their only defence.'

'We will return to the exact moment that we leave,' I assured him.

In time-free Heaven

My team assembled in my office and I repeated to them the instructions that Gabriel had delivered to Moses.

'In short,' I said, 'we have to find a way of dividing the Sea of Reeds so that the People can walk through the middle on dry land and then, I assume, return the water back to its usual place, over the heads of the Egyptian army.' I paused. 'We must be ready before the Earth's Sun reappears in the desert sky. Any questions?'

Maphrael spoke for us all. 'How?'

'That is what we are here to decide,' I told them.

'The heat of their Sun can dry up a large puddle remarkably quickly,' Hushael said tentatively. 'With enough energy, we could turn the whole sea into dry land.'

'That's not what we've been asked to do,' I pointed out.

Jeshaphael mumbled, 'We'd have trouble drowning the Egyptian army in a dry seabed.'

'A strong enough column of wind can push water out of its way,' Hushael tried again. 'In theory we could blow the water apart.' He fell silent. We all waited. Eventually he continued, 'But the speed of wind required would tear the humans to pieces.'

'I only want viable suggestions,' I stated, at the risk of upsetting Hushael. 'I would like to return to Moses as quickly as possible. The longer I spend here, the more I become out of touch with his situation.'

'We need a water expert,' Maphrael said. 'There must be an Angel who knows more about the stuff than we do.'

'I'm sure there is,' I said. 'Jeshaphael, go and find him, whoever and wherever he is. Maff, fetch Archangel Michael. I doubt that we will be able to do this without his help.'

While they were on their errands, I urged Hushael to consider everything that he knows about marine life.

'Perhaps there is some plant or animal that might help us,' I said.

Jeshaphael returned with a wild-looking Angel called Viathel, the carer Angel for the great whales which travel the length and breadth of Earth's bleak oceans – an Angel who was, in some ways, as frightening as the environment he works in. I was explaining our challenge to him when Michael and Maphrael arrived. I suggested that Viathel go off on his own to consider some options. I could see that he was no more comfortable in our company than I was in his.

'I have one idea,' I informed the rest of my team. 'We could form two walls of Angels, standing side by side across the lake, and hold back the water ourselves.'

The suggestion was greeted with dumb horror.

'The Angels in those walls,' Jeshaphael said slowly, 'would never work again. Even if they managed to hold themselves up against the effects of the water, they would be damaged beyond all usefulness.'

'I know,' I said solemnly.

'Then the idea is too ridiculous to consider,' Jeshaphael said harshly. Maphrael and Hushael had not yet emerged from their own silent terror.

'I didn't claim that it's a good idea,' I said carefully. 'Only one thing matters: Will it work?'

'I'm sure it would work,' Maphrael said, 'but who would you choose for such a suicidal mission?'

'I would ask for volunteers,' I explained. 'I will be the first to volunteer and I would hope that you three,' (I did not include Michael in this), 'would stand beside me.'

The reply came in three speechless stares. Two of them informed me that they would be there; the third did not.

'We have a plan then, Angels,' I said, 'terrible, but effective. All I hope for from you, now, is a better one, for all our sakes.'

I called Viathel back into my office.

'The only solution I can think of,' he informed us, 'is ice. If you freeze the surface of the lake, your humans will be able to walk across it quite safely. Then, when the other humans pass across – this *army*, whatever that is – all you need do is melt the ice and they will all fall into the freezing water.'

'That would fulfil two of our objectives,' I agreed, 'but it is not what our Boss told Moses. He said the water would be divided and the People would walk on dry land.'

'What you could do,' Viathel began again, 'is to freeze the entire body of water solid and then carve out a path through the middle.'

'That would destroy every living thing in the lake,' exclaimed an indignant Hushael.

'Preferable to destroying several thousand Angels,' Jeshaphael replied.

'There is a greater problem,' Viathel said. 'I don't believe you could achieve it in the Earth Time available.'

The room was momentarily filled by a chorus of disappointed grunts.

'This ice stuff,' Maphrael asked Viathel, 'could we make it in a hot desert, without having to touch the water?'

'If the air above the water is cold enough,' the wild Angel explained, 'the water on the surface will freeze.' He suddenly became animated. 'And here's the clever thing about water: when it gets very cold, it doesn't sink to the bottom like it should.'

The technical details of cold water were not something the rest of us wanted to hear about – with the obvious exception of Hushael.

'Is there anything else we *need* to know about making this ice?' I asked quickly.

'It helps to have a good wind,' Viathel added.

'I have an idea,' Maphrael announced triumphantly. 'Come on, Hush, Jeshaphael – I need your help.'

Hushael responded immediately. Jeshaphael did not.

'We'll manage without you,' Maphrael informed him, unperturbed.

'Where are you going?' I demanded.

'To try it out,' he said. 'If it works, then I'll explain it. To tell you now would only waste time.'

'Maff,' I called after him urgently. 'Keep well away from the Israelites and the Egyptians.'

'We'll go to the other side of the lake,' he assured me, and the two Angels departed.

'Michael,' I said as soon as they were gone, 'we had better assume that whatever method we use will be labour intensive. I need as many Angels as possible on standby for immediate deployment.' He nodded curtly and left.

While I waited for Maphrael and Hushael to return, I studied Jeshaphael's mind closely. I am concerned for him. At the start of

159

our campaign he was unswervingly obedient, almost too much so. Recently, he has become increasingly awkward. He has not worked on Earth before; the blight of human rebellion seems to have contaminated his spirit.

The uncomfortable silence between us was momentarily filled by the sound of Archangel Raphael singing his way up the corridor. He did not even glance in through my open doorway; he was completely absorbed in his music. The rich harmonies flooded into my office, refreshing my jaded spirit. Jeshaphael, I noted, found them irritating.

'It worked,' Maphrael announced gleefully as he bounded back into the room. 'What we need, Oriel, is to employ the services of all the Angel guardians of the Israelites and the Egyptian army.'

'I can't do that,' I said reluctantly but firmly. 'It would be quite wrong to take a soldier's guardian away from him the night before a battle. The Israelites particularly need their guardians tonight; they think they are about to die.'

'Then we can't do it,' Maphrael sighed, his enthusiasm fading like a dying star.

'I believe I can get you the majority of Michael's army, though,' I told him.

The fading star sprang back into life. 'Let's get on with it, then. There's not much point in explaining the whole thing. I'll tell you as we go. Viathel, would you like to come with us?'

The carer of Earth's whales declined the invitation.

I was encouraged by Maphrael's confidence. I sent the others ahead, staying behind to tell Michael what was happening. On the way to his office, I passed my Boss's door. It was open. Instinctively, I paused in his doorway. He looked up at me and smiled. I did not smile back, though somewhere under the enormous heap of concerns in my mind, I knew there was the potential for a smile.

The Sea of Reeds

I returned to the very point in time that I had left. Moses was considering his instructions from Gabriel, and the People – reassured by Hushael's cloud movements that their God had not abandoned them – were waiting to see what would happen next.

Moses spoke for the first time in the whole ugly confrontation. 'Come with me,' he instructed the crowd confidently. There was no hint of his stammer. His faith in my Boss's ability to do remarkable things is complete. He turned and walked the short distance to the water's edge.

Eight miles away, on the opposite shore, Maphrael was organising a vast army of Angels. He formed two long lines of Michael's troops above the surface of the water. Many more Angels were massed together in the desert sky beyond. By the time Moses had pushed his way through the tall reeds at the water's edge and was actually standing in the deadly stuff (irrationally I wanted to pull him back from such danger but resisted the temptation), Maphrael's avenue of Angels stretched right up to the shingle beach beneath me. Moses held out an arm, raising his gnarled wooden staff above the water. The dense reeds began to sway and bend towards us, pushed by a strong, cold wind from across the lake. The People watched in wonder as the reeds in front of Moses were flattened, giving the appearance of a short road that led onto the surface of the water. The wind billowed Moses' cloak behind him. He wrapped it around himself against the cold and turned back to the rescued slaves.

'Go back to your families and rest,' he ordered them. 'Meet me here at first light.'

The Israelites walked back through their disordered camp, while a large group of Angels took their place on the shore to deflect Maphrael's cold wind up into the sky and away from the People. Moses stood for some time, peering into the windy darkness, talking gratefully to my Boss. I left him there.

I crossed the sea to join Maphrael. He had the majority of his Angel workforce packed tightly together in the air above the eastern shore. Their task was to grab individual molecules of nitrogen and oxygen from Earth's thin atmosphere, suppress the level of their energy and then release them. It was a phenomenally labour-intensive operation but it dramatically cooled the desert air. Behind those Angels was a large squadron whose duty was to drive warm air, at considerable speed, towards the 'coolers'. The two lines of Angels above the water then channelled the cooled wind down onto the surface of the sea.

I found Maphrael in a position that was more typical of Hushael: bent down over the hazardous surface of the windswept water. Excitedly, he showed me the first thin crystals of ice as they stretched their fragile tentacles slowly outwards and interwove themselves with other crystals that grew towards them.

'It's working!' he cheered and leapt up, darting from Angel to Angel, encouraging them in their work.

'Is there anything I can do to help?' I asked, above the noise of wind and waves.

'Not at the moment,' he told me. 'Go back to your People, Oriel. I'll call if I need you.'

I did as I was told. Jeshaphael, for all his earlier reservations, had excelled himself, producing a display of fire that was warming the spirits of the Israelites. On the other side of Hushael's dark cloud, the mood of the Egyptian army was significantly cooler. I did not stray into Shlyphantel's territory, but watched from the edge of their camp as the Seraph of Egypt attempted to bolster Rameses' failing resolve. The stubborn king knows that his chances of defeating Moses are fading into the mysterious darkness.

I returned to the leader of my People. He was asleep, cuddled up under a fleece blanket with his two sons. Zipporah was sitting upright, attempting to divert her simmering anxieties by repairing a bald patch in Moses' cloak. I settled beside her. She is troubled by the stresses of leadership pressing on her husband. The torrent of abuse he suffered during the afternoon hurt her more than it did Moses. I spoke with her guardian, Yashenel, urging that he devote special care to her in the months ahead. I also suggested that he make contact with the guardian of Zipporah's father, Jethro. I encountered him when I first came to the Sinai desert; he is a man of considerable faith and wisdom.

I was dragged away from these domestic details by Maphrael.

'I have a serious problem, Oriel.'

As we crossed the lake, he pointed out that the wind was less cold than it had been. Then he showed me the reason. The vast cooling unit, made up of many thousands of Angels, had fallen into a fit of mindless giggling. The Angels were still attempting to do their work, but kept nudging and barging one another, which sent them into convulsions of meaningless laughter. This pointless jostling was accompanied by a cacophony of absurd songs and silly jokes. Their movements had become clumsy. I watched as one Angel repeatedly struggled to grab hold of a passing molecule, and then let it slip from his grasp as soon as he succeeded. Inside his mind, the Angel's thoughts were slipping and sliding their way round the pathways of his intellect.

'What's happening?' I asked.

'Here, take this.' Maphrael handed me a simple nitrogen molecule. 'See what happens when you squeeze the energy out of it.'

I suppressed the energetic vibrations that had been caused by the heat of Earth's Sun. The molecule became colder but I didn't notice anything else. I looked questioningly at Maphrael. He passed me another, and then another. Gradually I began to sense a faint hum in the extremities of my being.

'The energy that you are removing from the air,' Maphrael explained, 'is stimulating your spirit. These Angels have repeated this simple operation billions of times and it has made them highly excited. I don't know what to do. I need the air to be cold to freeze the lake, but if their productivity goes down any further, they will soon be warming it up.'

'What are you planning to do with this ice, Maff?' I asked, giving in to my rising unease about his whole plan.

'I'm not worried about that. I need cold air; lots of it.'

'Why don't you rotate the Angels around the different tasks?' I suggested. 'That would at least spread out the effects to a certain extent.'

'Until the whole lot of them are as high as Earth's Moon!' he replied.

'Do it anyway,' I said. 'I will ask Michael to restore some discipline to his troops.'

Michael was exactly where I expected to find him – carefully analysing the force of the Egyptian army.

'I need you,' I said. 'Your Angels have become intoxicated. If you don't control them, those chariots will overrun our Boss's new nation the moment their Sun rises into view.'

Michael was shocked by the state of his usually disciplined troops. The sound of his thundering voice quickly restored a level of order to the chaos. He drew his Angels into straight lines, and prowled back and forth among them, bawling at any individual who let out even a slight snigger. Maphrael introduced a basic rotation system but he was not optimistic about the effectiveness of the remedy.

'I don't think it will be enough, Oriel,' he confided. 'No matter how loudly Michael yells at them, their minds are still going to get fuzzier and fuzzier, and their work rate will go down. If this ice is not thick enough in just one place, your entire nation could be drowned, and a good many Angels will go down with them.'

'Do you need some time out?' I asked.

'I need another idea,' he said. 'I wish Viathel had come with us.'

At that moment, Gabriel appeared. He gave me a minuscule package. 'A present from the Boss,' he said.

I opened it: inside was one tiny molecule – two oxygen atoms linked to a nitrogen atom. I showed it to Maphrael.

'Make one of these, Maff,' I said. He did, and then looked up at Gabriel questioningly.

'Don't ask me for an explanation,' Gabriel said.

'Make some more, Maff,' I told him.

As Maphrael proceeded to make a series of the little triplets, a smile gradually crept over his face. Suddenly, he flung himself at Gabriel, giving the Archangel a huge hug.

'Michael!' Maphrael called urgently. 'Get your Angels to make these.' He raced over to Michael and showed him the molecules.

'When you combine the nitrogen and oxygen in this configuration,' he explained triumphantly, 'they absorb energy in the process. If we make loads of these, it will cool the air without affecting the Angels at all. It might even sober them up.'

The information was passed hurriedly through Maphrael's vast cooling factory. When the new process started production, a deep, drunken cheer went up from all the Angels who had been struggling to focus on their work under Michael's watchful eye. Before long, the cold wind was as cold as it had been at the start, and the Angels were labouring with a fresh sense of purpose. They began to sing. I did not see who started it, but they were singing Raphael's human-style song.

Go down, Moses, they slurred in imprecise unison, *way down in Egypt land. Tell old Pharaoh, to let my People go.*

Within a short space of time the entire company of Angels were singing together. Gradually, the song became less slurred and more tuneful. The Angels worked in time with the song's primitive rhythm, pumping out cold air to the relentless beat of the music. The production rate climbed, the wind was colder and the ice grew thicker.

Maphrael was now focusing all his attention on the ice itself, measuring its exact thickness all along the lake. I joined him.

'I have to go and practise something, Oriel.'

'Is it going to be ready in time?' I pressed him.

'I hope so,' he replied without stopping. 'I don't have time to talk. I have to work on the next stage.'

I returned to the merrily singing Angels, recovered from their uncontrollable giggles and just irrepressibly happy. I checked on Moses and the Israelites. They were asleep – so, now, was Zipporah.

Next I visited Shlyphantel.

'I am sure you have an idea of what will happen in the morning,' I said to him.

He nodded stiffly.

'I need the Angel guardians of Egypt's soldiers to give their charges unusually deep sleep tonight,' I explained, 'and prolonged sleep in the morning.' The Seraph accepted my instruction, knowing that it came with our Boss's authority.

Crossing the part-frozen lake, I saw that the first, deflected rays of Earth's Sun were penetrating the sky above the desert. I rushed to fetch Maphrael.

'The light's coming, Maff,' I told him. 'It's time to divide that lake in two.' Then I added, 'Though I still don't understand how you propose to do it.'

'You'll see,' he said. When we passed the Angels who were causing the wind he told them, 'On my signal, slow the air current down to a strong breeze.' Next we came to the coolers. 'When I give the signal,' Maphrael instructed, 'reduce your process to ten per cent of capacity. All we will need is to keep that ice from melting.'

Next Maphrael made his way into the middle of the lake and directed the channelling Angels to lower their two lines down onto the ice itself.

'It will not harm you in any way,' he assured them when they looked suspiciously down at the surface of the Sea of Reeds. 'The water has formed itself into a solid and is completely harmless. I am going to cut a line down the middle of the ice and I need you to make sure that the two halves of the ice sheet stay tightly together. If they do come apart,' he warned, 'the water will rise up from underneath and you will be standing in it. You don't want that to happen, do you?' This last comment guaranteed him a thoroughly diligent workforce.

Maphrael sped to the desert side of the lake and signalled to the Angels there to slow the wind. He then altered his Angelic brightness in a way that I have never seen done before. He produced a thin beam of pure red light, which he directed down onto the ice. The power of that sharp ray melted a straight cut through the frozen water. Maphrael worked his way carefully across the surface of the sea to the other side.

'Where did you learn to do that?' I asked.

He ignored me. When he had successfully sliced the whole ice sheet into two sections, he returned to the middle and gave more instructions.

'I need you to press the ice down in the middle,' he told the two lines of Angels, 'so that the sheets form a straight-sided valley. Always keep the two halves together.' The Angels did as they were told, each one anxiously checking that no water was emerging from between the sheets. The two vast platforms of ice dipped down to form a giant 'V'.

'Keep going,' Maphrael urged. 'When the ice below you touches the ground, hold it as near the base as you dare and carefully break it off to fit the shape of the seabed. We need a perfect fit between ice and earth.' Then he added, half to himself, 'I'll get them to increase the wind to freeze off any leaks.'

'I'll tell them,' I said. When I returned, a narrow alleyway had already appeared at the shore, though in the middle of the lake the ice still formed a deep 'V'. I watched, astounded at the outrageous brilliance of Maphrael's idea.

I was disturbed by a rich voice beside me. 'Superb work, Oriel.' It was my Boss.

'Don't give me the credit,' I replied. 'This is Maphrael's work.'

He nodded thoughtfully and then looked up at Jeshaphael's multicoloured light display, which was illuminating Maphrael's lengthening corridor. 'Jeshaphael has done well, too,' he said.

'He has,' I said with a certain reservation. 'But I am worried about him.'

'I know you are, Oriel.'

Maphrael had now managed to form a continuous path right down the middle of the lake from one shore to the other. He instructed the Angels to push the two walls of frozen water steadily apart to widen this road.

'How wide will it need to be?' I asked my Boss.

'I am quite sure that Maphrael has worked that out,' he assured me.

The sky was noticeably lighter.

'I must go and wake Moses,' I said.

The Israelites were already stirring. I shook Moses gently and he sat up. I prompted him to look round at the new highway through

166

the sea. What he saw swept him beyond the limited range of his emotions. He stared numbly at the divided lake. Hur joined him. As each human saw what Maphrael had achieved in a single night they gasped. I shook Moses from his paralysis. With Hur's help he sent a message through the camp for everyone to pack their possessions and be ready to leave in the traditional order of their tribal families.

Maphrael, his job done, joined me and asked if he could bring Jeshaphael down from his sentry post at the far end of the camp. He led Jeshaphael to the very centre of one ice wall and showed him how to monitor the integrity of its structure, searching for any signs of weakness. Maphrael did the same on the other side.

As soon as Moses and Zipporah had folded their blankets and loaded them onto the barrow, they set off. The Angels fell silent as our Boss's chosen nation proceeded down the eerie corridor of solidified water. The Israelites kept away from the cold walls. These people had never encountered the phenomenon, and wisely avoided what they couldn't understand. Their children, however, had no such reservations. They broke away and dashed towards the smooth white surfaces, only to be called back urgently. Apart from the occasional anxious shouts of protective parents, no one made a sound.

I made my way immediately behind Moses. He was holding his staff in one hand, with Zipporah holding onto his other arm. Aaron and Miriam had insisted on pushing the barrow, with the empty dough bowls now packed away. As I passed between the two lines of quietly triumphant Angels, I thanked them all. When I reached Maphrael, I could not find words to suitably express my gratitude.

'I cannot thank you enough,' I told him.

'We haven't finished yet,' he reminded me with a distracted smile. 'And I'm sorry to say that the most dangerous part is still to come.'

I crossed to the other wall and thanked Jeshaphael.

'Our Boss is full of praise for your part in this, Jeshaphael,' I told him. He smiled. I could not remember when I had last seen a smile on that face.

It took three hours for Moses and his family to cross the Sea of Reeds. The Israelites stretched out behind them down the entire length of the seabed path so that the last tribe was just entering the corridor as Moses and Zipporah climbed the opposite desert shore.

The time had come for Hushael to move his blanket of cloud and give the Egyptians their first sight of my Boss's dramatic rescue. Moses' guardian was noticeably tired from the effort of two consecutive shifts, thinning his Angelic form in the vacuous Egyptian sky, but he unquestioningly accepted a third session. I instructed him to lead the people far enough into the desert to prevent them from slowing down the progress of those behind them. As soon as Hushael's cloud moved from the shore, the Israelites could see Pharaoh's army, ready in battle formation. The morning Sunlight glinted off their polished chariots and pointed spears. Poised for attack, Rameses hardly stopped to wonder at the miraculous road through the middle of the sea; what concerned him was that his slaves were getting away. He shouted a command and the chariots rolled.

The descendants of Jacob's youngest son, Benjamin, were the last to leave. They were the first to see the charging cavalry. They screamed in panic, urging those ahead of them to move faster. Terror spread like a wave along the broad line of humans. People bunched up tighter, dragging their carts, hurrying their sheep, slinging little children onto their shoulders. The Egyptian army was rapidly gaining ground.

On the desert shore, the People hurried up onto the beach and fanned out in all directions to make space for those behind them. At the Egyptian shore, Rameses stopped at the wall of ice. He had heard travellers' tales about water that became hard like rock, but he had never seen it. His generals were uneasy. They urged their king to be cautious, but Rameses was insistent. He needed his slaves back; he could not finish his cities without them.

While the Egyptian advance was delayed, the Israelites were getting away. Those at the back anxiously looked over their shoulders, not daring to believe that the pharaoh would allow them to escape. Then the moment came that they were dreading: the Egyptian war chariots entered the frozen corridor. The people at the back abandoned their possessions and simply ran, but they could not match the speed of the chariots. When the last Israelites passed the midpoint of their crossing, the Egyptians were within bow-shot of their quarry. A volley of arrows flew up in the air and clattered against the hard walls of the lake just behind the terrified Hebrews. Then, without warning, the Egyptian advance faltered. The chariots at the front of the charge suddenly stopped and those following crashed into them.

My Boss whispered from behind me, 'I suggested that Maphrael leak a small amount of water onto the seabed. The chariot wheels are stuck in the mud.'

The Israelites were getting away once more. At the western end of the crowded corridor, Rameses was sending more and more of his troops after the slaves. At the eastern end, the first Benjaminite families were beginning to emerge. Some had even gone back to retrieve their carts and barrows.

Archangel Raphael arrived.

'What are you here for?' I asked.

'Maphrael's orders, my dear,' he said. 'He asked me to sing for him.'

'Maphrael seems to have thought of everything,' I observed.

'I must say, though,' the Leader of Heaven's Worship added, 'it is a rather unusual song.'

The last Israelites were now climbing the final ascent onto the beach. Behind them, the Egyptians had forced their way back through the thick mud and were retreating. To a man they concluded that it was better to face the anger of the king than to risk the wrath of the God of the Israelites. Once clear of the mud, their escape gathered pace. Maphrael rose up above the lake and addressed the two lines of Angels who were holding the ice walls in place. He also addressed the Angel guardians of the retreating Egyptian soldiers.

'When Moses gives the signal,' he instructed, 'rise clear of the ice walls as fast as you can. Do not hesitate for anything. There is no margin for delay.' He waited for assurances that everyone understood this. He then turned to the desert shore and called, 'Thank you, Raphael.'

Archangel Raphael joined Maphrael in the middle of the lake and began to sing. All he sang was one single, high-pitched note, far too high to stimulate the dull ears of the humans. Conducted by an intensely concentrating Maphrael, Raphael steadily increased the volume of this note. Maphrael repositioned himself beside Moses. Moses was shining brightly with an unshakeable belief that he and his People were safe in the hands of their God. Every Angel was watching him.

'NOW!' Maphrael screamed.

Moses swung his staff forwards over the lake. The ice wall shattered into a billion fragments. Two lines of Angels shot into the sky and liquid water engulfed the Egyptian army. There had indeed been no moment to spare. I looked across the churning water, littered with chunks of ice and broken chariots. One Angel had been caught by the returning water and Maphrael was desperately trying to pull him from the terrible liquid. I sped across to help, grabbed the struggling Angel and, together with Maphrael, pulled him clear of the lake.

It was Jeshaphael.

PART THREE

The Desert of Shur

After witnessing the demolition of Pharaoh's army, the Israelites collapsed on the ground, their minds and bodies exhausted by the stress and effort of their flight. It was still morning. Michael and his Angels returned to heaven to recover. Apart from the guardians of the People, the only Angels who remained with me on the eastern shore of the Sea of Reeds were Hushael, Maphrael and Jeshaphael. Jeshaphael's Angelic form was only slightly injured by the water. The greater damage was to his already fragile mind.

Moses declared that the People need travel no further that day; they would resume their journey next morning. The Israelites gathered in small groups and recounted, repeatedly, the details of their remarkable experience. Moses' family spent the day composing new words to a tune that Miriam remembered her mother singing. The new song tells of the violent destruction of Pharaoh's army and honours my Boss for such a dramatic rescue. When evening came, and the people were sitting around small fires in subdued mood, Miriam jumped to her feet, pulled up Zipporah and the two of them began to dance round the scattered camp fires, singing:

Sing to the Lord, for he is exalted.
The horse and its rider he hurled into the sea.

Many of the women and girls joined the dance and, before long, the atmosphere of numb relief had transformed into bold carnival: men clapped and smiled; women danced and sang; children jumped and skipped. The darkness has obscured the thin stretch of restless water that separates them from the Kingdom of Egypt. For the first time in three centuries the descendants of Abraham are daring to believe that they really are free – free after a lifetime of enforced labour.

The Angels are dancing too, led by Maphrael and Yashenel. The dancing of Angels is a thousand times more vigorous than the sedate hopping and skipping of humans. I might have joined them but I chose to stay with Moses and Jeshaphael. Jeshaphael is in no mood for dancing.

Watching the celebrations of both Angels and humans, I have

pondered the events of recent months. Moses, who had all but given up living his own life, has become a pillar of shining faith. For the first time he has begun to provide the father's love that he never received in his own childhood for his own two sons. In the same stretch of Earth's time, Jeshaphael, a bright Angel who was a devoted and reliable servant among the hosts of Heaven, has been buffeted and bruised by the vagaries of life on this small but significant planet. And a People who knew nothing in their lives but hard work and brutal whippings have escaped from successive generations of abuse and slavery. However, behind this modest achievement, there lies a long wake of human misery – the latest instalment of which is being washed up on the shore of the Sea of Reeds as I write.

*   *   *

Over the last three days, Moses has led his people eastward into the desert. At first, his sole objective was to get away from the lake and the borderlands of Egypt, in case Rameses should be foolish enough to continue his pursuit. By the second day, the specific responsibilities of his new role began to settle themselves in his consciousness. As he strode out with his family at the front of the People, following Hushael's pillar of cloud, deputations from various Israelite tribes informed him that their water supplies were becoming worryingly depleted. They wanted to know when Moses would get them to a substantial source of fresh water, because the water of the Sea of Reeds had been bitter and of limited use.

Neither Moses nor I were prepared for these demands. Until then, Moses had been feeling quite at home in the desert, spotting suitable patches of vegetation for the People's goats and sheep to graze. Hushael assured me that Moses knows a number of ways of extracting a small drink from the arid landscape, but it quickly became apparent that none of these were much use for a population the size of the one that is following him.

On the evening of the second day, I gathered my small team, including the partially-recovered Jeshaphael, and said. 'We need to find a large body of water.' The suggestion was greeted with blank silence.

'Not again,' Maphrael commented wearily.

'I don't want you to do anything to it, Maff,' I assured him. 'Just find it. These humans need to drink the stuff.'

'Sorry to appear stupid, Oriel,' Maphrael said, 'but how are we supposed to find water when we don't know where it is? It is hardly an activity we are trained in.'

'I thought you were quite an expert in the subject.'

'I have had my fill of aquatic entertainment,' he replied, 'especially after seeing what it did to Jesh.'

'I'll go,' Hushael volunteered.

Maphrael went with him. Jeshaphael could not have gone – even if he had wanted to – because his pillar of fire was needed to provide a focal point for the Israelite camp during Earth's night.

The two Angels returned in high spirits.

'We have found twelve holes in Earth's surface,' Maphrael informed me, 'and the horrible stuff oozes out of every one of them.'

'Excellent,' I replied.

'But I fear that they are more than a day's walk away,' Hushael added.

'Oh.'

Hushael continued in his unhurried way, 'If we take a rather longer route, there is a small pool that we could reach tomorrow.'

'We'll do that,' I decided. 'Hushael, lead the People there in the morning.'

Marah, in the Desert of Shur

The first group of humans arrived at Hushael's pool in the early afternoon – and we quickly learned the limits of Hushael's understanding of water. As usual, it was Joshua's little army at the front. They dipped their thirsty faces into the clear water, and instantly broke into a series of coughs and splutters. Hushael's pool is, apparently, quite undrinkable. Clan after clan of Israelites drew near to the promised pool in the hope of refilling their empty containers. There was not a cheerful face to be seen as the People stood around the edge of the bitter pond, grumbling to one another about Moses' incompetent leadership.

I called my team together for an urgent meeting. We were busy wondering how we might remove the offending salts from the liquid without injuring ourselves when Archangel Gabriel arrived and spoke to Moses.

He pointed out a length of parched wood that was lying among the rocks and said, *Throw that into the water and it will become drinkable.*

I grabbed Gabriel urgently and declared, 'It would help enormously, Gabriel, if you bothered to talk to me first, before putting ideas into Moses' head.'

'I was asked to deliver the message to Moses,' he replied.

'That may be so,' I said angrily, 'but we are the ones who have to put the plan into action. If you would only give a moment's independent thought to your work, you could give us some advance warning and save us from all kinds of problems.'

'If our Boss had wanted me to inform you first, then he would have told me,' Gabriel declared.

'*Think*, Gabriel!' I yelled. 'You were created with a mind. Use it. How am I supposed to make all this water palatable to petty human tastes when Moses has already lobbed some filthy lump of dead tree into it, which, for all I know, might have poisoned the pool even further?'

Maphrael was standing supportively beside me. Jeshaphael joined in: 'You just abandon us down here, expecting us to sort everything out, only showing up when it suits you,' he said.

Conducted in the complex language of Angels, this catalogue of frustration went on for some while. During that time, Moses was being similarly harangued by his fellow Israelites. The sorry scene was finally brought to an end by Hushael shouting my name over the top of Jeshaphael's latest complaint. When we were finally quiet, he said, 'Look at the pool.'

The ring of Israelites around the edge of the pool were all on their knees in the water, laughing, singing and cheering. They were busily filling water containers and emptying them into their mouths. The water, quite clearly, had become drinkable.

I looked up to Hushael, and asked, 'What happened?'

He pointed towards Moses. Our Boss had arrived and we had been so caught up in our argument that we had not even noticed. Gabriel and I were abashed. We quickly apologised to one another for our stupidity and waited for our Boss to finish his conversation with Moses. However, when he had finished talking to Israel's leader, our Creator departed without so much as a glance in our direction.

Elim

Today we travelled to Elim where there are *twelve* springs of water – and thankfully all twelve of them are pure and drinkable. The palm trees growing between the springs are laden with ripe fruit – enough for everyone to enjoy at least one portion – and there is fresh pasture for the goats and sheep. Moses' experience as a desert herdsman has been of great value. He knows how long the people and the animals need to stay here in order to gain maximum benefit from the water supply.

The Desert of Zin

The People moved on from Elim when Moses judged that the pasture could no longer sustain their livestock. They were reluctant to leave the security of the only regular water supply they had found since entering the desert, even though they were well aware that the grazing land was exhausted. During their stay, the Israelites ate from their flocks and herds, using the animals' skins to make new water containers. It was Moses' threat that these precious animals would become diseased if they stayed that persuaded them to move on.

The People are utterly dependent on Moses. On the evening of the fourth day out from Elim, he gathered the representatives of the tribes and explained that if they continued to slaughter their goats and sheep every time they were hungry they would soon have none left.

'What are we to eat then?' one of the leaders asked angrily. 'Did you bring us out here to die of starvation?'

Moses said nothing.

Another of the Israelite elders spoke up. 'We had plenty of food in Egypt.' There was a murmur of agreement round the gathering.

'What I wouldn't do for a large pot of Egyptian stew!' a younger man added.

Moses looked at him, wounded.

'You were slaves in Egypt,' he said.

'Better to be a well fed slave than a liberated skeleton,' the man mumbled to his neighbour.

'As long as you have your flocks, you have something,' Moses said sternly. 'You have milk every day, wool every year, and occasional meat and new skins. Without them, you will have nothing.'

Though this was true, he also knows that the Israelite herds are far too small to sustain so many people.

'You can't eat the desert grass,' he told the representatives, 'but your sheep and goats can.'

Moses turned his attention to a large group of women waiting for him. Some were brandishing desert plants and roots, and wanted to know if they could be eaten. Many had complaints against their fellow Israelites, most of which were disputes over ownership of livestock, or accusations of food being stolen.

Moses was occupied well into the night. When he finally returned to the simple tent that he had constructed for his family, Gershom and Eliezer were asleep. Zipporah was waiting for her husband, sympathetic but irritated. The morning came all too soon for them. They packed their possessions into their barrow, ate an inadequate meal and followed the patiently receding pillar of cloud which was Hushael. All through that day Moses was assailed by complaints, accusations, questions and grumbles. He was not able to take his turn at pulling the barrow with Aaron, or help Zipporah look after their children. He darted back and forth across the broad line of moving humanity, doing his best to deal with each problem. I considered the fact that these People only have Moses to believe in. They have not managed to see beyond him to their God.

That night, when he had settled the last dispute of the day, he returned to his tent to find Zipporah crying.

'I can't carry on like this, Moses,' she sobbed.

Moses did what he had been doing since early that morning. He listened to Zipporah's complaint and then suggested a solution.

'Maybe you should take the boys and go back to your father,' he said. 'I couldn't help you today and it won't be any different tomorrow. Our God has given me this People to look after. But they are not your people. You don't have to stay.'

'We'll talk about it in the morning,' Zipporah sniffed.

They didn't get the chance. They were woken by two men fighting over a goat.

'I caught him stealing my milk,' one accused.

'It's *my* goat!' the other asserted.

The men, father and son, each asserted their ownership of the animal. Before long there was a small crowd outside Moses' tent, most of whom were complaining about the shortage of food. Everyone blamed Moses for the problem.

Hur arrived with a deputation of tribal leaders. The people were refusing to travel any further.

'If we are going to die in this desert,' one man stated, 'then why bother moving on. It would be easier to die here.'

The crowd grew. A rumour was spreading through the camp that Moses had been paid by Pharaoh to lead the Hebrews out into the desert and starve them to death. The Egyptian chariots at the Sea of Reeds – so the rumour claimed – were there to chase the slaves away, not recapture them.

I was in my Seraphic position, behind Moses' right shoulder (following Shlyphantel's example). While Moses struggled to address each individual issue, I spoke with the complainants' Angel guardians, searching for any information that might help Moses in his replies. I was disturbed by an Angelic voice behind me.

'Ar'angel Oreel?'

I turned to see a large group of shabby-looking Angels.

'Got a special deliv'ry for you, guv.'

'I didn't order anything,' I replied.

'You are Ar'angel Oreel?' the same scruffy Angel asked.

'Yes.'

'This *is* the Desert of Zin?'

'Yes.'

'Then it's for you.'

'What is it?' I asked.

The Angel turned to face his crew. 'Which of you's got the docket?'

A note was passed forwards.

He read from it: 'Sixty per cent carbohydrate, 30 per cent fat, ten per cent amino . . .'

I interrupted: 'You will have to wait. I'm busy.'

'Can't do that, guv. We've got a load of Coturnix coturnix to fetch.'

I had sent Maphrael and Jeshaphael off across the desert in search of suitable food for the People. I now wished I hadn't.

'Leave it in Moses' tent,' I instructed the delivery Angel. 'I'll deal with it later.'

'Can't do that, guv,' he said dismally.

'Why, in all Heaven, not?' I demanded.

'Wouldn't fit.'

177

I was just about to explode with anger when Gabriel arrived.

'What are you doing here, Alael?' he exclaimed.

'Dropping off Oreel's whatsit.'

'You're too early!' Gabriel stated with exasperation. 'It's not due yet.'

'Yes, it is,' the deliverer argued. 'It's on me docket. Where is it? Here. Desert of Zin. Middle of the night. Look.'

'This is the middle of the *day*,' Gabriel laboured.

'Is there much difference?' Alael asked innocently.

'Yes, there is,' Gabriel bellowed. 'Go and fetch the other stuff and bring this lot back tonight.' He turned to me. 'I'm sorry about this, Oriel. I have the explanation here.' He waved a message for Moses. The delivery crew shuffled away.

I listened in as Gabriel passed on our Boss's latest instructions. The delivery had evidently been some specially formulated food-stuff for the Israelites.

Moses asked Aaron to explain the situation to the People. His own voice was strained from the effort of trying to negotiate with an angry crowd all morning. Aaron did not have much more success.

'Are you being paid by Rameses as well?' someone shouted at him.

While Moses and Aaron sought Hur's help in getting the people to be quiet, Maphrael returned looking worried.

'I've lost Jeshaphael,' he announced.

'What do you mean?' I asked.

'How can you lose an Angel?' Gabriel added.

'We were looking for human food, as you know,' Maphrael explained. 'We went in different directions, agreeing to meet at a particular place and time. Jeshaphael never turned up. I've looked around but can't find him. You know how dim he has been lately.'

This was true. Jeshaphael's brightness has been diminishing since we left Egypt, not helped by his dip in the Sea of Reeds. I had dismissed it as being a consequence of dimming himself into the pillar of fire every night, even though it was evident that Hushael was not showing any similar symptoms. I was not surprised by Maphrael's news, but I was disturbed.

'Maff,' I said, 'swap places with Hushael. He knows this desert very well. He may have a better chance of finding Jeshaphael. I'm sure you can manage a pillar of cloud.'

Maphrael did as I asked and the sudden change in the appearance of the Heavenly cloud had a beneficial side effect. The Israelites noticed it, became quiet, and began to listen to Aaron.

'I must be off,' Gabriel told me. 'Alael should be back shortly with his first consignment. Sorry about the mix-up.'

He left and I listened to Aaron passing on Gabriel's message to the People: *God is going to teach you to follow his instructions,* Moses' elder brother told them. *Tonight he will send you food from Heaven. You will gather it in the morning, two litres per person. There will be enough for everyone, for one day. Your God has heard your grumbling.*

Moses took over. 'The God of your ancestors has spoken to me. He said, *Tell the People that they will eat meat this evening and bread in the morning. Then they will know that I am their God.*'

A voice piped up, 'So are you now telling us that we *should* slaughter our livestock?'

There was a murmur of approval at this question, punctuated by a scattering of accusations that Moses had changed his mind. Moses and Aaron tried to regain the People's attention, but with little success. The two brothers struggled to make themselves heard for some while until the Israelites gradually quietened down of their own accord. They stopped shouting at Moses to look at the sky behind him. I turned to follow their gaze. What I saw was Alael and his delivery crew herding a vast flock of small birds across the desert sky. They drove the creatures down among the Israelites who cheered excitedly and ran in all directions, trying to catch them. In the briefest measure of time the whole camp had joined the sport, everyone abandoning whatever they had been doing to run around trying to catch some meat for their supper. Maphrael and I watched in delight as dark human dissatisfaction gave way to joyous hope.

An Angelic voice intruded on our observation. 'Ar'angel Oreel? Could you sign 'ere please?'

Next morning

Unfortunately, the arrival of more meat than they could possibly eat did not stop the Israelites from squabbling. They fought over who got which bird first. They argued over whose bird was the biggest. And, when they finally settled down to preparing their supper, they squabbled over whose turn it was to pluck the next one. Moses was called upon to settle numerous trivial disputes. When he finally returned, hungry and exhausted, to his own tent, it was empty. Miriam found him, bewildered and alone, at the entrance, clutching a message from his wife: *Have taken your advice. The boys and I have gone home. Z.*

Moses did not move, but the arrival of his sister prompted his face to droop down towards his chest. His shoulders shuddered, and he began to cry. For so many years, Zipporah had been there for him. She had always welcomed him, embraced him, encouraged him and looked after him. Now she had gone. The fact that it had been his own idea only made his pain worse. He hated himself; he hated his job; he hated the Israelites who had kept him away from his family.

I felt as incapable of helping Moses as he was of helping himself. Miriam put a loving arm round her distraught brother and guided him gently towards the small tent which she shared with Aaron.

'I've saved some quail for you,' she told him.

* * *

During the Earth night I discussed Jeshaphael's disappearance with Maphrael, who had successfully changed from a pillar of cloud to a pillar of fire. Hushael had not reported back about his search. Maphrael and I agreed that it would be in character for Hushael to keep looking until he found the missing Angel. While we continued to consider this matter, I received a third visit from Alael.

'Right, guv,' he said, 'where do you want yer stuff?'

'Could you deposit a pile outside each tent?' I asked.

The Angel emitted a long, low whistle. 'Wouldn't have the time,' he replied.

'You wouldn't have to,' Maphrael suggested. 'You could weave in and out of time and deliver a pile to each family at exactly the same moment.'

'Never done that,' Alael recoiled. 'Don't even know if it's allowed. It's either one big pile at the edge of the camp or we sprinkle it all over the place.'

I suggested the single pile. Maphrael overruled me.

'The way this People are at the moment,' he said, 'bringing them together will only cause more arguments. Best send them all in different directions.'

It was good advice. There were an awkward few moments

during which Maphrael and I expected Alael to get on with his work, but he didn't move.

'Do it then,' Maphrael urged.

'The deliv'ry is to Ar'angel Oreel,' Alael told us. 'I can only act on 'is orders.'

'Please, Alael,' I said deliberately, 'will you deliver the whatever-it-is for me?'

'How d'you wan' it?'

'SPRINKLED,' I bellowed.

From then until shortly before the Israelites woke up, Alael and his crew spread the small, hard granules of food evenly across the camp. Just before Earth's Sun appeared over the desert horizon, Hushael returned. Alone.

'I found him,' he told me, 'but he refuses to come back. He says he has had enough. I did my best to . . . What's all that white stuff?' He stooped down to pick up a round grain of the seed-like substance and studied it carefully. 'Very clever,' he observed. 'Very clever, indeed. Was this your idea, Oriel?'

'No, it wasn't,' I said.

'I didn't think so,' he said distantly. 'As far as I know, there is only one person who could produce something as clever as this.'

He didn't say who that was, and we didn't ask. Hushael took over from Maphrael in the sky above the camp and Maphrael returned to his usual brightness.

Five days later

These last few days, the Israelites have continued their slow progress across the desert. Alael has sprinkled a fresh load of whatever-it-is every night. The Israelites have boiled it into porridge or baked it into bread every morning. Hushael repeated his judgement about the designer of the substance, after we noted that those who rush out and sweep up as much as they can in the early morning never have a grain more than those who go last and have to pick their way round the rocks and dirt of the desert. Another intriguing feature of Alael's daily delivery is that whenever any of the Israelites have tried to put some aside for the following day to save themselves from the morning traipse around the camp to collect the stuff, it has become putrid overnight.

Every day all the Israelites have to gather their food and cook it. Every day, each one of them finds all that they need to feed their family. Every day, they only have enough for that day. This is my Boss's work.

Jeshaphael has not returned. All of us – Hushael, Maphrael and I – have visited him and urged him to join us again, but he has declined. Tonight, while I was waiting for the sixth daily delivery, I decided to return to Heaven to discuss the matter with my Boss.

In Heaven

'You must let him go,' my Boss said, after I had explained the situation in some depth.

I was shocked. 'But I don't want to lose him,' I pleaded. 'He is a greatly talented Angel who has played an important part in our work.'

'I know.' A profound sadness was etched into my Boss's face.

'Well, can't you do something?' I exclaimed.

'What is freedom, Oriel?' my Boss asked me.

'It is . . . er . . .'

'What is freedom for the Israelite People, Oriel?'

I had not had much opportunity to consider such wider issues. I waited for my Creator to answer his own question.

'The Israelites are now free to complain without fear of being whipped,' he explained. 'They are free to follow Hushael's cloud or to stay where they are. They are free to stay in their camp and die, or to flee back to the security of slavery, or to follow Moses to the fertile land that I promised them through Abraham. It is their choice, Oriel. That is the beginning of freedom.'

'But they are only humans,' I stated. 'Jeshaphael is an Angel.'

'Jeshaphael is not my slave,' my Boss said solemnly.

'Couldn't you speak to him?'

'Jeshaphael knows that my door is always open if he wishes to speak with me.'

The conversation was not going very well.

'Perhaps if the right Angel were to talk with him?' I suggested.

My Boss looked at me with pained eyes. The lines of sadness on his face grew deeper. 'I created an Angel with great skill in the arts of persuasion,' he told me, his voice heavy with sadness. 'An Angel whose task was to talk with troubled Angels and gather them back into the community of Heaven.' He stopped talking but I was sure he had not finished.

'Why don't you send that Angel to Jeshaphael?' I suggested.

There was a thick silence.

'That Angel, Oriel, is Lucifer.'

The implications of this information sank slowly into my darkening consciousness.

'Perhaps,' I proposed feebly, 'Jeshaphael will stay on his own in the desert and Lucifer won't bother with him.'

My Boss did not reply. But his eyes told me how foolish that hope was.

'I had better return to the Israelites,' I said, no longer able to bear the weight of my Master's sadness.

I made my way to the door, turning to look once more into his grieving eyes. He held up a message.

'For Moses,' he said.

Back in the Desert of Zin

The moment I arrived at the Israelite camp, Alael turned up.

'You're earlier than usual,' I observed.

'Can't chat,' the Angel replied. 'This load's heavy.'

He and his crew started to pour the Heaven-sent food over the camp. Maphrael was watching from his night-time post above the temporary settlement.

'You're spreading it much too thickly, Al,' he called. 'If you keep that up, you'll run out half way round.'

Alael turned to me. I was following his progress closely and had made the same observation.

'Tell him not to call me Al,' he said.

'I'll do that,' I said, 'but he's right. You're leaving it twice as thick as you usually do.'

Alael shouted to one of his staff, 'Eh, Chaff, bring us the docket.' The Angel shambled his way over to us and gave Alael a crumpled delivery note. Alael studied it, then handed it to me. It referred to Earthly weights and volumes, neither of which meant very much to me. Alael spotted my confusion. 'Chaff!' he called after the Angel, who had returned to his work.

'Have you still got yesterday's?'

For the second time, the Angel abandoned his huge bundle of white granules and, after a search, produced another screwed up delivery note. I compared the two. Quite clearly they had been asked to deliver twice as much.

'Do you know why?' I asked as I returned the paperwork.

'No.'

I remembered the message for Moses which I had not yet delivered, as he was asleep. I opened it: *Tomorrow will be a day of rest for the whole community. It is a day set aside for God. Tell the People that today they must gather and prepare food for two days. Tomorrow will be a special day.*

When the Israelites woke and began the daily chore of gathering and cooking their Heavenly food, Moses told everyone to pick up twice as much as usual and that the seventh day was a day for rest.

'What do you mean: rest?' they asked.

'A day with no work,' Moses explained patiently.

'Why?'

Moses wasn't sure how to answer this one. I did my best to help him. 'It's a day for parents to play with their children,' I suggested. Moses accepted the idea and passed it on. 'A day for husbands to talk to their wives,' I continued. He seemed less convinced by that one but still passed it on. 'A day for everyone to talk to their Creator; a day for weary limbs to recover; a day when wives and mothers don't have to cook or clean.' Finally I added: 'A day when busy leaders don't have to deal with endless enquiries.' To my surprise, Moses did not announce this last one.

The following day – the seventh day – a number of the People ignored Moses' instructions and set off around the camp to search for their daily gleanings from the desert floor. They did not find a single grain.

'How stupid can they be?' I asked Maphrael. 'They have been given a day to rest and insist on working. They have plenty of food in their tents but are still looking for more.' I made my way round the camp, giving instructions to the Angel guardians. Whenever I found one of the Israelite men improving his tent, or cleaning his barrow, I said to his Angel, 'If our Boss says that he needs a day's rest, he needs a day's rest. Tell him to stop.' I said the same for every woman that I found making clothes or tidying her tent. 'They can do that another day,' I insisted. 'Today is for resting.'

By the end of the day it was quite clear that the Israelites simply do not know how to rest. It is something they have never done. Those who were not blatantly ignoring my Boss's instructions quickly became bored and started arguing. Most of them could not resist the temptation to get on with one job or another.

As the Sun's light faded, I was with Moses outside his tent, where the usual queue had assembled to demand that he resolve their assorted arguments and difficulties. Despite Miriam's best efforts to send them all away, Moses had insisted on doing his duty, claiming, 'If I don't deal with this lot today, I will have twice as many tomorrow.'

Travelling south towards Sinai

The Israelites continued their haphazard progress southwards towards the mountains where I first found Moses. Their lives have begun to settle into the regular pattern of six days of work and travel followed by a day of rest. They quickly learned that there was no gain from rushing out of their tents on the morning of the seventh day because there would be nothing to collect. Learning to rest, however, has been much harder for them – though there is a noticeable difference when they do.

It was Maphrael who pointed out that, from his night-time vantage point above the camp, he can tell which ones have made best use of their rest day.

'Look at them, Oriel,' he said excitedly. 'The ones whose spirits shine brightest, I guarantee, are the ones who have taken a day off.'

I looked into tent after tent of those with shining spirits. Maphrael was right.

Moses has continued to hold his court session every day. This concerns me. It is not good for Moses and it is not good for the future of the People. They need some means of resolving their own problems. They also need to recognise the one who is their ultimate leader: my Boss.

*   *   *

Each day, after Hushael has been relieved from his daytime cloud duty, he sets off across the lifeless landscape in search of water

185

and vegetation, in order to plan his route for the following day. Two mornings ago he had found neither. That was not a great problem because the People now carry spare water. But yesterday was the same and this morning Hushael failed once again to find a suitable water supply. I am expecting increased complaints for Moses.

*　*　*

I was quite right. As Moses and Aaron pushed their barrow at the front of the Israelite advance – just behind half of Joshua's small but growing army – a succession of individuals and tribal leaders arrived to complain that their water skins were either nearly or actually empty.

Last night I accompanied Hushael. We searched the entire plain between the camp and the Amalek hills. We found numerous patches of grazing land for the goats and sheep, but no wells, springs, pools or streams. We returned to the camp to discuss the situation with Maphrael. As we often do, we followed Hushael's advice. He assured us that there would be plenty of water in the hills and suggested that we lead the People across the plain as quickly as possible, travelling at night to reduce water consumption.

*　*　*

This change of plan instantly confused Alael, who took a while to understand that we needed him to deposit the food at the place where the Israelites would be arriving in the morning and not where they had camped the previous day. The Israelites, on the other hand, were quick to understand that, if their pillar of fire was moving away during the early evening, they needed to follow it. Hushael and Maphrael's pillars have become one of the few fixed points in their nomadic lifestyle. Although they readily journeyed during the cool, dark, night-time hours, vaguely associating the pillar of fire with the God who has cared for them every step of their way since leaving Egypt, this didn't stop them from grumbling at Moses.

After two nights, everyone's water supply was exhausted. At the start of the fourth night's journey, when the Amalek Hills were already looming over them, the people began to riot. They clambered out from the shade of their tents, dizzy with thirst. Though not one of the whole population was ill, their mouths were swollen with dryness. They resorted to their usual complaint: 'Did you bring us out of Egypt to die?'

If their mouths would have allowed it, many others would have joined the protest, but they needed to conserve their energies. Instead, Hur, the nominated spokesman of the tribal leaders, whispered threateningly to Moses, 'If anyone round here is going to die, you'll be the first.' His words chilled my spirit.

Moses looked up at the sky in the direction of Hushael's cloud and shouted, 'Lord, what shall I do with these people?'

At that moment, Archangel Gabriel arrived with a big, beaming smile.

'Everyone enjoying themselves?' he asked.

I suggested coolly that he get on and deliver his message.

Take the tribal representatives ahead with you to the rock at Horeb, Gabriel instructed Moses. *Take your old shepherd's staff as well. When you get there, strike the rock with your staff at the spot I show you.*

When Moses had accurately repeated the message within his thoughts, Gabriel handed a message to me. It had no words. It was a detailed picture of a desert rock face with one particular point carefully marked.

I stayed with Moses, Hur and the other tribal leaders, sending Hushael ahead with the picture of the rock face. Maphrael, the pillar of fire, followed behind, leading the People at their usual lumbering pace. When I arrived at the rocky hillside identified in the picture, Hushael was marking the exact spot on the rock that had been pointed out, murmuring to himself, 'Very clever. Very clever indeed.'

I attempted to direct Moses towards Hushael, but he ignored me. 'Ah,' he said to the leaders when they were close to the sheer cliff, 'I have come across this before. All I have to do is find the right place.'

The Israelite leaders, having spent their entire lives on the flat and well-watered delta of the River Nile, were quite perplexed by the whole situation. There was no sign of water, nor of any live vegetation. Moses was excited. He strode over to one end of the cliff, jammed his staff under his arm and worked his way carefully along, feeling the rock with his fingers in the darkness. He was concentrating his attention on a line at which two different types of rock met. I did my very best to draw his attention to the place where Hushael was patiently waiting for him. But Moses continued his moonlit search, methodically and in silence.

While Moses made this unnecessarily slow progress along the bottom of the dry cliff, the People began to arrive, led by Maphrael. Everyone waited and wondered what was happening. Most of them wondered whether thirst had driven Moses mad, and whether they would all die at the foot of this forbidding cliff. Just a few wondered what wonderful thing their God might do next.

Eventually Moses made it to the place that Hushael had been marking all along. His mind was deaf to the voices of three Angels, all telling him that he had finally arrived; he was only listening to his fingers. Exactly where Hushael had been pointing, he found what he was feeling for – a small patch of salt crystal on the surface of the rough rock.

'Here it is,' he announced quietly. He stepped back, took the staff from under his arm, held it with its base pointed at the patch of crystal and slammed the end of his staff into the rock.

Nothing happened.

He did it again, and again. On the third blow a small trickle of water emerged from the dry rock. Moses didn't stop. He continued to hammer away, and with every blow the strength of the trickle increased. Suddenly, a large lump of rock gave way and a torrent of water gushed out, soaking Moses and the tribal leaders. Israelites near the front cheered and rushed forwards, clutching their water skins. Above the roar of hoarse voices, Moses attempted to shout, 'We camp here.' He didn't need to. They had worked that out for themselves.

Rephadim

The Israelites have stayed some time at the foot of this gushing cliff. They soon regained their strength, and the desert floor has flourished with abundant plantlife for the goats and sheep to chew. At one stage, Moses became ill, exhausted by his unrelenting work. Aaron did his best to deal with the endless procession of complaints and squabbles, while Miriam tried to keep Moses from attempting to run things from his bed.

The presence of so many people and animals has caused considerable anxiety among the mountain herdsmen of Amalek. Last night I received a visit from their Seraph. Reuggael is a rather ragged and surly Angel, which surprised me. I had assumed that all Seraphs had the same smooth sophistication of Shlyphantel.

'Got some bad news,' he growled.

'How can I help you?' I smiled in return, wondering to myself whether this Angel had spent too long among the rugged mountain herdsmen.

'My lot have declared war on your lot,' the Seraph informed me bluntly. I was shocked. 'Stupid thing to do seeing as your lot are the Boss's chosen ones, but what can an Angel do?'

This short, growled speech raised so many questions in my mind that I didn't know which to ask first.

'How do you know about them being our Boss's chosen ones?'

'He's been talking about it for centuries,' the gravelly voice told me.

'Talking about it to whom?'

'Us Seraphs.'

'What has he been saying?'

'That your lot are going to set an example to all the others: show 'em the Boss's way of doing things. I'm all in favour. These Amalekites are as stupid as their sheep.'

I wondered at this grunting Seraph who cast such a different light on my own Seraphic responsibilities.

'Do you know Shlyphantel?' I asked.

'Meet him occasionally. Too posh and poncey for my liking. You'd think the rest of the world was just there as a backdrop for Egypt, the way he goes on.'

I allowed myself a restrained smile.

'Your lot gave them a good kicking, I heard,' he continued.

'My *lot* didn't have much to do with it,' I assured him.

'And now my Amalekites are lining up for the same treatment,' Reuggael said, disregarding my disclaimer.

'When and where is this war going to happen?' I asked.

'They'll come down onto the plain tomorrow and attack the day after,' he mumbled. 'I've told them they're being stupid, but they won't listen. They think their silly little god can do anything.'

'Who is their silly little god?'

'They haven't really got one. Just a twisted tree branch one of them found in the desert and slapped some gold on.'

We were getting off the subject. I was worried by the prospect of a battle against an army of hardened hillmen.

'What do you want me to do?' I asked.

'Give the Amalekites a thorough thrashing,' my visitor stated. 'They deserve it. Probably won't knock much sense into them though.'

With that the Angel wandered off, leaving me to ponder the prospect of more human suffering. I didn't know what frightened me most: the thought of Joshua's inexperienced army being hacked to pieces by Amalekite battle axes or the idea that the constantly-grumbling and complaining Israelites were supposed to set a good example to other nations.

While the Israelites were gathering their daily ration of Alael's nightly delivery, small groups of young Amalekite men began to climb down the steep mountain slopes onto the desert plain where Moses and his People were camped. The Amalekites were armed with crude weapons they had made for themselves. Their spears were little more than straight branches, sharpened to a point at one end. Only a few had metal-headed axes. The rest had strapped shaped stones onto rough wooden handles. As their numbers grew, so did the anxiety of the Israelites.

'What should we do?' Maphrael asked me.

'I don't know, Maff,' I admitted. 'Their Seraph is expecting us to defeat them, but Joshua's little army is already outnumbered and not one of them has experienced a real war.'

'You have to do something,' Maphrael insisted.

'I've sent for Archangel Michael.'

* * *

Michael didn't come. When the tribal representatives marched up to Moses' tent in the middle of the day and insisted that he do something about the hostile-looking Amalekites, I did not know what to advise him. Moses told them to go away and find Joshua, then return with him.

Moses, like me, knew that Joshua's small militia would be no match for the Amalekites. He sat down in the entrance to his tent and called out to God for inspiration. I expected Gabriel to arrive with instructions. He didn't. I looked to Maphrael for some advice.

'You're the Seraph,' he said.

'Tell Joshua to get his fighters ready,' I suggested, 'and get them to recruit some more – only volunteers though. Make sure every man understands what he is getting himself into.'

There was a real possibility in my mind that the Amalekites

might rout the whole camp. I didn't want to risk Moses getting caught up in that.

'Climb to the top of that cliff,' I told the Israelite leader. 'Take your staff with you – that always seems to come in useful – and pray hard to God to rescue your People.'

It fell far short of being a full battle plan, but they seemed sensible precautions to begin with. The tribal leaders, led by Hur and Joshua, resolved to raise the largest fighting force they could. For the rest of the day, separated by a mile of empty desert, the two armies organised themselves for the mindless bloodletting to come.

During the night the Israelite camp hummed with the sound of fervent prayer. Most of the prayers were so contaminated by selfishness that they were of little value, but some rang clear with generous love for others than themselves. I was encouraged. Shortly before dawn, Archangel Michael arrived with an Angelic army that exactly matched the number of Joshua's soldiers.

'Oriel,' he commanded, immediately taking control of the situation, 'take Moses up the hill. I'll look after things down here. And tell Hushael to keep his pillar of cloud exactly as usual.'

Michael turned to his Angelic troops and distributed more orders, assigning each of them to a particular Israelite soldier.

'What, exactly, is your plan, Michael?' I asked.

'My plan,' he said, annoyed at me for questioning his orders, 'is for you to encourage Moses' prayers and for me to deal with the battle.'

'I am not moving from here, Archangel Michael, until you have explained to me, in detail, what you intend to do with my People,' I retaliated.

Michael sighed impatiently.

'It's very simple, Oriel. Moses will pray for the safety of the People. He will hold up his staff in the air as a symbol of those prayers. The staff will be a sign to my Angels to guide the Israelite men through the battle. As long as Moses prays, Joshua will have the most effective fighters this planet has ever known.'

'And if Moses stops praying?'

'They're on their own.'

I shuddered.

'Anything else, Oriel?' the Leader of Heaven's Army asked pointedly.

'What do you want Maphrael to do?'

191

Michael paused. Maphrael was evidently not part of his plan.

'Oh, yes,' he said, suddenly remembering something. 'Gabriel asked me to give you a message. Tell Maphrael to go and fetch Zipporah. The Boss wants her and Moses back together.'

After giving Hushael and Maphrael their instructions, I returned to Moses. I suggested that he take Aaron and Hur with him up the hill. Aaron has been the main inspiration in the development of Moses' prayers over these past months. And I judged that it would be wise for Hur, as the appointed representative of the tribal leaders, to be actively involved; it might avert some future grumblings.

At first light, Moses and his two companions climbed slowly up the side of the great cliff that was still producing a steady supply of fresh water. When Earth's pale Sun emerged over the eastern horizon, the Amalekite herdsmen formed themselves into a long, curved line that enclosed the Israelite camp against the rock face. They began to clash their axe handles against their spears while repeating a rhythmic grunt.

Joshua arranged his silent and fearful force into a similar line, facing outwards at their grunting enemy. The rest of the Israelites retreated to the foot of the cliff where they cowered, clutching their children and their most valued possessions. Joshua took his position in the very middle of his army, surveying the vicious herdsmen of Amalek. From time to time he glanced behind him to see if Moses had yet reached the top of the cliff. His instructions were to wait until Moses lifted up his staff.

At some unseen signal, the Amalekites stopped their chant. There was a sickly silence. Moses panted his way to the top of the cliff. Reuggael, the Amalekite Seraph, appeared beside me. Below us, Archangel Michael was standing at Joshua's side and, in the same way, an Angel warrior accompanied every one of Joshua's thinly-spread army.

'As I said,' came Reuggael's growling voice, 'we're in for a thrashing.'

Moses steadied himself after the exertion of the climb, then slowly and deliberately took his staff in both hands, gripping its base, and lifted the much-travelled length of wood high above his head.

'NOW!' Joshua yelled – and the two armies ran at each other. Axes swung. Spears jabbed. Men screamed in anger and pain. Blood flowed. Soon there were fighters from both armies lying in lonely agony on the desert floor, their bodies damaged beyond repair. I counted them as they fell, both Amalekites and Israelites. Despite the greater numbers of the mountain men, and the ferocity of their warfare, more of them had died.

'When will it end?' I asked Reuggael.

'When one side runs away,' the Seraph told me.

'The Israelites have nowhere to run to,' I observed.

Reuggael grunted.

I have never before seen human warfare at such close quarters. I had foolishly assumed that it would be over quickly. Not so. The long lines gathered into clumps of mortal fury. When a gap opened up, Israelite women led by Miriam scurried among the scattered corpses to drag wounded Israelites to safety. The bleeding Amalekites they left to die. I turned to my fellow Seraph and apologised for this partisanship. He grunted.

As the battle dragged on, I focused my attention on young Joshua. Archangel Michael had a firm grip on each of Joshua's arms and moved them swiftly into position each time a spear or axe was jabbed or swung in his direction. Michael also guided him in attack, pointing out the place and moment when his enemy's guard was lowered. But then, without warning, Michael moved aside and left the inexperienced general to his own devices. The same thing happened across the battlefield. The Israelite men lost their confidence, jumping backwards to avoid the blows of the Amalekites. The line of battle edged towards the Israelite camp.

I looked round at Moses. He had dropped his staff and was vigorously shaking his arms, which had seized with cramp. In that terrible moment I realised that I had been distracted from my own task. I was supposed to be supporting Moses' prayers, not watching the carnage. I urged him to pick up his staff once more. As soon as he did, Michael's Angels returned to the fray and the Israelites began to push the Amalekites back.

After that, I devoted my attention to Moses, asking Reuggael to update me on the progress below. I tried to ignore the screams wafting up from the plain, and focused on the silent screams of the muscles in Moses' arms and shoulders. There was no way he would be able to hold the staff above his head for as long as the fighting seemed likely to require. I spoke encouraging words into his mind, and took some of the weight of his staff to relieve the pressure on his arms. I even tried singing a few verses of Raphael's song – much to Reuggael's amusement.

Moses' whole body was becoming tired. It seemed strange that Joshua should still be fighting so vigorously below us, yet Moses, who only had a light staff to wield, should be struggling.

There was a large rock not far from where Moses was standing. I suggested to their guardians that Aaron and Hur should roll the boulder to the top of the cliff so that Moses could sit on it. This took some time. Twice while they were moving it, Moses lowered his arms to relieve cramp. On both occasions, the Amalekite army rallied and drove the Israelites backwards. During the second of these episodes the Amalekites in one of the battle groups completely wiped out their opponents and ran to the next group to join their fellow herdsmen.

At last the boulder was close enough for Moses to be able to sit down and still see the battle. Immediately, his prayers redoubled and Joshua's army gained the upper hand. They had fought through the hottest part of the day and both armies were considerably thinned. The men were now wearily swinging their axes whether or not there was an enemy in range. Hur suggested that he and Aaron each hold up one of Moses' arms. Then the Amalekites were driven steadily back.

Not until Earth's Sun was descending in the western sky did the last remnant of the Amalekite herdsmen turn and run, limping, towards the hills. Joshua's troops did not pursue them; they simply sank, exhausted, to the ground.

'That's that done,' growled the scruffy Seraph.

Moses, Aaron and Hur lowered the staff, watching carefully to ensure that the Amalekites did not suddenly return when they did.

A cheer of celebration rose from the Israelite camp, but it did not last for long. Every family had sent at least one of their men into the battle. Many of them will have to bury their dead before nightfall.

*   *   *

Ten days later

There has been no rest for Moses. The battle against the Amalekites threw up all manner of additional problems that the

People brought for him to solve. There were squabbles over the possessions of those who had died. There were arguments over who should be caring for those who had survived. There were claims for compensation, and accusations against those who had not volunteered to fight. Each day the plaintiffs arrived shortly after sunrise and, when the sky finally went dark, Moses dismissed those who were remaining, telling them to return the next day.

Today's proceedings were interrupted by two Israelite men storming through the camp in such a fury that everyone in the relatively orderly queue scuttled out of the way.

'He won't let me kill his son,' the first man declared indignantly.

Moses studied the men carefully. There was no doubting the intensity of their anger. He invited them to sit down on the mat which he used for this daily court.

'He won't let me kill his son,' one repeated.

Moses looked to the second man who curtly nodded his agreement.

'Why should you kill his son?' Moses asked patiently, assuming that this was dramatic language for something much simpler.

'Because he killed *my* son.'

Again Moses looked to the second man, who replied with a single nod.

'You killed his son?' Moses asked.

Another nod.

'He broke my rib,' the second man spoke for the first time.

'This man's son broke your rib?' Moses has learned to be rigorous in gathering all the facts before he delivers any judgements.

'No, Eliab did.'

'Are you Eliab?' Moses asked the first man.

'Yes.'

'How did you break his rib?'

'With my battle axe.'

'Why?'

'He punched me in the face.'

'Who did?'

'Ziph,' Eliab replied, pointing to the second man.

'You broke his rib with a battle axe because he punched you in the face,' Moses checked.

Eliab nodded proudly.

And why did you punch him, Ziph?'

'He stole my goddess,' Ziph replied.

'It was *my* goddess,' Eliab argued.

'I paid for that goddess,' Ziph shouted.

'You paid my son,' Eliab retorted. 'But it was my goddess.'

'Wait!' Moses intervened.

Eliab explained. 'My son, Perez, stole my goddess and sold it to Ziph. I was only taking back what's rightfully mine.'

'I caught him red-handed,' Ziph added.

'You've been trying to get your hands on my goddess for weeks,' Eliab accused.

'That's not true!' Ziph insisted.

'Quiet!' Moses demanded, taking back control of proceedings. 'Eliab, why did your son steal your goddess and sell it to Ziph?'

'He was angry with me.'

'Who was?'

'Perez.'

'Your son?'

'Yes.'

'Why?'

'Because I wouldn't let him play with his friends, because he wouldn't get out of bed to help me collect the whatever-it-is in the mornings.'

'I understand,' Moses said cautiously. 'And what exactly is this goddess?'

'It's a small Egyptian fertility charm which my wife and I use for . . . for . . . you know . . .'

'Do I?'

'Well, you're a married man!'

'I see,' Moses said hastily. 'You were telling me about the theft . . .'

'The goddess is solid gold and we keep it in a secret compartment in our money casket. Nobody, not even our son, knew about it.'

'But you said Ziph had wanted to own it for . . . for a while?'

'Well, he found out about it, didn't he,' Eliab said, becoming somewhat reticent.

'How? You said the goddess was a secret between you and your wife.'

Neither man wanted to answer this question. They looked briefly at one another and then resolutely at the ground.

'I need to know,' Moses insisted.

There was a long and uncomfortable silence. Eliab and Ziph both kept their eyes fixed on the desert floor.

'Tell me,' Moses demanded forcefully.

'I got injured in the battle,' Eliab began.

'And he couldn't . . .'

'My wife got . . .'

'It was just a neighbourly enquiry,' Ziph said defensively.

'I should have seen it coming, months ago,' Eliab reflected.

They stalled.

'I need to know,' Moses demanded.

Ziph made a brave attempt to get to the heart of the story.

'Abihail, Eliab's wife, told me about his injury and everything, and she showed me the goddess and said how it wouldn't be much use to them any more because of what happened to him in the battle. He was off milking the goats at the time, and Perez was playing with his friends, and – God knows – there was nothing else happening because it was the seventh day . . . you know, the stupid rest day . . . and there was just her and me in their tent, and . . .'

'Spare me the rest of the details,' Moses said wearily.

'But that's not the problem here,' Eliab claimed. 'That sort of thing is happening in every other tent across the camp. The problem is that he won't let me have his son.'

'Enough!' Moses sighed. He looked up into the morning sky while his mind and spirit sought some Heavenly guidance.

I attempted to sum up the case for him. 'Eliab disciplined Perez for being lazy. Perez stole the goddess from Eliab and sold it to Ziph. Ziph caught Eliab stealing the goddess back and punched him. Eliab attacked Ziph with a battle axe. Ziph murdered Perez. And now Eliab wants to kill Ziph's son to settle the score. But none of this would have happened if Ziph and Abihail hadn't . . .'

'Moses, my boy!'

My summary was brought to a sudden halt by the arrival of Moses' father-in-law Jethro, striding across the Israelite camp followed by an extensive entourage of servants, wives, children and grandchildren. Among them were Zipporah, Gershom and Eliezer.

Moses welcomed the distraction. Before running to greet his wife, he said to the two miserable men, 'Until I make a decision about your case, neither of you may kill, punch, attack, worship or lie with anyone. Do you understand me?'

Eliab and Ziph nodded obediently. For all the complaints that the Israelites have made against Moses since their rescue from slavery, their acceptance of his leadership is total. As I watched those two sorry men return to their shattered families, I realised that the Israelites are still slaves in their hearts and minds. It's only their bodies that have been freed.

Moses went to meet his own family. Gershom ran ahead and jumped into his father's arms. Moses embraced his son with tears in his eyes. The feel of his son's limbs wrapped tightly around his waist gave a new perspective on the case that had so recently been absorbing him. Moses prised his son off him so he could reach out to embrace his wife.

'Moses!' Zipporah exclaimed with horror. 'What has happened to you?'

The minor details of a human's body are of little interest to me, but in the moments that followed I realised that they revealed, to Zipporah, clear indications of the poor state of Moses' mind and spirit. She saw that her husband had lost weight, that he had less hair on his head and more lines on his face, that he stood with his shoulders drooped and his back bent. I had observed all these things myself but had failed to grasp their significance. Zipporah immediately understood that he is worn out – wearied by the constant demands of the People, and the pressures of leadership.

Miriam arrived, embraced her sister-in-law, was introduced to Jethro and his family, and guided them away through the queuing Israelites to the relative privacy of her own tent.

'What are all these people doing here?' Jethro asked.

'This is just what I told you about,' Zipporah informed her father. 'They come to Moses with all their difficulties and differences.'

'Crazy!' the old man observed as he slipped off his sandals to enter Miriam and Aaron's home.

*   *   *

In the cool shade of Miriam's tent the family have exchanged greetings and news. Jethro has quizzed Moses about the precise sequence of events since he gave up being a shepherd to become the leader of his People. Zipporah, meanwhile, quizzed Miriam about Moses' eating habits and the intricate details of his daily routine. All the while, Zipporah held tightly onto Moses' hand. The boys ran off in search of their friends.

As the day drew to its close, Zipporah and Miriam busied themselves preparing the food that Jethro's wives had brought with them. Hur entered the tent and courteously reminded Moses that there was still a large number of Israelites waiting for him to judge their cases. Moses went out to dismiss the people, his father-in-law with him.

'Why do they come?' the older man asked.

'They come to seek God's will,' Moses replied.

'And so they should,' Jethro said, 'but do they all have to come to you?'

'When there's a dispute,' Moses explained, 'I decide between the parties and then I teach them God's law in such matters.'

While Moses was telling the people to return the next morning, I said to Maphrael, 'Maff, what's this about *God's law*? Our Boss hasn't given them any laws, as far as I am aware.'

'Not laws as such,' Maphrael concurred.

'So where is Moses getting this *God's law* from?'

We were both thoughtful. I recollected all the visits we've had from Gabriel, wondering if there have been messages I missed.

Moses did his best to send the people away but there were several who said, 'I know you asked us to come back tomorrow, but . . .'

'It's you, Oriel,' Maphrael suddenly announced.

'What's me?'

'The Giver of God's law.'

'WHAT!' I exclaimed with shock.

'It's obvious,' Maphrael said cheerfully. 'You help Moses out with the disputes. So when you put ideas into his mind, he assumes they are from the Boss.'

'But . . . well,' I struggled. 'They are, inasmuch as I am allocated to Moses by our Boss. But this is terrible. We can't have him thinking that I'm his . . . Oh, Maff, the very thought of it! What should I do? I can't let him carry on thinking that I'm . . . It's too dreadful to mention. I shall have to go to Heaven and sort out the misunderstanding.'

'That would be good,' Maphrael said, with a mischievous smile. 'The two of you could have a God-to-god chat.'

I was so appalled by Maphrael's humour that I could not find suitable words to admonish him.

In Heaven

I popped into my own office first, to comb out my tangled mind before visiting my Boss. It felt very comfortable to be seated behind my desk again. I flipped through several files that were awaiting my attention. The affairs of Heaven are so much clearer than the murky business of humanity. I was tempted to deal with a few matters, just for the simple pleasure of achieving something. In the life of a Seraph, I have discovered, achievement is a very difficult thing to measure. I worked through file after file: approving new postings for Angels, writing references, resolving rota clashes. Every time I picked up a new file, it seemed so much easier to deal with the routine administration of Heaven than to go the short distance that would lead me to my Creator's all-knowing stare.

Eventually, he called me.

'I'm waiting, Oriel.'

I looked longingly at a request for training from an Angel whose planet is on the brink of developing primitive life-forms.

'You and I need to talk.' My Boss's voice rang around the room.

I dragged myself along the corridor and peered cautiously round my Boss's doorway.

'Have you lost the distinction, Oriel,' he asked seriously, 'between what is you and what is me?'

'Not at all, sir,' I replied quickly. 'The very reason I came here was to clarify that distinction.'

'Then you have no need to be afraid. Come in.'

My Boss smiled as I entered his room.

'It's Moses who has lost the distinction between what is me and what is you,' I explained.

'He is human,' my Boss said. 'What he hears is the voice of Heaven. He is not capable of defining it more accurately. Most humans give no consideration to Angels whatsoever.'

'I have noticed that,' I said.

'Those few humans who are aware of my Angels,' he continued, 'sometimes become so obsessed with them that they ignore me altogether.'

'Are they really that stupid?' I asked.

My Boss looked at me with a look that displayed both amusement and pain. I moved the conversation on.

'Moses thinks that you have been giving him laws,' I explained.

'I have.'

'When?'

'Almost every day.'

My thoughts suddenly darkened. A flash of anger shot across my mind. 'It would help a great deal if you arranged for someone to tell *me* what you are telling Moses,' I complained.

My complaint was met by a disarming smile.

'I did not think it necessary to ask you to tell yourself what you had only just told Moses,' he said.

'I don't understand.'

'Yes, you do, Oriel. I have given Moses my guidelines for living, through you.'

'So it *is* me?' I said, my mind spinning with confusion.

My Boss looked intently into my eyes. 'I trust you, Oriel.'

'But I get things wrong. I wouldn't dare to trust me with anything as complicated as human laws.'

'I do trust you, Oriel,' my Master insisted. 'I made you the acting Seraph for Israel because I know that you will give Moses good advice. My People do not have a formal system of law. They have you instead – for now.'

I said nothing. I was trying to take this all in and to assess what I might have done differently if I had understood all this before.

'But you are quite right,' my Boss announced, calling me out of my thoughts. 'The Israelites need clear guidelines and established patterns for living, so that they can resolve their own problems and enjoy the fullness of their humanity. Only then will they be able to show the wisdom of Heaven in their rebellious world.'

'The guidelines would need to be very simple,' I suggested. 'The only law the Israelites understand is: Do what you're told or you'll be whipped.'

'Oriel,' my Boss said, in a tone which informed me that our conversation had taken a significant turn, 'it is time for you to bring Moses back to the mountain where you found him. I will then give him and his People the guidance and advice that they need. Tell Hushael to lead them into Sinai tomorrow.'

I knew our discussion was completed and headed for the door.

'And Oriel,' my Boss added, 'I would greatly value your suggestions about what form that guidance and advice should take.'

I returned to my office, relieved that I was not guilty of impersonating my Creator, but weighed down by the responsibility of speaking on his behalf. I resisted the temptation to hide in my mountain of Heavenly paperwork. I have to take Moses to the mountains of Sinai.

⁂

The Desert of Sinai

The following morning, when the People woke up, they immediately saw that Hushael's pillar of cloud had moved up into the hills. They collected their daily ration of food quickly, and began to dismantle their tents. For some who had lost loved ones in the battle against the Amalekites, it was a welcome relief to move on from a place that now held so many painful memories. The People were too busy to pester Moses with their complaints. Instead, Jethro sat with him on his judgement mat and explained that he would do better to devolve his responsibilities to the tribal leaders, clan leaders and family leaders.

'Choose people who are capable and who respect your God,' Moses' father-in-law told him, 'those the People trust, and know to be honest.'

'But they won't know how to resolve situations like the one I had to handle yesterday,' Moses pleaded.

'Of course they won't,' Jethro said disarmingly. 'Teach them how to deal with the simple issues; train them to bring any difficult cases to you. Trust me, Moses. You and your People are wearing each other out. If you follow my advice, then you will be able to handle the strain, and the People will be much happier.'

The prospect of the People being happy and not constantly grumbling won Moses over to Jethro's plan.

'And,' Jethro smiled in a way that was reminiscent of my Boss, 'my daughter will have her husband back.'

By mid-morning the Israelites were winding their way up into the hills above Rephidim. They passed through the Amalekite area without incident and came to the bleak rocky mountains that used to be Moses' home.

It was good to see Moses and Zipporah walking together at the front of the People again. At their first rest stop, Moses summoned the tribal leaders and explained Jethro's system of family, clan and tribal judges. They agreed to nominate suitable candidates but were more interested to know where Moses was taking them.

'We are going to the place where God first spoke to me,' he told them. 'This is what he told me to do.'

'What are we going to do when we get there?' Hur asked.

'I'm not sure.'

Mount Sinai

The People didn't enjoy their journey across Sinai. They had never experienced mountains before. They complained about the cold nights and the chilling wind. They complained that it was hard to find suitable places to pitch their tents. They complained that their feet were sore and their legs tired from climbing. There was, however, one significant difference in their complaints. They were not all complaining to Moses; they took their problems to the clan leaders.

This evening the Israelites finally reached the mountain where Gabriel and I first found Moses. Now Moses is sleeping deeply, his body tired from a long and arduous day's walk, but – more importantly – his mind is clear. He has not been pestered by the People's squabbles; his wife and sons are at his side; and the homely sound of the wind howling among the ancient rocks sang him to sleep. I spent the night with Maphrael and Hushael, considering what guidelines and instructions these People will need in order to make a success of life outside slavery.

We all agreed that the instructions should be brief and memorable. I proposed that we work our way through all the individual cases that have been brought to Moses over recent months, and categorise them into a basic code for community life.

Maphrael said, 'Why don't we just look at that row between Eliab and Ziph? Those two have got just about everything wrong.'

It was certainly a good place to start. We have already spent numerous nights discussing this case, which Moses has still not resolved, despite daily visits from the two adversaries.

Maphrael got us started. 'It's all pretty obvious,' he told us. '*No stealing, no lies*, and *no worshipping idols*.'

'And *no inappropriate use of our Boss's name*,' I added. 'And what about the most obvious of them all: *no killing*.'

From that point our task became more complicated.

'But what about killing in a battle?' Maphrael asked. 'I don't see how we can rule that out without ruling out warfare altogether.' He was right. 'And might there not be some situations in which it could be right to kill another human?'

'Like what?' I asked.

'Well, they kill their animals when they become injured or diseased.'

'I'm not getting into that,' I said quickly. 'Can't we leave it at, *no murder*, for now?'

All agreed.

'We all know how the Eliab and Ziph saga started,' Maphrael went on. '*No adultery* needs to be on the list.' We approved that. Then he asked, 'How many rules are we looking for, anyway?'

'Twelve,' I said immediately. But then, remembering that my suggestions were liable to be mistaken for my Boss's decisions, added hastily, 'It's just an idea: one law for each of the Israelite tribes?'

'Seven more to go, then,' Maphrael informed us.

'*No worshipping other gods*,' I said. At that point we ground to a halt.

'What about your favourite one, Oriel?' Maphrael asked.

'What favourite one?'

'You're always trying to stop them from working on the seventh day.'

'I don't think that issue is quite in the same league, do you?' I replied.

I realised that Hushael had not yet made a contribution, even though he was thinking intensely about the matter. I encouraged him to share this thoughts.

'It seems to me,' he said cautiously, 'that what's at the heart of most of their squabbles is that they want to have for themselves what other people have got.'

'You could never enforce a ban on that!' Maphrael said dismissively.

Hushael did not respond. I have developed such a respect for this unusual Angel that I was reluctant to ignore his opinion.

'If enforcement is a consideration,' I replied to Maphrael, 'I think we'll have to remove the ban on adultery from the list.'

This led to a long silence. I thought about how chaotic the lives of the Israelites have become, and I wondered if they would ever manage to follow any of these instructions for more than a few days.

'Maybe we should include something really basic,' I proposed, 'like . . . *no grumbling*.'

Maphrael let out a raucous laugh. 'This lot couldn't keep that up for an hour!' he snorted.

He was right.

'What if we took the opposite approach,' I said, 'and aimed at the very heart of their problems? Hushael went that way with *no jealousy*. How would it be if we simply said, *Love God*?'

'And you could follow that with, *Love each other*,' Maphrael added.

We considered this for a long while. I liked it. If we were not able to fence in the behaviour of the Israelites, perhaps we could focus their attention on a single central point.

Our deliberations were about to be brought to an end by the arrival of dawn. Hushael said, 'Be patient.' I wasn't sure whether he meant it as an instruction to Maphrael and me, or as a law for the Israelites. At that moment the Sun's outer rim emerged over the rocky horizon, and we each went to our daytime duties.

* * *

During the morning, while the Israelites were busy re-pitching their tents more securely (it had been almost dark when Hushael's guiding pillar finally stopped at the foot of the mountain), Moses wandered up the mountainside in search of the place where he had seen the incandescent bush and heard my Boss's voice. While he stood, remembering that day, Archangel Gabriel arrived.

He read my Boss's words to Moses: '*If you obey my instructions and keep your part in the arrangement between us, then, out of all the nations in this world, you will be my treasured possession.*'

When Moses was confident that he had heard the entire message correctly, he scrambled back down a goat-track to the camp, where he found Hur and asked him to assemble the newly-appointed clan and tribal leaders outside his tent. When all 70 leaders had gathered, Moses explained Gabriel's message. The experience of receiving, rather than delivering, the People's complaints, had prompted these men to be much more sympathetic towards Moses. 'We will do what the Lord has said,' they agreed unanimously.

Moses sent them back to their separate sections of the camp to tell the People that they would soon receive God's special instructions, and that they will be his chosen nation. Moses climbed back up the winding track to the bush. Confident that he would be heard, he spoke out aloud, informing my Boss of the leaders' decision.

Gabriel was ready with the reply: *'I am going to come to you in a thick cloud. The People will hear me speaking to you and will learn to trust you.'*

Having lived with the Israelites for the past few months, I was surprised to hear that such trust could be achieved so easily.

'Tell them,' Gabriel continued, *'to prepare themselves. They should wash themselves and their clothes. In three days' time, I will come down to this mountain. Mark out limits around the foot of the mountain to prevent the People from going up it. Anyone who strays up the mountain will die'*

Moses noted these instructions carefully.

'I have a message for you too, Oriel,' Gabriel said. 'The Boss is throwing a party for all Israel's Angel guardians. Come to the top of the mountain on the night after tomorrow. He says it's time to celebrate the weaning of his nation.'

I was thrilled. My Boss is going to show himself to the Israelites, and the period of their infancy is over. The Israelites are about to become an independent nation. I followed Moses back to the camp and passed on my Boss's invitation to every Angel I met.

*　　*　　*

The following day the Israelites were busy washing, drying and mending their clothes. They were excited but tense. There were many quiet conversations, as they wondered what it would be like to hear the voice of God. The more they talked about it, the more the idea disturbed them. When night came, children were sent to bed early, and adults lay awake in their tents, worrying.

When the last human had been lulled to sleep, I called the Angel guardians to come with me to our Boss's party. They didn't need to be asked twice. Before leaving, I visited Maphrael, who is the only Angel to miss the celebrations. He has to maintain his nightly vigil as a pillar of fire above the camp. He was grumpily resigned to his loss.

'What should I do if Lucifer and the Opposition attack the camp while you are all away?'

'I don't think they would be stupid enough to do it when our Boss is quite so near,' I said.

'Have a dance for me, Oriel,' Maphrael said dismally.

'I'll have seven,' I assured him.

*　　*　　*

The party was wonderful! My Boss greeted each Angel by name and thanked them for their work among the descendants of Abraham. He then announced that he is going to give the Israelites a law of their own so that they can govern their own affairs. Then the singing and dancing began. In my Boss's presence, the tyranny of time has no sway. While he was with us we were free from its stifling constraint. It was a holiday. Archangel Raphael's choir provided the music and we cavorted around the mountain top until we had danced out every irritation and frustration. As is common with such events, the party ended in laughter. One by one we abandoned our songs and dances, and simply laughed. We chortled, giggled and boomed until the first light of Earth's Sun bounced down on us from the pale blue sky. At that moment, our Boss addressed us a second time.

'Tomorrow,' he announced, 'my People will become my nation.'

We cheered and whistled in delight.

'As you all know,' he continued, 'every nation is led and served by a Seraph. Therefore, when Moses gathers the People together before I establish my binding promise to them, I shall inaugurate the Seraph of Israel.'

A murmur of enquiry shivered round the gathering, wondering who it would be. Numerous faces turned to me, asking the same question that was in my own mind: Does he mean me?

The guardians returned to their charges in the Israelite camp. I waited for an opportunity to have a private word with my Boss.

'Who is going to be the Seraph?' I asked.

'That is up to you, Oriel,' he replied.

'I don't understand.'

'You may choose. If you wish to be Seraph, the job is yours.'

'No other nation has an Archangel for a Seraph,' I pointed out.

'Israel is not like other nations.'

'Who would look after all my work in Heaven?'

'Which is the easier task, Oriel?' my Boss asked me. 'To sit at a desk in Heaven organising rotas and training sessions, or to lead this nation through their role in human history?'

* * *

In the Israelite camp, the People were assembling along a line of stones that the leaders had laid out around the base of the mountain.

Maphrael joined me and said, 'You lot were making a racket up there last night. Even the People could hear the music booming.'

I smiled. 'Did anything interesting happen here, Maff?'

'One thing,' he said. 'Jeshaphael paid us a visit. He wandered through the camp in the middle of the night, looking at all the People. He didn't say anything or do anything.'

'On his own?' I asked, anxious that my lost Angel might have joined the Opposition.

'Yes,' Maphrael assured me. 'I called to him numerous times, but he ignored me. Then he faded back into the desert.'

The Israelites had all left their tents and were waiting at the foot of the mountain. They had strict instructions that they must not, on any account, cross the line their leaders had marked out, but the warnings were unnecessary. Raphael's choir had started again, and the human ears, not able to hear the music nor see the Angelic dance, heard only a loud booming like thunder.

When everyone was in place, there came a sound like a trumpet from the obscured mountain top. This was Moses' signal. The People watched in awe as the man they had endlessly criticised but still followed, climbed up towards the unknown terror above them. He disappeared into the smoke engulfing the top of the mountain – smoke so thick that it made Hushael's pillar of cloud look like the brief wisp from an extinguished candle.

Moses was not gone long. He emerged from the darkness and strode back down the track to where the 70 leaders were assembled. He reminded them that the people must not cross the line, and asked Aaron to join him. The two brothers disappeared from view. I followed.

I accompanied Moses and Aaron to the dell where Moses had corralled his sheep when I first saw him. Gabriel was there, as were Raphael and Michael. Ahoshal, Aaron's guardian, was with us, and Hushael, as Moses' guardian. The Angel choir were still singing energetically above us while we waited for our Boss to arrive. Hushael and I concentrated hard on Moses, knowing that the briefest glimpse of the Creator would destroy his fragile human life. Michael informed us that the cloud and smoke had been especially constructed to keep Moses and the Israelites from seeing anything that would harm them.

My Boss arrived and spoke to the two men. He passed on the instructions and guidelines that he had prepared for his People. This included all the shreds of advice that I had given to Moses since he led the Israelites away from the brickworks. My Boss didn't give the laws to Moses in blunt human words. He unfolded the themes, philosophies and principles with which he had created the human race. It was as though my Boss was singing complex melodies, letting Moses put together the words. The laws formed in his mind like the perfect lyrics to my Boss's song. Aaron also heard my Boss's voice and he too found words to express the inexpressible speech of Heaven. By midday, Moses had committed to memory as much as his human mind was able to hold. Then my Boss stopped speaking.

I capitalised on this pause in proceedings.

'Master, you asked for my suggestions in this matter. Maphrael, Hushael and I concluded that there should be just 12 instructions. The first should be: Love you. The second: Love each other. After that, the laws should be: don't worship other gods; don't make idols; don't misuse your name; don't murder; don't commit adultery; don't steal; don't lie; don't long for what other people have; don't grumble; and . . .'

'Be patient, Oriel,' my Boss demanded. 'Let Gabriel speak.'

I shrank with embarrassment. Gabriel read to Moses: '*Tell the Israelites, You have seen for yourselves that I have spoken to you. Do not make any gods besides me, and do not make images of gold or silver. Only worship me. Now go back to the People, write these instructions down, and read them to the Israelites. I am going to establish a permanent arrangement between myself and the nation of Israel.*'

I apologised for my untimely outburst before following Moses and Aaron back to the camp. At the bottom of the mountain they walked straight through the line of frightened and bewildered Israelites and went to Aaron's tent. There the two men spent the rest of the day discussing, debating, and finally writing down the instructions and guidelines that they had heard on the mountain.

* * *

The next morning, when the Israelites emerged from their tents to gather food, they saw Moses at the foot of the mountain assembling an altar from an assortment of large rocks. Joshua was helping him. When the rough altar was completed, they stacked up a series of flat rocks to form 12 tall pillars, one for each tribe. Moses then sent instructions for all the People to assemble in their tribes around the altar. It took some time to gather the entire Israelite population. Ahoshal and I waited with Moses and

Aaron beside the altar. At the moment when the last straggler joined his clan, a hush spread across the camp. My Boss had arrived. The People could not see him; it was the Angels who quietened the empty chatter of the waiting Israelites.

Moses explained to the People, as best he could, what had happened on the mountain the previous day. He showed them the calfskin scroll on which he had written my Boss's instructions, and told the People that he would read it to them shortly. But first he sent young men – a representative of every clan – to fetch 12 young bulls that they could sacrifice on the altar in honour of the God of Israel.

While the People waited for the bulls to be brought, talking among themselves, my Boss turned to me and said, 'Oriel, it is time for you to decide. If you choose to return to Heaven, I will be delighted to have my affairs in your capable care. If you choose to lead this People, I will be delighted that they have your wisdom and insight to guide them.'

'If I take the Heaven option,' I asked, 'who will be Seraph?' The answer to this question might influence my decision.

My Boss smiled. 'I do not answer *what ifs*, Oriel.'

'What will happen to Hushael?'

'That is between me and him.'

'Can I wait to see how they respond to your guidelines?' I enquired.

'No. Israel's Seraph must be a witness to the agreement that I am establishing today. Oriel, you must decide now.'

'Can I slip out of time to consider the matter in more detail?'

'Do you need to?'

I looked across the forest of human bodies standing, sitting, crouching and waiting around Moses' altar. I saw their confusion; they simply do not know how to manage the basic responsibilities of freedom. I saw the shallowness of their spirits; they are so easily distracted by the physical appetites of their shadowy bodies. I saw their anxiety about the time that lies before them – which they cannot see – and their fear for that lack of sight. These people certainly needed a Seraph.

'Are you sure I am capable of doing this?' I asked my Boss seriously.

'I trust you, Oriel.'

I had thousands more questions, but that declaration from my Master silenced them all.

'I will be Israel's Seraph,' I said.

My Boss stood on top of Moses' altar and called to the assembled spirits of Heaven.

'My Angels, I am pleased to inform you that Archangel Oriel will be the Seraph for Israel.' A vast, song-like cheer rose up from the Angel guardians. Other voices joined in the burst of celebration. Directly above me, Archangel Raphael led his choir in a rousing chorus. Gabriel embraced me, sweeping me into a brief dance, whispering mischievously, 'Are you sure you want to tangle up your life with the tiresome affairs of these humans?'

I stopped dancing. 'There is something special going on here, Gabriel. I'm not sure what it is, but I catch glimpses of it when our Boss allows me to look into his mind.' Michael joined us. He gave me a swift, congratulatory nod.

Our Boss called me up to stand beside him on top of the altar. The young men had returned, dragging the anxious bulls and carrying bundles of dry desert scrub for a fire. The desiccated remains of once vibrant plants were piled onto the altar and the fire lit. The marginal increase in temperature on the Altar did not affect me, though the humans were forced to back away until the blaze was less intense. The young men wrestled their bulls to the ground and, one by one, Aaron sliced the animals' throats. He collected the blood in a large bowl. I have seen numerous such rituals before and find them tedious and uninspiring. Then I looked at my Boss. His attention was not on the physical butchery but on the faint spirits of the People. Connections were forming in their minds. They were beginning to understand the significance of their dramatic rescue from the clutches of Pharaoh Rameses. They knew that their God had done all this for a reason, and they were inclined to trust him.

'This next bit is important, Oriel,' my Boss informed me.

Aaron had handed the bowl of bulls' blood to his brother, and Moses carried it up to the altar. Using a sprig of some plant, Moses walked round the fire, flicking large amounts of blood directly at me.

'Does he have to do that?' I asked my Boss, quite disgusted to discover that the blood was splattering over both of us.

'Yes.'

'Why?'

I enjoyed another brief and indescribable moment of revelation; this daubing with the life-juice of dumb animals is also part of my Boss's greater pattern. When Moses had finished, my Boss and I were liberally covered in the stuff. The heat of the fire gradually burnt it away, and the young men threw the dismembered carcasses of the 12 bulls into the flames.

Moses put down the half-empty bowl, wiped his bloody hands clean and opened up the newly-written scroll. He invited the People to settle down on the desert floor while he read my Boss's guidelines to them. With the help of their Angel guardians, the People listened to every word. They had never before had laws of their own; it excited them. These practical instructions were a great improvement on the crude and cruel demands of their Egyptian slave-drivers.

The very first section considered the fair treatment of slaves: all slaves must be freed after six years of service. This was greeted with a great cheer.

Next came instructions relating to the wide variety of situations that had arisen since the Israelites left Egypt. They were answers to questions that most families had asked at some stage. Before being given these laws, the People had turned to Moses. Now they would be able to deal with most problems on their own. This was good. They were given guidelines regarding compensation after accidents, security of personal property, social responsibility, poverty and worship.

When the reading ended, my Boss spoke into Moses' thoughts words to be repeated to the whole assembly. Holding an arm around me as he spoke, my Boss said, 'See, I am sending an Angel with you, to care for you, and to bring you to the land that I have prepared. Listen to what he says. If you do, I will be an enemy to your enemies and will oppose those who oppose you.' Moses repeated every word.

I looked round at many thousands of Israelite faces, all listening intently, all bright with a solid trust in my Boss, all inspired by what they had seen and heard.

Moses held the leather scroll above his head and declared, 'These are the terms of a lasting covenant between you and God. Will you ratify this covenant and will you keep to it?'

'We will!' the People shouted in unison. Their voice was like the roar of an exploding star. Their spirits shone with renewed brightness.

'Will you live by these laws?' Moses demanded.

'We will,' came the unanimous reply.

'Will you follow the Angel our God has appointed to us?'

I waited excitedly for their reply.

'We will do everything the Lord has said,' the People affirmed.

Moses picked up his bowl of blood once more. This time he splattered the red liquid over the People. They seemed less squeamish than me about it. The arrangement was sealed. The blood had become more than the spilt fluid from a few dying cattle; it was a symbol of unity, binding Heaven and Earth in a mutual promise. The Angels cheered and the Israelites joined them. I was delighted to be associated with such determined humans.

*   *   *

Later that day, when the fire had died down and my Boss and the other Angels had departed, Hushael called me up to his daytime vantage point above the camp.

'Oriel,' he asked, 'what should I do? Am I still Moses' guardian, now that you are formally his Seraph?' There was a touch of sadness in the eyes of this most loyal Angel.

'I don't know,' I said. 'I'm not responsible for the guardians any more.'

'Do your People still need me to show them the way now they have you to follow?'

'You have been a comfort and an inspiration to them,' I assured the quiet Angel. 'Please don't leave us just yet.'

A short while later, my People watched from behind their line as Moses and the clan leaders climbed up towards the dark smoke that still engulfed the upper half of Mount Sinai. At the edge of the cloud, Moses stopped. The People could not see what their leaders were looking at but they saw each one of the 70 elders fall on their face in worship. Then Moses and Joshua left the others and walked on into the obscuring cloud. The People watched and waited.

Moses took Joshua to the place where he had now twice heard the voice of his God. Some time later, Joshua emerged briefly into the Sun's light. 'Wait here until Moses returns,' he told the leaders. 'If there are any disputes you cannot resolve, take them to Aaron and Hur.'

Joshua vanished into the smoke again. The leaders sat down where they were, half way up the mountain, and waited. The People below them did the same. When evening came and neither

Moses nor Joshua had reappeared, everyone drifted away to their tents.

At the mountain top

When Moses had dismissed Joshua, he climbed up to the very top of the mountain. There, where my Boss had established his Heavenly court, time had no meaning. There Moses heard the unrepeatable music of my Boss's voice speaking directly to him; there he witnessed the eternal worship of the Angels. The cloud and smoke protected his fragile human form from the full glare of Heavenly brightness, but still Moses saw and heard things that no other human has ever known.

What happened in that meeting of Earth and Heaven cannot be explained in clumsy human words so I shall not attempt to do it. However, at one point in this timeless encounter, my Boss said to me, 'Oriel, we must provide Moses with a simple summary of my guidelines that people can learn and remember.'

'Maphrael, Hushael and I have already worked on that,' I told him.

'I know,' he said. 'Could you write down your suggestions for me?'

I peeled two slices of rock from the surface of the mountain, and wrote into them the list we had compiled. I began with the double call to love, and listed the others in order of diminishing importance. At the end, I was still not quite sure whether the call for patience had been intended by both Hushael and my Boss as a law for Israel or just a comment to me. I wrote it in rather small letters.

My Boss studied the list intently, looking into my mind as much as at the words on the rocks.

'These must be instructions for all humanity, for all their time on Earth,' he said. 'I do not think that *grumbling* and *impatience* need to be mentioned here.'

I wiped away the last two commands. 'I wasn't sure about those two myself,' I explained. 'I also wondered if *jealousy* was in the same category.'

'You have a great respect for Hushael's opinion,' my Boss observed, looking into my mind. I nodded. 'And rightly so,' he said. 'Let it remain.'

'I had thought there should be 12 commands in all,' I said. 'One for each tribe.'

My Boss hummed to himself for a while and then said, 'Be patient, Oriel.' He drew my attention to the first two requirements, *Love God* and *Love one another*. 'You cannot include those here,' he said.

I was astounded. 'But surely,' I spluttered, 'they express the very root of everything that you created the humans for?'

Again my Boss hummed thoughtfully. 'Indeed, Oriel, they do,' he said, 'but this is not the time or the place for them.'

My thoughts dived and stumbled through a billion memories but I could find no sense in what he had just said.

'Why not?' I asked.

'These,' my Boss said, indicating the whole list, 'are commandments, Oriel. But love cannot be commanded. Love can only be invited. No one, in Heaven or on Earth, can be coerced to love. They must choose it.' I pondered this idea.

'You are right, Oriel,' he continued, 'that, more than anything in this Universe, I long for humans to love me, just as I have always loved them. You are right that, for them to care for each other with the same devotion that they apply to themselves, is the fulfilment of their humanity. But I cannot command that love.' Then, after a long pause, he added quietly, 'Not yet.'

That last comment confused me even more. It was reluctantly that I removed those first two commandments from the stones. We were down to eight.

My Boss and I studied the remaining commandments.

'There are two missing,' he said softly. I waited for him to tell me.

'Children should respect their parents.' The words appeared in the smooth face of the stone as soon as he spoke them.

'But isn't that commanding love?' I asked.

'No,' he assured me. 'I long for all children to love their parents, Oriel, but not all parents are lovable within the limited capacity of a child's love. It is, however, important that they respect their parents, even if they cannot love them.'

'And the tenth?'

'It isn't the tenth; it is the fourth.'

I was intrigued. This would be the first commandment after those relating to the worship of other gods and the use of my Boss's name.

'My People must rest for one day after every six that they work: they, their children and anyone staying with them. That, Oriel, is my command.'

'I had not thought that one was quite so important,' I said lamely.

My Boss looked at me, smiled, and said, 'You were wrong.'

I smiled back.

'Now,' he said, 'take these two pieces of rock and give them to Moses. It is time for him to return to our People. I must speak to Hushael.'

I watched for a moment while my Master spoke to my studious assistant. I could not hear what was being said, but I saw Hushael's face beam brighter than I had ever seen it shine.

I picked up the two slices of stone on which my Boss's ten instructions were now neatly inscribed in a consistent script, which was certainly not mine. I carried them to where Moses sat, enraptured by the never ending, never repeated worship of Heaven. He saw me coming. For the first time he actually *saw* me. I smiled at him and he bowed respectfully. It was a wonderful moment. A new dimension of my life as a Seraph opened up before me. Rameses had never looked into Shlyphantel's eyes, I am quite sure. But Israel is no ordinary nation; they are my Boss's treasured possession. The prospect of relating directly with Israel's leader – Angel to human, human to Angel – was exciting. I was going to enjoy being a Seraph.

* * *

Our Boss joined us. 'The People you brought out of Egypt have been quick to turn away from me. They are an obstinate People. Leave me. I must contemplate my anger against them.'

My optimism vanished. 'What's happened?' I asked.

'You will find out,' my Boss replied. His face was dark with fury and sadness.

'What are you going to do?'

'My anger is not quickly roused, Oriel. I have deep compassion for these People, after all that they have suffered. I have been gracious to them. I have cared for them. I have forgiven their selfishness and stupidity. But those who are guilty cannot be left unpunished.'

Moses heard all this. 'Lord,' he said, 'why should you be so angry with these People? It was you who brought them out of Egypt. Must the Egyptians be left saying, "Their God took them

216

out of Egypt to kill them in the mountains?" Be patient with us. Remember the promise you made to Abraham.'

Moses looked at me. I was the only one that he could see. I, in turn, looked to my Boss, who was looking at Moses. I followed his gaze. Moses was radiant with profound love for the Israelites and with an unshakeable trust in my Boss's promises. Such spiritual strength, I was sure, would outweigh whatever petty stupidity the Israelites had got up to in his brief absence.

Moses' love and faith engaged with my Boss's anger and justice. I saw some of my Boss's thoughts. He considered destroying the Israelites and starting again with Moses, just as he had with Noah. But he resolved – as he would have said to Abraham four centuries earlier, if Abraham had persisted – 'For the sake of one righteous man, I will not destroy them.'

I guided Moses towards the track that led down to the Israelite camp.

In the camp

Our path down the mountain took us past the place where Moses had dismissed Joshua. Joshua was waiting for him.

'There is the sound of war in the camp,' the young man said, with understandable concern.

Moses listened, his ageing ears as clear as they had been in his youth. 'That isn't the sound of battle,' he announced. 'It's singing.'

We were puzzled. Moses and I were forearmed for trouble; neither of us had expected to hear the People singing. The two men strode purposefully down the hillside. When we emerged from the protective cloud into Earth's Sunlit day, we had our first glimpse of the rebellion that our Boss had warned us about. The Israelites, singing and dancing, were engaging in some sort of worship, modelled on the religion of the Egyptians.

Aaron came running out of the camp and up the slope towards us. He fell, breathless, at Moses' feet.

'Don't be angry, my Lord,' he said. He had never before addressed his brother so formally. 'You know how weak these People are,' he said. 'They thought you were dead. They said to me, "Make us a god we can see, like the gods of Egypt." So I told them to collect the gold jewellery that the Egyptians had given them. I built an altar and threw the gold into the fire. When the fire was burned out, the gold had formed into the shape of a calf.'

This last detail was a face-saving lie. I could see the truth in Aaron's mind: he had shaped the calf himself.

Aaron continued. 'The People said, "This is your god, Israel. This is the god who brought you out of Egypt."' There was an uncomfortable pause. Aaron added weakly, 'We thought you were dead.'

With this information, the scene became clearer. The People were singing and dancing around a small gold figurine. They had been feasting on roasted meat, taken from their herds and flocks. They were in the tired and bloated later stages of a major religious festival – all in honour of a badly carved lump of metal.

When the full horror of what had happened dawned on Moses, he looked at the two pieces of stone that he had treasured all the way down the mountain. *You shall have no other gods before me,* my Boss's script read, and *You shall not make for yourself an idol in the form of anything in Heaven above or on the Earth below. You shall not bow down to them or worship them.*

Moses glanced again at the revelling Israelites. He hurled the first stone angrily to the ground. It smashed to pieces. Aaron and Joshua both looked on in horror as Moses raised the second stone above his head and flung it down with all the force he could muster. It shattered into so many pieces that not a single word of my Boss's inscription remained intact.

He stepped over the wreckage and paced furiously down the track. Aaron and Joshua had to run to keep up. Word of Moses' return had spread through the camp. Scattered groups of revellers abandoned their madness and ran to the foot of the mountain to greet their leader who – I discovered – had been missing for more than a month.

'Whoever is on the Lord's side,' he boomed, ablaze with anger, 'come and stand with me.'

The People were confused. They didn't know what to make of it all. Some of Moses' relatives, members of the tribe of Levi, crossed the short distance to join the man who had led them to safety through the middle of the Sea of Reeds. Other Levites followed. The rest stayed where they were standing.

'Fetch your weapons,' Moses ordered the descendants of Levi. He made no attempt to conceal his instructions. 'Go through the camp. Hunt down the ringleaders, perpetrators and promoters of this insanity, and kill every one of them.'

The Israelites scattered. The Levites chased after them. The air filled with yells and screams as crude justice was administered. Moses walked into the camp and up to the golden calf, which was mounted on a smooth rock. It had been deserted. It looked ridiculous there, alone and surrounded by the dismal refuse of human festivity. The figure was small and badly formed, undoubtedly the work of Aaron's inexperienced hands. Moses grabbed the thing and ground it against the rock, grating it like a cheese. The intensity of his rage was such that he did not stop until there was only a small ribbon of misshapen metal left in his hand.

'Sweep it up,' he ordered Aaron, 'every speck.'

Moses' brother crawled round the base of the rock, gathering the shreds of gold into the front folds of his tunic. Joshua helped. Moses surveyed the human ruins of his People. The camp was now littered with dead and dying Israelites.

Gabriel arrived. 'I have a message from the Boss,' he told me, rather uncertainly.

'Well, hand it over then,' I snapped.

He passed the message to me, though it was addressed to Moses. *Tell each Levite to take up his sword. Order them to go through the camp, from one end to the other, each killing his brother, friend and neighbour.*

'You're too late,' I told Gabriel.

'I know,' the Archangel replied.

When I first realised what my People had done, I descended into shocked numbness; I had neither thoughts nor feelings. I simply observed and remembered. I witnessed the deaths of nearly three thousand foolish humans. I watched as Opposition spirits arrived to carry away the spirits of the dead: shamed human spirits, taken to timeless nothingness to await the day when their lives will be judged by my Boss. I saw guilt, remorse and indignation. I saw tears of sorrow and of grief and of contrition. In the middle of this mayhem, Moses marched his brother to the one and only water supply for the entire camp and insisted that he empty the grated gold into it so the People would be forced to drink their own stupidity.

That night the camp was silent. Moses did not sleep. He walked among the Israelite tents like a disembodied spirit, pausing whenever he encountered a telltale pool of drying blood.

My mind was still locked. I stared emptily across the camp

where, 40 days earlier, the Israelites had pledged their allegiance to my Boss and I had chosen to become their Seraph. I watched as Alael and his crew delivered the daily supply of food. There were three thousand fewer mouths to feed. A thought floated through my mind – the first thought I had experienced since the moment when Moses shattered my Boss's commands. I thought: *Even though he is distraught with anger against these People, my Boss still feeds them*. The dark night then seemed a little less dark.

After the People had eaten their morning meal, Moses assembled them at the ruins of the altar he had built on the day when they promised to follow my Boss's guidelines.

'You have done a dreadful wrong,' he told them. 'But I will go back up to the Lord. Perhaps I can make some atonement for what you have done.'

His announcement was met by several thousand shamed and silent faces. Now that Moses had returned, the whole episode seemed nothing but foolish to those who had taken part in it. There were some among them, I discovered – Moses' family included – who had taken no part in the revelry. They had stayed in their tents and ignored the mocking taunts of their neighbours. Aaron, it should be recorded, took no further part in the events once he had made the golden calf.

Moses turned and climbed again up the mountain. I went with him. Maphrael joined me.

'What are you going to do?' he asked me.

'I don't know,' I replied. He understood the fragile state of my mind and said no more.

'What did you do?' I asked him in return.

'I did everything I could, Oriel, honestly I did,' he said. 'But, once the humans had set their hearts on one particular course of action, there was nothing that the wisdom of Angeldom could do to make them do otherwise.'

Moses reached the familiar place where he had spoken to my Boss before.

'What a stupid thing these People have done!' he cried out. 'But now, Lord, please forgive them, or otherwise wipe me off the face of the Earth with them.'

'Those who have rebelled I will blot out,' my Boss replied, appearing visibly, through the smoke, to Moses for the first time. 'But you, Moses, must lead my People to the land that I have promised to them. My Angel will go with you.'

I looked at my Creator. He looked back at me.

'I'm not so sure,' I said.

He observed the struggle raging in my mind. Then he spoke.

'Leave this place, Moses. Take the People you brought out of Egypt. I will send an Angel with you, and you will come to a good and fertile land. However, I myself will not go because they are a stubborn People and I might destroy them.'

'Then I'm not going either,' I declared. I had not exactly made a decision about this, but I could see no better sense than to follow my Boss's example.

A second time, my Boss did not respond to my statement.

Moses spoke up. 'You have told me to lead this People,' he said. 'Remember, Lord, this People is *your* nation.'

'I will always be with *you*, Moses,' my Boss replied, 'but I will not be associated with that rebellious and disobedient People.'

'Me neither,' I said. I was ignored again.

'If you won't come with us,' Moses insisted, 'then I am not moving from this place. How can you be with me and *not* be with my People?'

My Boss looked into the deepest parts of Moses' being. There his love was shining, as was his unshaken trust in his God, and his anticipation of the fulfilment of the promises made to his ancestors. Moses waited for an answer. I marvelled at the difference between the man standing beside me now and the one that I had failed to distinguish from his sheep when I first found Moses at this same place.

'I am very pleased with you, Moses,' my Boss said. 'I will do what you have asked.'

Moses needed to be sure. 'If you are pleased with me, Lord, forgive our stupidity and rebellion. Accept us as your People and come with us.'

I was amazed at his courage. Moses was confronting his Creator and demanding that he change his intended course. I could never be so bold.

'I have made a promise to my People,' my Boss declared. 'I will keep it. Now, Moses, return to the camp and chisel out two pieces of stone like the first ones which you broke. Bring them to the mountain-top in the morning, and I will write on them the same words.'

Moses was satisfied. He turned and set off down the now familiar goat track.

'Oriel,' my Boss said, 'are you not going to return with Moses?'

'I don't know,' I said.

He looked into the formless pain dominating my mind.

'Oriel,' he said, 'go back to the camp and return with Moses tomorrow.'

I did as I was instructed – obeying is so much easier than choosing – but I didn't stay with Moses. I couldn't bear the brightness of his love for my Boss and for those foolish Israelites. I spent the rest of the day in solemn silence, perched on the remains of the stone altar where I had been splattered with the blood which sealed the promise between my Boss and his People. Maphrael sat with me.

When Earth's Sun set and Maphrael took up his night-time position, I wandered through the camp. I listened to children swearing at their parents. I watched as men betrayed their wives in the arms of younger women. I heard prayers being offered to the petty gods of Egypt; I saw the shadowy figures of young men sliding in and out of the tents of sleeping strangers, stealing whatever took their fancy.

I knew that I had no patience with these People. Unlike Moses and my Boss, my anger at their disobedience was not tempered by love. I was simply angry. The People were determined to follow their own desires. There are a few who are loyal, who explain to their children the advice of their Creator; but these dedicated individuals are the butt of their neighbours' jokes. They are ridiculed for their loyalty, not respected.

I could not lead the Israelites. In the morning I went up the mountain ahead of Moses.

'I cannot be Seraph of Israel,' I informed my Boss. 'I have nothing but anger against these People.'

He said nothing.

'I have let you down,' I said.

'I gave you a choice, Oriel,' he replied.

'I don't love them,' I explained.

'I do not command love,' he told me.

'Am I lost?' I asked.

'You are loved.'

That was not a direct answer to my question. 'What should I do?' I enquired.

'I invited you to choose between Seraphic duties here and Archangelic duties in Heaven,' he reminded me.

'Do you still want me in Heaven?'

'If you will not lead Israel, Oriel,' he said, 'I command you to Heaven. Do you resist my command?'

'No.'

'Then you are not lost.'

That was what I most needed to hear. There was a timeless silence between us, a silence in which I knew I was loved, even though I am incapable of such love.

'Who will be Seraph for Israel?' I asked.

'That is not your responsibility, Oriel,' my Boss informed me gently.

Again silence. My awareness of Earth's time returned when I saw Moses clambering up the goat track, carrying two freshly cut pieces of stone.

'I shall return to my office,' I told my Boss.

As he has done before, he allowed me to start to leave and then called me back.

'Oriel,' he said brightly, with a smile that was deliberately revealing. 'On your way to Heaven, could you please tell Maff that I need to speak to him?'

PART FOUR

In my office in Heaven

Since leaving Mount Sinai I have not attempted to follow the progress of Moses and the rebellious Israelites. My mind has been fully occupied in the intricate routines of Heaven; I have left the affairs of humanity to those who have the patience for such things. On a few occasions, in the distance, I have seen Maff visiting my Boss with his fellow Seraphs, but I did not speak to him. A short while ago, however, I was called to my Boss's office. He informed me that there was one more task for me to perform concerning Moses.

'Oriel,' he said, 'I would like you to collect Moses.'

'I don't understand,' I said.

'Moses is preparing to die,' he explained. 'When his body finally fails, I would like you to collect him and bring him here, before the Opposition get their hands on him.'

This was a most unusual request. 'That Moses is going to die is, of course, expected,' I said, thinking aloud. 'But surely, if I bring him here, the brightness of Heaven will destroy his spirit. His life has been far from pure and blameless.'

'Oriel,' my Boss said patiently, 'if the brightness of Heaven was likely to burn up Moses' spirit, would I ask you to bring him here?'

My mind was whirling, desperately trying to recall all my experiences in the desert of Sinai and on the plains of Egypt. I reminded myself that my Boss never asks his creatures to do things they are not capable of.

'No,' I said apologetically.

After a gently forgiving smile, he said, 'Moses' spirit has grown, Oriel. He will not be able to live the life of Heaven fully – not until Israel's work has been completed – but he will survive here.'

I was still uncomfortable about the idea of bringing a human into Heaven. It has only been done once before and that was in the very early years of the species. My Boss knew my struggle.

'Moses has lived 40 Earth years since you last saw him, Oriel.'

I reflected on how Moses' spirit had grown dramatically in the very few years that I knew him. It was possible that he could have grown enough to enjoy a reasonable existence in Heaven.

'Where will I find him?' I asked.

'On Mount Nebo.'

My Boss handed me precise details of the time and place for Moses' death. I studied the map. I was surprised to discover that he would not be dying inside the territory that had been marked out for Israel since the days of Abraham.

'Have they already been thrown out of the land that you promised them?' I asked.

A darkness clouded my Boss's face. 'No, Oriel, they have not yet arrived.'

The Israelites had been due to move into their new home just a few months after leaving Sinai.

'What happened?' I exclaimed.

'They continued very much as they had started while you were with them.'

I was suddenly greatly relieved that I had chosen to return to my desk.

'How many Seraphs have they got through?' I asked.

'Maff is still looking after them, and doing an excellent job in difficult circumstances.'

That was good news. 'As I remember your plan,' I said, 'Moses was scheduled to lead the Israelites into their new land. Why am I collecting him from Mount Nebo? They're nearly there. Couldn't we wait until he gets over the river?'

'Moses disobeyed me,' my Boss said. All such memories are painful to my Master. His eyes filled with disappointment.

'Oh!' I exclaimed. Whatever Moses had done would complicate the process of naturalising him into Heaven. Rebellion and Heaven do not mix.

'You need not concern yourself with those matters, Oriel,' my Boss assured me, knowing what I was thinking. 'Those details are all covered in my plan. But, until that day, it is necessary for Moses to atone for his rashness. For that reason he will only see the Land of Canaan; he will not enter it.'

'What did he do?' I asked.

'He smashed the rock with his staff to get water from it.'

'I was there,' I said hurriedly. 'You told him to!'

'It was a different rock, a different time. Moses knew that there was water in the rock, but I knew that if he hacked it out, like he had before, many of the Israelites would conclude that he had magical powers. I asked him to stand by the rock and order the water out with a spoken command, leaving the rest to me.'

Here my Master's sadness became more intense. 'He had already decided what he was going to do. He ignored me.'

I considered whether I should plead Moses' case – in the same way that Moses had done for the Israelites on Sinai – and tell my Boss that the punishment did not match Moses' crime. I could refuse to collect Moses until he had been allowed to cross the River Jordan and step onto the ground he had hoped for all those years. My Boss brought my thoughts to a halt.

'Oriel,' he said sternly, 'you are an Angel. Moses is a human.'

There was something in the way he said this which made me feel, just for a moment, that he values humans more highly than Angels. I ignored the idea. 'I'll go and fetch your . . . your human,' I said.

'Just one other thing, Oriel,' my Boss said. 'Conceal Moses' physical body. If the Israelites find it, they will be tempted to start worshipping him.'

The idea of disposing of a human corpse did not appeal to me. 'Couldn't Maff do that?' I asked.

'Maff will be busy with Joshua.'

<hr>

Mount Nebo

I returned to Earth just before Moses' scheduled departure and visited Maff. He was helping Moses through the official hand-over of power to the now mature Joshua. It was a surprisingly complicated process. All that Israel's Seraph had time to say to me was, 'He's all yours, Oriel,' as Moses turned and walked solemnly out of Joshua's tent.

I followed Moses to his own tent and waited while he embraced his elderly wife, Zipporah. 'I'm going up the mountain, my dear,' he told her. He had to shout to make himself heard.

'What do you want to go all the way up there for, you old fool?' his wife asked affectionately.

'I'm going to look at the land,' Moses explained.

'You'd better put an extra cloak on,' Zipporah said. 'It will be cold on the mountain.'

'I'll be fine,' Moses laughed.

'You go carefully, now. I wish you'd let Gershom go with you.'

'Stop fussing, woman,' Moses shouted, pulling his wife into a familiar embrace.

'I don't like to think of you – all alone on that mountain.' Zipporah pushed the white hair away from her husband's eyes.

'Dying's not that difficult,' Moses muttered under his breath.

'I can't hear you.'

Moses laughed, kissed his wife and extracted himself from her arms. Holding her at arms' length, he looked directly into her eyes.

'I won't be coming back,' he said earnestly.

They kissed once more and Moses backed out of the tent. 'Thank you, Zipporah,' he said, 'I could not have done it without you.'

'Get on and leave me in peace, you soppy creature.' Tears flooded Zipporah's eyes as she watched her husband turn and walk away.

Moses walked in silence to the edge of the Israelite camp. Nobody took much notice of him as they went about their daily business. When the camp was behind us and he had begun his slow but determined ascent of the mountain, he suddenly said, 'It's good of you to look after me for these last few hours, Oriel.'

'I didn't think you could see me,' I said, surprised.

'I can't,' Moses said. 'But I know you're there. I remember you from Sinai.'

This was so unexpected that I didn't know what to say to the man.

'There's not much for you to do though,' he continued. 'I suppose you can make sure I reach the top. I've been told the view will be rather special.'

I wasn't sure it would be wise to explain the reason for my arrival. I didn't want the Opposition to overhear and then cause trouble. We climbed the mountain in silence. Moses required all his energy to force his ancient body up against the drag of Earth's feeble gravity. It took a long time. When he eventually reached a place where he could see across the Jordan Valley to the mountains and plains of Canaan, his lungs were close to collapsing from the effort and his heart was beating dangerously fast. His keen eyes soaked in the rich greens that are fruit of the land's vibrant fertility.

'That will be lovely,' he gasped, slumping breathlessly against a large boulder.

'I have come to take you somewhere far lovelier,' I whispered into his spirit.

228

Then two Archangels arrived. Lucifer appeared first.

'He's mine now,' Lucifer barked, approaching Moses.

'Tell Michael that,' I replied, pointing to the Commander of the Angelic Armies who had appeared immediately behind the leader of the Opposition.

Lucifer spun round and his spirit faltered at the sight of Heaven's greatest warrior. I left the two of them to their struggle and concentrated my attention on Moses. His bodily organs were only functioning sporadically and his breathing was shallow, but his eyes were fixed on the lush green plain of Jordan where his People will be able to live and grow their own food.

'That will be lovely,' he repeated.

I expected his body to collapse at any moment, but his lungs continued to breathe, and his heart kept beating while he stared, with unblinking eyes at the fields and forests below. Behind us, both Lucifer and Michael called up reinforcements. Their argument became a tussle. More Angels and Opposition spirits arrived. A serious fight was developing. Lucifer was determined to carry Moses' spirit away to Death. Michael had orders to prevent it.

'What are they squabbling about?' Moses asked me through snatched breaths. 'They're as bad as the Israelites.'

'They're fighting over you,' I said.

Moses giggled. 'Am I worth it?'

I didn't reply. Mount Nebo was now awash with battling spirits. Lucifer and his forces were trying to position themselves close to Moses, to be there at the moment when his body finally lost its struggle. Michael and Heaven's Army held them back. Such violent confrontations between spirits are costly to both sides. Heaven's casualties are sometimes rendered incapable of any further productive service. Lucifer, though his resources are limited, is a ruthless commander; he will sacrifice large numbers of his spirits in order to interfere with my Boss's work. I scanned the faces of the Opposition troops to see if Jeshaphael had been assimilated into Lucifer's army. I couldn't see him.

Moses was still hanging on to Earthly life. At times he drifted from consciousness into detailed dreams about the Israelite tribes settling into their new life as farmers and fruit growers. In these dreams, the People continue to turn their backs on their God.

His physical condition deteriorated further. Lucifer was becoming frantic. Michael ordered his strongest warriors to form

229

a tight ring around Moses and me. I could not see through the brightness of this Angelic shield. Moses' shallow breaths were becoming rarer. As his physical vision began to fade, his spirit became increasingly aware of the shining Angels around him. On several occasions I wondered if he had breathed his last breath, until his body forced in another lungful of air.

Eventually that next gasp failed to happen. Moses' tired muscles relaxed and his spirit, lithe and energetic, emerged from its decrepit shell. He was, however, far from clean. The detritus of his long and selfish human existence clung to him, but the strength and stature of his spirit was outstanding.

A howl of, 'No!' went up from the ranks of the Opposition. I held Moses' spirit firmly by the hand and lifted him up from the mountain. The battle quickly faded. I looked down at the exhausted and wounded spirits below me and saw the thin and wizened form of Moses' old body. I still had to deal with that. Much to Archangel Michael's annoyance I took Moses back down to Earth. The Opposition resumed their assault while I snatched the limp corpse from the ground. I hurried to a deserted valley, scooped out a small trench in the soil and dropped Moses' Earthly remains into it. Moses watched and said nothing as I unceremoniously pushed the loose soil over his grave.

'What happens now?' he asked.

I turned to take a good look at Moses' spirit. Though bright and strong, it was strangely naked without its body, and badly stained. He did not look like an Angel, neither did he look like a man. He seemed, somehow, incomplete.

Heaven

Moses and I were met at the door to the Great Gathering Place of Angels by Archangel Gabriel.

'The Boss has organised a modest party for Moses,' he explained. 'But we must be careful that we don't overload him.'

I could hear the sound of singing. I opened the door and guided Moses through. In the far corner, Raphael was leading a septet of Angels in a song of celebration written especially for the occasion. We crossed the vast hall, and Gabriel introduced Moses to a collection of Angels who had played significant parts in his life, including the Angel guardians of both his mothers. Our Boss was not present. Though Moses was given a quick glance of God on Mount Sinai, his damaged spirit is not in a fit state to survive an encounter with the true Heavenly brilliance of his Creator.

I spoke briefly to Hushael. He has been commissioned to work on the initial plans for an entirely new universe. All the other talk around me was about Egypt and the Israelites, so brought back uncomfortable memories. I looked across at Moses. He seemed to be at home in the company of Angels, laughing and chatting. I even noticed the beginnings of a dance as his spirit responded to the intoxicating rhythms of Raphael's music.

Maff arrived. The tempo of the occasion instantly increased. He and Moses embraced like long-separated friends, and Maff swept his former charge into a manic dance, spinning together around the vast space, cheered and applauded by the other Angels.

I didn't stay. I slipped quietly out of the Gathering Place, content to leave the affairs of Earth in the hands of other Angels. The sounds of high celebration faded as I made my way down the corridor that leads to my office. I closed the door behind me, ready to settle into the duties allotted to me.

There was a message on my desk. I recognised the script; it was from my Boss. It read, simply, 'Oriel, thank you'.

An excerpt from ORIEL'S DIARY:
An Archangel's Account of the Life of Jesus

27AD

Jesus announced today that he is leaving the family business at the end of the financial year and moving to the small fishing community of Capernaum on the northern shore of the Sea of Galilee.

We have been waiting for this moment for many years. Our real work now begins. For security reasons we have not been able to talk or write about Jesus' future. It is only in the most secret places of Heaven that our Boss's plan has been discussed. But now the flag is up and the Opposition will most certainly have heard the news. I have called an Archangelic Council immediately and before it starts I must speak with my Boss.

Later

This was the first discussion I've had with Michael for many Earth years. Throughout Jesus' human life so far, Michael and his troops have been maintaining a 'spirit exclusion zone' around Nazareth to enable Jesus to grow up without any unusual spiritual interference. Michael arrived at the meeting in a festering grump.

'Capernaum is a ridiculous place for him to live,' he asserted. 'It is very close to the border between the Jewish and non-Jewish territories and, to add to the problem, he has chosen a waterside location which is very hard for us to defend.'

Having raised this exact issue with our Boss earlier, I was equipped to handle Michael's outburst with the same reply I had received. I calmly said, 'That's right.'

Michael was too distracted by worry to pick up the point.

'Why, for everyone's sake, does he not move to Jerusalem? Which is, after all, the obvious place for him to go.'

'He chose Capernaum,' I stated.

'Why?' Michael persisted.

233

'For all the reasons you just explained.'

Michael is an excellent warrior but he is rarely quick to understand the workings of his Boss's mind. There was a long silence while the Commander of the Angelic armies struggled to comprehend what was happening.

'Are you telling me,' he said slowly, 'that the Son wants to live in a place where he is utterly open to the attacks of the Opposition at a time when they are concentrating all their resources against him?'

'Yes.'

'So what do I do?'

'Watch carefully and wait for orders,' I explained. 'But, most important of all, make sure that none of your forces interfere without authorisation from either myself or the Boss.'

Michael was quiet. Next it was Gabriel's turn and I suspected that he would not like his instructions either.

'Jesus' arrival is not going to be announced in the usual Angelic fashion,' I explained.

'Our Boss wants to leave everything in the hands of the humans he has chosen. Our role is to watch carefully but keep our hands and mouths to ourselves. Gabriel, the job you usually do will be done by Zechariah's son, John. You already know the family.'

He nodded.

'I want you to lead John out into the Judean desert and help him to proclaim the message outlined here.' I passed him the file our Boss had given me. Gabriel took it with an air of resignation.

'Remember,' I continued, 'as with Michael, you must keep out of sight and let the humans do the work.'

Gabriel pulled a dissatisfied face. He likes to be where people can see him and enjoys his earthly reputation as *the Angel of the Lord*. Several months or years spent unseen in an earthly desert, watching a human attempt at proclaiming our Boss's message, is not an assignment he would have chosen.

'The leader of the Opposition will mash him!'

Michael's sudden outburst surprised us all.

'Jesus is only a mortal man now', he continued. 'He doesn't stand a chance.'

An excerpt from ORIEL'S TRAVELS: An Archangel's Travels with St Paul

In my office – free from the unrelenting pressure of time

'I have a challenge for you, Oriel,' my Boss said to me after a thought-filled silence. The word 'challenge' swept through my Angelic being like a great wave.

Serving the author of all creations is a challenge in itself. I shuddered to think what it might be that even he calls a 'challenge'.

'After your excellent work looking after my Son,' he began, glancing at the Heavenly man seated beside him, 'I would like you to look after another human for me.'

I have been responsible for Heaven's Angel guardian scheme since the very first humans stumbled across planet Earth. However, only once have I been a guardian myself and that was for Jesus himself, during the last months of his Earthly life.

Father and Son looked intently at me while I digested their request.

'Who is it?' I asked, suppressing a rising tide of excitement.

'I have been looking for someone to travel to Rome,' my Boss explained, 'and tell its citizens about Jesus.'

I glanced at the Son, seated beside his eternal Father.

'What's so special about Rome?'

'It is the centre of the world's most powerful empire, at the particular moment in Earth's story that we are considering.'

I nodded thoughtfully. 'Who have you chosen?'

'A man called Saul, from Tarsus in Turkey.'

I was confused. 'You have picked a Turk to tell a Jewish story to the citizens of Rome?' I asked. I knew it was unwise to question his judgement but there was nothing to be gained from keeping my thoughts to myself; my Boss always knows them anyway.

'You know me, Oriel,' he replied with a disarming smile that invited me to ask further.

'What is it that makes Saul the right man for this job?'

'That is for you to discover,' my Creator replied, his eyes twinkling.

The Son joined the conversation. 'Saul is a Jew – he got *that* from his mother. And he's also a citizen of Rome – he inherited *that* from his father.'

This was an encouraging start. I waited for more.

'He has spent the last three years studying at the Rabbinical University at Jerusalem.'

'I like the man already,' I interrupted enthusiastically. 'I always said you should choose some followers from the university!'

'You did indeed,' the Son said. Now he was the one with a twinkle in his eyes. 'That's why you are clearly the Archangel for the job.'

'Where and when will I find the man?' I asked.

The communication that holds Eternal Father and Son in perfect unity is too deep for any Angel to fathom, but they allowed me to glimpse a ray of playful amusement that passed between them. I recognised it at once, and it set my spirit on alert. It warned me that there is something about this Saul that does not match the picture I was forming in my imagination. I shall just have to travel down to Jerusalem and meet the man to find out what.

More bible-based fiction titles from Scripture Union

Letters to Kate
Claire Bankole

Through letters, postcards and emails, Claire helps Kate in her struggle to live the God-life amid the stresses of exams, college and a gap year project.

Dear Bob
Annie Porthouse

Uni student Jude writes a diary to her imaginary future husband as she searches for what it means to be a Christian. For older teens and 20s.

Love Jude
Annie Porthouse

In this sequel to **Dear Bob**, we follow Jude's comic antics as she struggles with life in her second year at uni – hilarious and realistic insight into student life and culture.

For information on these and all our titles:

- phone SU's mail order line: 0845 0706006
- email info@scriptureunion.org.uk
- fax 01908 856020
- log onto www.scriptureunion.org.uk
- write to SU Mail Order, PO Box 5148, Milton Keynes MLO, MK2 2YX
- or call into your local Christian bookshop

Help with reading the Bible

SCRIPTURE UNION produces a wide range of publications, many of which help people understand the Bible.

You might like to **request free samplers** from our range of quarterly personal Bible reading guides:

CLOSER TO GOD – experiential, relational, radical and dynamic, this publication takes a creative and reflective approach to Bible reading with an emphasis on renewal.

DAILY BREAD – to help you enjoy, explore and apply the Bible. Practical comments relate the Bible to everyday life, combined with information and meditation panels to give deeper understanding.

ENCOUNTER WITH GOD – provides a thought-provoking, in-depth approach to Bible reading, relating Biblical truth to contemporary issues. The writers are experienced Bible teachers, often well known.

SU also produces Bible reading notes for children, teens and young adults. Do ask for details.

- phone SU's mail order line: 0845 0706006
- email info@scriptureunion.org.uk
- fax 01908 856020
- log on to www.scriptureunion.org.uk
- write to SU Mail Order, PO Box 5148, Milton Keynes MLO, MK2 2YX
- call into your local Christian bookshop

Scripture Union
USING THE BIBLE TO INSPIRE CHILDREN, YOUNG PEOPLE AND ADULTS TO KNOW GOD